OF THE
SOCIAL CONTRACT
&
DISCOURSE ON
POLITICAL ECONOMY

DU
CONTRACT SOCIAL

OU

PRINCIPES

DU

DROIT POLITIQUE

PAR J.-J. ROUSSEAU

Citoyen de Genève

fœderis œqua
Dicamus leges
Æneid., XI.

A AMSTERDAM
CHEZ MARC MICHEL REY
MDCCLXII

OF THE
SOCIAL CONTRACT
or
Principles of Political Right
&
DISCOURSE ON
POLITICAL ECONOMY

by
Jean-Jacques Rousseau

*Translated from the French
with an
Introductory Essay and Notes by*

Charles M. Sherover

1817

HARPER & ROW, PUBLISHERS, New York
Cambridge, Philadelphia, San Francisco,
London, Mexico City, São Paulo, Singapore, Sydney

This work was originally published in French under the title DU CON-
TRACT SOCIAL OU PRINCIPES DU DROIT POLITIQUE

OF THE SOCIAL CONTRACT, OR, PRINCIPLES OF POLITICAL RIGHT &
DISCOURSE ON POLITICAL ECONOMY. Copyright © 1984 by Charles
M. Sherover. All rights reserved. Printed in the United States of America. No part of this book may be used or reproduced in any manner
whatsoever without written permission except in the case of brief quotations embodied in critical articles and reviews. For information ad-
dress Harper & Row, Publishers, Inc., 10 East 53rd Street, New York,
N.Y. 10022. Published simultaneously in Canada by Fitzhenry &
Whiteside Limited, Toronto.

FIRST EDITION

Designer: Jane Weinberger

Library of Congress Cataloging in Publication Data

Rousseau, Jean Jacques, 1712–1778.
    Of the social contract, or, Principles of political right & Discourse
on political economy.

    Translation of: Du contract social, and Discours sur l'oeconomie
politique.
    "Perennial Library."
    Includes bibliographical references and index.
    1. Political science. 2. Social contract.
I. Rousseau, Jean Jacques, 1712–1778. Discours sur l'oeconomie politique. English. II. Sherover, Charles M. III. Title. IV. Title: Principles
of political right. V. Title: Discourse on political economy.

JC179.R86 1984   320'.01   84–47673
ISBN 0–06–080719–9 (pbk.)

---

84 85 86 87 88 10 9 8 7 6 5 4 3 2 1

Contents

Preface

This volume contains the two essays by Jean-Jacques Rousseau that constitute his explicit contribution to the development of political philosophy—which, in *Emile,* he described as "my *principles of political right.*" This is, in fact, the subtitle of his prime theoretical essay, *Of the Social Contract* (1762), a title which suggests, as he himself confirms at both its beginning and its end, that it is not complete. Designed to develop basic principles of a free society, it is perhaps overly succinct, as it provides few examples of how these principles might be applied in concrete situations. For this reason, the essay *On Political Economy,* which appeared in Diderot's *Encyclopédie* (1755), is a crucial supplement; subsequently published as an independent essay, it might well be referred to as the Third Discourse. Having worked out his basic principles in this essay by addressing some of the tangible economic and social issues of his time, Rousseau has provided us here with the kinds of public policies he had in mind as the consequent of the principles he was to develop in the more theoretical and comprehensive work of 1762: for example, public education, taxation by consent and on what he called a "proportionate" basis. By using the earlier essay as a key to, or elucidation of, the later and more famous one, we may hope to resolve some of the controversies about Rousseau's intended meaning.

These essays are presented here in new translations which seek to bring the English into the closest possible approximation to the original French texts—with resultant clarification of many ambiguities and possible misunderstandings. Because an author's idiosyncratic capitalization and punctuation, as well as paragraphing, often affect the precise meaning of his statements, an attempt has been made to keep these as close to the original French as English usage permits. Paragraph numbers, however, have been *added* to facilitate reference.

This new translation of *Of the Social Contract* is based on the French edition edited by Maurice Halbwachs of the Sorbonne—the text of the original edition of 1762 together with Rousseau's notes that were added to the posthumous edition of 1782; although completely redone, it builds in part on my previously published modification of the Tozer translation. *On Political Economy* is newly translated and incorporates the same translational and editorial maxims.

Of the Social Contract has had an unusually deep impact on the development of democratic thought—yet it remains controversial even today, when we generally take many of its essential points for granted. Just why this should be so is not immediately clear. Perhaps it stems from the overly concise text Rousseau has presented to us: reading his essay with care is not as easy as his readable style suggests. Often he seems to have reflected in his text the paradoxes that marked his life. His eloquent presentation of a new thesis or insight often seems overly simple until, in the knowledge that he had no actually functioning democratic practice on which to draw, one considers the application he had in mind or the later development of the point at issue. For these reasons, detailed Notes which seek to elucidate the text as sympathetically as possible can be helpful to the teacher, and the student, who prefers to face the issues presented (and consider possible contemporary significance) rather than merely focus on analyses of particular passages. As a complement to the Notes, the Introduction presents an overview which seeks to bring into focus some of the basic principles and fundamental concepts that structure this attempt by Rousseau to develop that set of interrelated concepts which he believed must necessarily function as the presuppositions of a free society.

The Introduction and the Notes presume that Rousseau believed each essay to be a coherently unified whole; they are designed to elucidate the texts as sympathetically as possible, not to criticize them—although they do suggest the direction which constructive criticism might take. But if such criticism is to be meaningful it must first come to terms with what Rousseau tried to do, by facing the texts in their full integrity and facing them whole.

The prime references in the Notes to these two essays are to each other and to *Emile*, which was published concurrently with *Of the Social Contract* and is complementary to it, as it suggests an education for free citizenship (called for in the earlier essay—see *On Political Economy*, 37–40) in the kind of society Rousseau was proposing. (References to other writings would but open controversies as to how his many writings before and after these two should be related to each other.)

All references to *Of the Social Contract* are identified as SC, to *On Political Economy* as PE—and in each case reference is to the *paragraph numbers in this volume;* references to *Emile* are identified as E and cite the page number in Alan Bloom's translation, published by Basic Books in 1979. Other authors referred to are either those whom Rousseau cited or writers who have since made use of some of his concepts.

The translations of five French words require special comment. (1) *Bourgeois* presents a question of contemporary meaning: it is not immediately clear that this word, which Rousseau used in its traditional reference to an urban middle class, was intended to have the rather pejorative meaning it has been accorded by some participants in contemporary political discussions; hence it has been translated by the more neutral "burgher." (2) *Liberté* can be translated as either "liberty" or "freedom"; many English-speaking thinkers distinguish between these two words: "liberty" in the negative sense of an absence of restraints, and "freedom" in the sense of positive opportunity. I have used the word "liberty" in the translations because it is the French derivative and also because the editorial decision to substitute "freedom" would prejudge the text—only when "freedom of the will" is clearly meant has the word "freedom" been used instead. But this stylistic decision (challenged by some of my notes) obligates the reader to determine in each of the many passages in which the word appears just how it is to be understood. (3) *Moeurs* can be legitimately translated as "customs," "manners," "mores," or "morality"— but Rousseau clearly used *moralité* in contradistinction to it. Consequently, following a suggestion by Halbwachs, this word has been taken as referring to "customary [or] habitual conduct" rather than to principles of morality as such and has usually been translated in this way or as "moral custom(s)." (4) *Patrie* has been translated literally as "fatherland." But this must *not* be taken in any chauvinistic sense—for Rousseau did not believe in aggressive nationalism or war (see PE 53). Rousseau invariably used this word, in distinction to "country" or "nation," to connote an emotive feeling of affection, loyalty and, as suggested by passages in Plato's *Crito,* to which Rousseau's principles owe much, an expression of gratitude for cultural ancestry and upbringing. (5) *Propriété* has often been translated, especially in *On Political Economy,* as "ownership" rather than "property," though both are justifiable, because Rousseau's interest there seems to be more focused on use and control than on mere legal title (see PE 42, n. 6).

For whatever merit this new edition may have, I am deeply indebted to several colleagues who have been kind enough to work closely with me in its development:

With regard to the translations, Professor Victor Goure-
vitch (Wesleyan University) and Professor Hilail Gildin
(Queens College) have reviewed my drafts, clarified important ambiguities, and made valuable suggestions which have
been incorporated into the texts. Michael Alix has worked
closely with me in preparing this final version, and its textual
fidelity to the French original is in no small part due to his
meticulously critical care.

Professor Howard R. Cell (Glassboro State College),
Professor John Lachs (Vanderbilt University), Professor
James Gouinlock (Emory University), and three students—
Donald Jenner (who used these Notes in his own teaching),
Enrique A. Garcia (who reviewed an earlier draft with me),
and Michael Stein (who has also helped me with clerical
details)—have made detailed and important suggestions for
the Notes and the introductory essay—as have students in
several of my classes.

Much as I am gratefully indebted to each of them, individually and together, the responsibility for what does and does
not appear here must be mine alone.

Introduction

Jean-Jacques Rousseau's proud boast, even in exile, was that he had been born a *citizen* of the free city of Geneva. And the meaning of citizenship, as embodying both responsibility and freedom, was to become the central concept he bequeathed to us.

His Geneva birthplace and first home was a small house literally in the shadow of the Cathedral of Saint Pierre— once John Calvin's pulpit and since then a shrine of the Protestant Reformation. Born on June 28, 1712, Rousseau died near Paris on July 2, 1778. He was buried two days later—on the second anniversary of the American Declaration of Independence, and eleven years and ten days before the storming of the Bastille, which set off the French Revolution and the consequent collapse of the decaying feudal order.

During his sixty-seven years, he lived in several Swiss cities, in northern Italy, and in England, but mostly in France. He lost his mother at birth and his father found it necessary to abandon him at the age of eleven. As he never found it possible to settle in one place and felt almost continuously persecuted because of the many controversies in which he engaged, his life, as related in his own *Confessions,* was not a happy one. He knew most of the luminaries of his time—Diderot, Voltaire, Hume—and quarreled with each of them. Yet his impact has been decisive: though its author was largely self-educated, *Emile* would have a definitive impact on the development of educational theory and practice; *Of the Social Contract,* published almost concurrently, in 1762, would revolutionize political history and political thought.

A son of the French Enlightenment, Rousseau yet dissented from some prime features of its outlook at the height of its popularity. Though he took up its new freedom of discussion, his conceptual roots seem more deeply planted in the earlier Age of Reason. For he opposed the French Enlightenment's rarefied deism, its predilection for a mechanistic materialism, its denigration of emotive values, its dogmatic belief in inevitable progress, the elitism embodied in its adherence to the values and customs of an aristocratic culture and paternalistic government, its faith in benevolent despotism. Championing the essential goodness and moral worth of the common man, the primacy of freedom and its requisite degrees of equality, man's oneness with nature and the consequent conviction that education should liberate natural potentialities instead of suppressing them, Rousseau set himself on a collision course with the "enlightened" views of his time. Despite his feeling that he had been defeated, his work was soon to serve as a major source of the new romanticism in literature and music, the idealism in philosophy, and the development of democratic theory in political thought that would mold nineteenth- and thereby twentieth-century thinking.

Although he was ostracized by his contemporaries, Rousseau nevertheless received the honor of having a Paris street named after him eight years before his death. Although he condemned the prevalent institution of absolute monarchy, he was offered asylum when he fled from Paris by the two enlightened despots of the time—Frederick the Great of Prussia and Joseph II of Austria—and the Queen of France later paid quiet homage at his grave. He opposed violence and believed that education, not the revolution he anticipated, was the key to the development of free societies

—yet, together with his antagonist Voltaire, he was enshrined in the Pantheon as a prime prophet of the French Revolution.

He was a prolific writer whose fame and contemporary importance derive from his political essays, but he earned his meager living by copying music. Indeed, music and the arts were a continuing interest. He first journeyed to Paris in 1741 in order to advance a new mode of musical notation; its rejection prompted him to write the *Dissertation on Modern Music,* which was published in 1743 and brought him to public attention. After a year in Venice as secretary to the French ambassador, he returned to Paris and became involved with the *Encyclopédie,* the project of his friend Diderot, to which he contributed several articles. At Diderot's urging, he entered an essay contest sponsored by the Academy of Dijon, won the prize, and in 1750 published his first political essay, generally referred to as the First Discourse, the *Discourse on the Sciences and the Arts*—which called their moral value into question. The next five years saw him write an opera, *Les Muses Galantes;* a play, *Narcisse;* and an opera, *Le Devin du Village,* which was produced and published, as well as the *Letter on French Music.* In 1755 he published the Second Discourse, the *Discourse on the Origin and Foundation of Inequality Among Men,* prefaced by a lengthy "Dedication to the Republic of Geneva," his idealized portrait of his native city.

The famous *Encyclopédie* (1755) contained his article "On Political Economy," which was later published separately, and might well be referred to as the Third Discourse. Generally ignored, this article anticipates *Of the Social Contract* in many ways. It demonstrates that it was in response to living issues of his time that he developed his philosophic principles; this earlier article thus illuminates the later essay by showing us the specific kinds of governmental policies he felt his principles called for; by thus providing concrete examples, it helps us to flesh out the later philosophic statement. Almost all of his subsequent works were devoted to social questions, although the continuity of his musical interests is manifested by a musical dictionary published in 1767 —five years after *Of the Social Contract,* which had established him as one of the most influential thinkers of the new age.

In many ways, Rousseau's *Of the Social Contract* marks the great divide between the old order of political and moral thought and the new. More than any other single work, this essay, written in Bourbon France when absolutism was universally respectable, and publishable only in Holland, has served to make popular democracy into the ideology of our time. Unlike many crucial writings which synthesize or focus different developments of thought, Rousseau's work, although reaching back to Plato, is a prophetic beginning. Goethe remarked, in contrasting Rousseau's work to Voltaire's that spoke for the Enlightenment, it is with Rousseau's not "the ancient world that finishes, but a new world that begins."

A fruitful beginning must have roots, and Rousseau drew richly on the political and philosophical heritage. However, our prime concern here is not Rousseau's intellectual genesis but the meaning of the statement he has given us, and so close scrutiny of those influences is not crucial here. For Rousseau's intent in *Of the Social Contract* was not to comment or speculate on the history of political thought or to sum up his own age; it was to initiate a new age, the one that has become ours.

This essay has been controversial from the beginning. Just why it should still be so is a question of academic interpretation, to which we will turn. But its initial reception clearly recognized its revolutionary nature. All shipments of the book from Holland to France were seized upon receipt; banned in France, pirated editions nevertheless promptly surfaced. The Parlement of Paris issued an order that both *Of the Social Contract* and *Emile* were to be burned in the Palais de Justice by the public executioner, and also issued a warrant for Rousseau's arrest. Escaping to Switzerland, he learned that both books had also been condemned and burned in his native Geneva and that a warrant for his arrest had been issued there as well. His biographer tells us why: "the seeds of freedom contained within [the books] were to start a revolution in Geneva. The two books were to stir up fresh quarrels over the question of liberty."[1]

Liberty or freedom is the issue Rousseau raised to the fore. Without qualification or equivocation, he insisted that the only justifiable base for any political state is its open acknowledgment that developing the meaning of freedom must be its prime commitment to the society it governs. Any other foundational principle, he argued, is illegitimate, devoid of any moral justification and thereby of any moral claim on the loyalty of its subjects. But how is freedom possible? What are the operating principles that define the responsive government of a free society? His concern here, in contrast to earlier speculations on historical development, is, as Kelly noted, "not history but logic,"[2] the social logic of freedom. His concern is to demonstrate the possibility of a free society (see SC 56–57, 130, 265) by spelling out the presumptions such a society must incorporate, the fundamental principles by which it must be guided, and the particular limitations of liberty (or freedom) such principles entail. *Of the Social Contract* is designed to elicit those principles of social organization necessary to the functioning of a social order if that social order is to be free, if it is to be constitutionally governed, if it is to secure the greatest possible freedom for its members and promote their destiny as free moral beings.

The key to understanding *Of the Social Contract* is, then, its

1. Jean Guéhenno, *Jean-Jacques Rousseau,* trans. J. and D. Weightman (New York: Columbia University Press, 1966), vol. II, p. 92; see also pp. 80–81.

2. George Armstrong Kelly, *Idealism, Politics and History* (Cambridge: Cambridge University Press, 1969), p. 55.

subtitle, "Principles of Political Right," all too frequently ignored. Although the "social contract" was a popular notion of Rousseau's time, it is the subtitle that points to his distinctive meaning of that term—and to his quest, not for the historic genesis of the state, but for the grounding principles of a free and thereby just or "right" society. As such, the subtitle points to the heart of his debate with other writers—and it is the title by which he himself referred to this essay.[3]

Rousseau's several references to John Locke in *Emile* suggest that both it and *Of the Social Contract* were at least in part prompted by his dissent from Locke's views on the kind of education needed in a free society and on the nature of such a society. Whereas Rousseau saw Locke arguing for the education of "gentlemen," Rousseau had called (in PE 37–39) for universal public education for democratic citizenship. Rousseau saw Locke, in his *Second Treatise of Civil Government*, as having argued for parliamentary, not popular, supremacy, for a social contract that though it might be construed as normative was presented as historical, with a human society little more than an aggregate of the particular individuals who happen to compose it, each of whom is seen as possessing certain inherent rights to "life, liberty, and estate" as essential personal attributes which he brings with him into society for his own protection. If each individual is somehow prior to his own community and his individual rights are regarded as prior to any conception of the common good, then the common good can only be defined as their protection. Any such doctrine seems to suggest a theory of laissez-faire individualism; two immediate and seemingly unanswered problems are, first, just how these inherent rights can then be adjusted in concrete social situations, and second, by what right they can be subordinated to a principle of absolute majority rule. If each individual's spe-

3. See *Emile, or On Education,* trans. Allan Bloom (New York: Basic Books, 1979), p. 85n.

cific rights are prior to the common interest of the society as a whole, it would seem that a just society is extremely limited in pursuing any conception of a common good, its main function being reduced to that of a policeman or guardian of the presumably inviolable rights of its members.

Rousseau may have borrowed the general notion of the "social contract" from Hobbes and Locke, but his radical reformulation of its basic meaning has pervasive implications. Forging the thesis that the interests of the community are always paramount, Rousseau's developed view is an incisive examination of the essentially social nature of man —a view that may be read as if Aristotle's system of governmental classification (cf. SC 182–189) and especially Aristotle's concept of "polity" were lurking in the background of Rousseau's thinking.[4]

Rather than posit any particular event from which to trace the development of human rights and obligations, Rousseau examines the broad expanse of classical history, where the modern concepts of republican government and democratic practice were first developed—but he does this only after first determining the principles to use as the key to his analysis of the human political situation. As he explained: "Before observing, one must make some rules for one's observations. One must construct a standard to which measurements one makes can be related. Our principles of political right are that standard" (E 458).

He then starts with a first principle, and seems to have

4. Paul Ricoeur, an outstanding contemporary French philosopher, has argued for both Rousseau's contemporary importance and his fundamental relationship to Aristotle: "The great, invincible idea of the *Social Contract* is that the body politic is born of a virtual act, of a consent which is not an historical event, but one which only comes out in reflection. . . . Rousseau, at bottom, is Aristotle . . . in voluntarist language. . . . Where Aristotle speaks of 'nature' and 'end,' Rousseau uses 'pact' and 'general will'; but it is fundamentally the same thing; in both cases, the specific nature of polity is reflected in philosophical consciousness." *History and Truth,* trans. C. A. Kelbley (Evanston: Northwestern University Press, 1965), pp. 251–53.

employed a procedure akin to the deductive method developed by seventeenth-century rationalism to determine what subsidiary principles of social organization follow from it. Following the analogy of mathematical reasoning, they had sought no empirical, contingent, or accidental point of departure, but a first principle, or a body of incontrovertible and logically necessary first principles, to serve as a rationally defensible standard by which to be guided in future experience.[5]

The first principle from which Rousseau proceeds is his opening declaration: "Man is born free"—meaning that man's essential nature is that of a being with the capacity for freedom (SC 5).

This principle, which could have been taken from Aristotle, is not an inductive generalization but posits a thesis of essential, thereby defining, potentiality; it is an a priori statement which, as Rousseau implied, could not be disproved by any particular experiences: for if free man, as he went on to say, is "everywhere . . . in chains," the empirical evidence would *seem* to deny the truth of his assertion. In beginning with this seeming paradox, he effectively dismissed the relevance of empirical descriptions of contemporary societies—just because there was no society in his time based on the principle of human freedom. His first principle is a statement not of factual description but of value, a claim to metaphysical truth, a normative standard akin to what Kant would soon call a "regulative idea"—a concept we use as a

5. Indeed, Rousseau's developed doctrine may be seen as bringing together, in social application, the thrust of Descartes's method of geometric reasoning from a first principle (the *cogito ergo sum*), Spinoza's conception of freedom (as self-determination), and the harmonized pluralism of Leibniz's monadological metaphysics (whereby all individuals participate in the life of the whole, which is reflected back into their individual selves). For but one indication of this, see Ernst Cassirer, *The Question of Jean-Jacques Rousseau,* trans. P. Gay (Bloomington: Indiana University Press, 1963), pp. 112–13.

yardstick to evaluate existing social institutions and practices. What Rousseau clearly set out to establish was not a
description of actually prevailing social conditions but a set
of principles by which reason can determine what is right,
what is wrong, what ought to be—what conditions must first
be met if a free society of free citizens is to be developed.
"I seek," he said in an early draft, "right and reason and do
not dispute about the facts."

His instrument—for developing the principle of "Man is
born free" into enabling principles of free society—is the
concept of the social contract, taken *not* as a historical event
but as a body of generally accepted operating principles
logically presupposed in an actually functioning free social
order. Such a "contract" includes the political procedures of
a society, but also the accepted ways in which its citizens
regulate their family lives, education, business affairs, and
private interests. The "social contract" is that body of im-
plicit and explicit agreements concerning its notion of the
common interest and the public good which binds a given
society together into one cohesive whole. Its opposite is the
notion of a "state of nature," again pictured here not so
much as a historical condition but as a useful fiction by which
one may understand what the absence of operative social
agreements would mean. As Rousseau seems to use it, the
social contract is that body of operating rights and obligations by which a society defines its own nature, and the
restraints its members accept as the price for the freedoms
they enjoy because of it.

The traffic light on the corner serves as a useful, if preliminary and simplified, illustration of the way in which these
concepts elucidate Rousseau's concept of a legitimate social
order. It expresses the general agreement that traffic should
be regulated so that both drivers and pedestrians can use the
street with reasonable safety. As each driver stops for the
red light and each pedestrian waits for it, they implicitly
recognize the entire series of social regulations ensuing

from the social agreement, which makes that inherently impotent and arbitrary light a means of regulating the use of the street for the common good. Should a recalcitrant driver ignore the light, his ticketing would accord with the regulations necessary for the use of the street and the principle that the law applies to all. Should many drivers ignore the light, the regulations governing the street become unenforceable: chaos, a miniature "state of nature," ensues and the use of that street by anyone becomes hazardous or impossible. In every use of the street according to the laws governing its use, each driver and pedestrian is participating in the general agreement concerning its use, acknowledging the social contract which sets out the procedures for translating that general agreement into specific rules, giving tacit consent to these rules, limiting his own liberty to drive or walk at will, and taking for granted the resulting positive freedom to use that street as a means of driving or walking in comparative safety.

If we conceive the social contract in the light of this elementary example, then Rousseau's argument becomes fairly straightforward. A contract is essentially a voluntary agreement which specifies certain reciprocal rights, obligations, and modes of resolving disputes. Its purpose is to assure the contracting parties of specific opportunities or freedoms to undertake specific kinds of acts and to spell out the obligations that are to be recognized as their price. It presumes that each contracting party has freely entered into the agreement, and that the contracting parties as a body have freely chosen to seek their mutual advantage or common good together, recognizing their contract as their means by which to do so.

Just as an argument is logically absurd if its conclusion contradicts its premises, so the social contract is illegitimate if it denies its essential presupposition of human freedom. Thus a society predicated on a repressive relationship of master and slave, as opposed to a society of free citizens, has contradicted the principle of a contract and is thereby illegitimate; it may be governed by force but not by right, and its government then has no moral claim on the loyalty of its subjects. Free persons are not merely subjects of their state; they are citizens—members of their society and constituents of it (see SC 46, 273). They can be legitimately bound only by their *own* acts of will: a legitimate social order then rests on the freely given or tacit consent of its citizens that it function as it does. However originated, a legitimate society at any moment of its development thus expresses the general agreement concerning the values or goals incorporated in the notion of the public or common good its members share as a group, and it conducts its affairs according to specified procedures for decision. It is these general evaluative and procedural agreements actually operative in a society that may be described as the contract binding its members together into one social order.

Using this idea of a contract, Rousseau tried to formulate normative principles by which one can discriminate a free or legitimate society from a repressive one. His underlying thesis (SC 55–57) is the proposition that individual freedom is necessarily grounded within the context of a free society, which recognizes the essential freedom of men by opening opportunities for the free development of its citizens. Positing no ideal system of government, he recognized that the specific requirements of different societies can vary greatly (see SC 138, 245ff.), and suggested that different forms of government may be necessary under differing circumstances. Rather than indulge in idle utopianism by painting a picture of one ideal social order for all, he concerned himself with the more serious business of seeking out those operational principles or rules which are the necessary conditions of maximal freedom in *any* society and for *any* form of responsive government. As long as such operational principles of human freedom are embodied in a given social order, it is of secondary importance whether it chooses to function under what we would today term a constitutional monarchy or a republican form, a parliamentary or a presidential system (see SC 307, 312; PE 45).

More important than the particular governmental form, or any specific laws enacted, is that there be a set of procedures by which social decisions are freely discussed and made; any specific law must not only be in accord with the general agreement or "general will" concerning the goals or values of the society; they must also have been adopted by agreed-upon constitutional procedures: only such fundamental constitutive conditions requisite to a society of free citizens can legitimate whatever governmental system is preferred (see SC 104; PE 45). Where such conditions are operative, the general intent of the citizens—that the society function for their common good—is manifested; the common good is then identified with their freedom *as* members of their society. One crucial condition for a free society, then, is that it rest on a *de facto* recognition that sovereignty —the justifiable claim to the right to rule—belongs to the people as one whole, as a corporate body (see SC 46, 67, 80). Working out the meaning of this concept of popular sovereignty—never before in modern times proclaimed so forthrightly—is one major task of this essay. The intent of the essay then, is to discover the functioning principles which are requisite norms of *any* free society: to elicit the functioning contract of a given society is to discover just how it organizes its freedom.

Of the Social Contract does *not* invoke a doctrine of specific innate or inherent rights. The only "inalienable" or universal right which Rousseau seems to define is the right to participate, as a free and politically equal member, in a free social order, which entails the concomitant right to "resign" and emigrate without punishment if one prefers to do so (see SC 80, 314, 327; E 455).[6] The implicitly developed

---

6. See Plato's *Crito,* 50–54, for the source from which Rousseau appears to have derived this principle.

thesis is that there is no list of specific rights which a society should *always* guarantee its members regardless of the needs of the society at the time; specific rights are contingent and are dependent on the general agreement concerning the fundamental values or goods in terms of which the society defines its working notion of the common interest; the needs of the society-as-one-whole are always paramount and may, in varying circumstances, justify particular limitations of individual liberties (see SC 60, 82, 87) (provided they are accordant with general societal will or intent—see below).

All specific rights, Rousseau argued, are social rights. They arise only within the contemporary context of civil society; they pertain to human relations within it and always entail social obligations. The first priority is always the common good, as the society freely conceives its common good, which *is* the *raison d'être* of the society itself. Individual rights are those individual claims or opportunities which the society deems useful to protect for the sake of the common good, and then is bound to protect for *each* citizen. But specific claims on the protection of the social whole which may be useful at one stage of development may be detrimental to the common good at another stage (see SC 137). And the society as such cannot legitimately claim from its citizens obligations which it does not deem necessary to its common good (see SC 79–88).

A sparsely populated agricultural society may indeed prefer a minimal government whose prime function is the protection of "life, liberty, and estate" (as Locke suggested). But today we see that a more complex industrialized society requires more positive government and certain degrees of community interference with the particular claims of individuals to use their liberty and property wholly as they see fit. The need for pollution controls in contemporary America and Europe, the miseries that attended the Industrial Revolution in nineteenth-century England, attest to the need for the community to restrict the functioning liberty of some in order to assure the greater freedom of all.

One problem with reading Rousseau is his preoccupation (like Aristotle) with the dying city-state—with a preindustrial economy prior to today's mass society. Many of his strictures—such as citizens knowing each other—make no contemporary sense. To see why he has something to say to modern societies (which he would not have recognized in either their political form of nation-states or economic form as industrialized complexes) requires an imaginative extension of thought. Yet, like Aristotle, his principles were worked out "in the small," and their extension to "the large" is a matter of history. By taking his broader principles we can see many of them operative today. For example, any modern free society regards itself as having the right (if not always the prudential wisdom) to interfere with the property rights of its citizens (by taxation, eminent domain, health and fire regulations, zoning rules for neighborhoods, and, only recently, by pollution and environmental controls); with their right to negotiate their own working conditions (by minimum wage and maximum hour laws, collective bargaining, social security, and unemployment insurance requirements); with their freedom of speech (by laws concerning libel, slander, incitement to riot or treason, and endangering the public safety); and with their personal lives (by laws concerning marriage, divorce, abortion, compulsory education, and military service). By common consent, such community interferences into the supposedly inherent liberties of individual citizens are necessary for the common good and the concrete freedoms the society enables all citizens to enjoy.

In seeking the need for flexible standards of specific individual liberties, freedoms, or rightful claims and obligations in terms of the social context of his time, Rousseau effectively anticipated and set the philosophic ground for the rise of the positive state which the complex economic and social conditions engendered by the Industrial Revolution were to make necessary. As Einaudi has noted:

To have anticipated the crisis of the Industrial Revolution before that revolution occurred, and on the basis alone of a speculative image of the nature of man to have offered a criticism of the premises of utilitarian individualism [before Bentham and Mill developed them]—these are two of Rousseau's greatest achievements and a main reason why we read him today.[7]

Rousseau's insight is that if man's essential capacity for freedom is to be made concrete and socially real for each individual, his freedoms and obligations must be defined in specific ways within the context of a specific social order—and in the terms by which his society defines its conception of its common good—which is, in the final analysis, the good of *each* citizen *in his capacity as a social participant*. To be concretely meaningful, those justifiable claims or rights, those opportunities a society secures for its members, must be specified in the conviction that their permissible exercise contributes to the good of the society-as-one-whole.

This common good is the *intent* of the society-as-one-whole; it is defined by the general agreement that binds the society together. Rousseau's term for this intent was "the general will." It is the *operating* consensus, the implicitly presumed working notion of the common good, the unifying social values of the society as a collective or unified entity, in which all citizens participate—not as a mere aggregate of individual wills but as members of one body. A citizen participates in forming that general will, first, by recognizing that his own individual good and the individual goods of fellow citizens depend upon the good of the community as such; and then by asking for himself as a citizen-member only what he asks for all fellow citizens (see SC 85).

Just how the general will can be known has long been a matter of contention—ever since Rousseau himself raised the question (see PE 19, 23). Much of the discussion, how-

7. Mario Einaudi, *The Early Rousseau* (Ithaca: Cornell University Press, 1967), p. 150.

ever, loses its mystery and awesomeness when we translate
the question into more contemporary terms by asking how
we determine, not the general will, but the operating value
consensus of a given group or society. For indeed any group
or society is united by some sort of fundamental concerns,
by an active consensus regarding the social values to be
sought in public activities, basic conceptions of the public
good, and commitments to operational procedures by which
to resolve specific differences and debates concerning public
policy. For example, we hold elections and select our officials by the principle of plurality or majority vote (see SC
328, 331); no matter how bitterly contested the election
campaign may be, the general consensus is that the person
receiving the largest vote is acknowledged, even by his
opponents, as rightfully occupying the office that was contested. It would then seem fair to say that the general will
is that contested elections be resolved by majority or plurality vote.

But then, even if a majority, the voice of the majority is
not necessarily the voice of the whole (SC 76). In the 1920s,
for example, the United States enacted legislation to prohibit the sale of alcoholic beverages. By virtue of the constitutional amendment and subsequent ensuing statutes, there
can be no doubt that this was the voice of the majority. But
it was *not* the general agreement, the consensus, the general
will of the whole. The active refusal of a sizable minority to
acquiesce in what it apparently regarded as illegitimate legislation brought the Prohibition "experiment" to failure.[8]

8. Comparison of the different fates accorded to the Sixteenth and
Eighteenth amendments to the American Constitution is instructive.
The Sixteenth authorized Congress to levy an income tax; the Eighteenth established Prohibition and authorized Congress and the states
to enact enforcement statutes. Notably, neither was a change of the
constitutional structure; each but added a new authorization to governmental power. In contrast to the Prohibition "experiment," the principle of the income tax—incidentally, akin to Rousseau's proposal for
"proportionate" taxation (see PE 64)—has been accepted, despite con-

Indeed, the general will is *not* to be equated with a popular vote; as Rousseau has stated, the result of "the public decision will be one thing and the general will another" (PE 16—but cf. SC 330!). If the general will is not identical with a public vote, it is certainly not to be confused with rule by mere majority or rule in the name of the majority; it is not a preface, as some have maintained, to justification of the tyranny of the majority or tyranny in the name of the majority. One test of the general will is, even if reluctant, common consent despite particular disagreements; a specific law not generally regarded as accordant with the unifying values of the society is illegitimate and is thereby unenforceable or requires widespread repression for its enforcement. No matter how strongly a majority may feel on a given issue, those who disagree are also legally equal members of the society, and respect for their views is essential to the health and legitimacy of the society-as-one-whole.

Rousseau's then-radical insistence on the doctrine of popular sovereignty by means of the doctrine of the general will is a way of resurrecting Aristotle's thesis (embedded in his notion of polity) that true popular rule means that the people-as-a-whole, and not merely their preponderant or most vociferous members, must be taken into account; that a "true" or legitimate form of government is rule *for* the common good of the society-as-one-whole and not merely for the particular number (even if a majority) who succeed in sharing power.

Those who oppose what is widely deemed good or progressive at the moment, as well as those who favor it, are also members of the society; their voices, too, must be heard, protected, and respected. They, too, participate in forming the common agreement or active value-consensus of the society, the general will of the whole.

For the necessary concomitant of a free society is the

---

tinuing debates about taxation *rates,* as fully accordant with the general will of the American people and thereby as legitimate.

general civic equality of all citizens (SC 135–37); this means the civic equality of *each*. Whatever rights and freedoms a society may accord to its citizens, any citizen may justifiably claim them for himself providing only that he does not seek to deny them to others. As a member of the society, each citizen deserves the same respect from the whole:

> . . . is the safety of a citizen no less the common cause than is the safety of the whole state? . . . if one understands . . . that the government should be permitted to sacrifice an innocent man for the safety of the multitude, I hold this maxim to be one of the most execrable that tyranny ever invented, the most spurious that could be advanced, the most dangerous one can allow, and the most directly opposed to the fundamental laws of society. (PE 32)

Any individual citizen is, in principle, a test case of the validity of constitutional and statutory legislation. Laws must dispense equal justice to all, and it is from this universality of law that justice and freedom ensue. So a key to the embodiment of the general will is the administration of equal justice in a society of free men. In sharpest contrast to utilitarian doctrine, it is not the "greatest happiness of the greatest number" (which conceivably could justify exploitation of a minority) but the good of *each* individual citizen that becomes the legitimate test case. (Hence the import of individual extenuating circumstances which most statutes authorize being taken into account.) If each citizen, as such, participates in forming the general will for the common good, then each citizen should be enabled to participate in the common good itself.

Yet we find the notion of the general will to be a focus of attack. To a large extent, such attacks stem from the third chapter of Book Two, entitled "Whether the General Will Can Err." There Rousseau tells us that the general will "always tends toward the public utility" and that "the general will is always upright" (SC 75; see 83, 141; PE 12). Yet too many translations have rendered this to read "the general will is always right" and too many commentators—forgetting that the French *droite* means "right" in the sense of upright, rightful, righteous, lawful, or legitimate, and *not* in the sense of "correct"—have charged Rousseau with claiming that it is infallibly correct (see PE 16)! But what Rousseau seems to be saying is that the general will, by setting out the value commitments of a society, defines the operative concept of justice for that society and the legitimacy of any particular claims within it. By such misreading, some commentators then suggest that modern totalitarianism—but see SC 254, 257, 258, 309; PE 32—can be traced to this "glorification" of the general will: for totalitarian governments in our own day have claimed to speak in the name of "the whole people" and dictators have claimed that their repressive governments are for the good of their societies. One might extract quotations from qualifying context to buttress such interpretation (see, e.g., SC 108), but doing so clearly violates Rousseau's clearly stated intent and meaning. For Rousseau was quite clear that the rightful power of sovereignty must be limited, that it is bound by the limits of "public utility" (SC 80–82, 439), that beyond the concerns appropriate to the community as such, "each individual, as a subject, has a personal and independent existence" (E 463) and, in a real sense, his citizenship itself is but a means to the realization of his own "personal and independent" concerns.

Perhaps most crucial is the last point: the general will is *not* to be equated with a majority vote. For the passions of the moment can often detract people from their true intent (see SC 75 and 401 comment). And rule by mere majority, without let or hindrance, often degenerates into tyranny (as in a lynch mob) when the equal claims to social freedom on the part of those in disfavor or dissent are overlooked or deliberately flouted (see SC 256). If it is legitimate to see the principle of the general will as embodying the thesis that *each* citizen has equal claims on the intent of the whole, then any repressive dictatorship, even if it claims to rule in the name of the majority, is foreclosed as illegitimate (SC 80–82).

The first principle stated in *Of the Social Contract* is that *every* man is essentially a free being, that the justification of a society is the enhancement of the concrete freedoms of its citizens. To this end, Rousseau insisted on *civic* equality (which is presupposed in the right to vote) as a necessary condition. The equality that is necessary to freedom is equality *in* freedom; it is not the equality of being enslaved—whether by an autocrat, a political party, or a dictatorship of one class or group of the whole society.

Just because of the import Rousseau places on civic equality, it is crucial to note that it is *as a means* requisite to freedom and not as a self-justifiable goal. "The first of all goods," he declared, is nothing other than "freedom" (E 84). Without it we would not be "able to live" (PE 36). And of the kind of equality that is requisite to freedom, he tells us, "it is necessary not to understand by this word that every degree of power and of wealth should be absolutely the same" (SC 136). Warning against a society divided between the very rich and the very poor, he urged, as Aristotle had done before him, that the health of a free society depends on a predominance of moderate or middle-class status (SC 136n.). For the "right of ownership . . . [is] the true foundation of political society" (PE 77) and "is the most sacred of all the rights of citizens" (PE 42). Absolute equality would foreclose the freedom to acquire and to use property, and property itself is a means of exercising and defending freedom. But specific rights to the acquisition and use of property, as any other rights, are social rights, which give the citizen a vested interest in his society; they are within society, not against it, and are conditioned by the general will of the society itself, which confers such rights together with the conditions for their exercise (see SC 40, 63, 65, 136; PE 42, 58, 73, 76, 77; E 461).

Thus arguing against what in the nineteenth century was known as Social Darwinism—"let the fittest survive and the rest perish"—Rousseau is, indeed, a progenitor of the theory of the positive state; for he urged that the state, as the agency of the community, must undertake those tasks for the common good which the community believes it requires. He suggested (perhaps seeking to democratize the mercantilism of his time) that the state should intervene in the economy in order to forestall and correct gross inequities (SC 136–37; PE 35). He was one of the first to argue that the general will requires concern for the economic subsistence of its citizens (PE 35, 41–2), and that public education, which interferes with family prerogatives, is "one of the fundamental maxims of popular or legitimate government" (PE 37). But the operating principle of such positive action must be, at all times, the needs of the common good, as delineated in the positive freedoms to be enjoyed by the individual citizens. In doing this, Rousseau saw beyond his time; for it is largely out of his conception of the nature of civil society that thinkers such as Immanuel Kant in the late eighteenth century, T. H. Green in the nineteenth, and John Dewey in the twentieth developed the modern conception of a free society that seeks to avoid undue paternalism while exercising an active concern for the welfare of its citizens.

The theoretical justification of the positive state is the organic conception of society (see SC 163, 249), which also finds its modern philosophic roots in Rousseau's essay (although it has received somewhat divergent development by Kant, Burke, and Hegel). Rousseau, possibly inspired by musical concepts (and perhaps by Leibniz's metaphysics of functioning harmony), did see society in organic or harmonic terms. Each man, as Aristotle had insisted long ago, is a citizen before he is truly a man; a man is essentially a social being who finds his own self only in the context of a social order. However alienated he may conceivably find himself, he reflects the language, thought patterns, and values of his society. Like a note in a melody, he finds his own meaning (even if negatively) in his relations to the whole. And society, like a melody, is nothing without the individual elements that constitute it. A society presupposes not only the diversity of its members, in their division of labor, divergent outlooks, and uses of their privacies, but also their basic functioning harmony, which unifies their differences into one coherent, interrelated, meaningful whole.

Our freedoms, Rousseau insisted, are always social freedoms and are within society, not external to it. The organic theory of the state recognizes that a society is, in a sense, an individual, a corporate person with a will and a history of its own. But a society's corporate existence is inseparable from that of the community of citizens who compose it. Each citizen derives meaning from, and frames his life in terms of, the ways in which he participates in aspects of his society —his family life, his education, his job, his church, his club memberships. He finds meaning in the contributions he makes to these subsocieties (most of which are not political in nature) and thereby to the social whole which protects them and gives them meaning (see SC 78; PE 15). But his contributions to his society are inseparable from the contributions the society makes to him. The relationship is reciprocal. As Rousseau saw it, the organically interrelated society is not then an external master; it is that to which the citizen belongs as an inherent element, and the society itself is inseparable from his own functioning being. No matter how tightly knit a society may be, the individual citizen is an individual who finds his own individuality in the specific freedoms he enjoys by virtue of his societal membership. One test, then, of a society's fidelity to its harmonic or organic nature is its avoidance of a master-slave totalitarianism and its encouragement, within its unifying framework, of the diverse individualities of its members (SC 80).

In this sense, Rousseau's essential thrust for the modern age can be understood as propounding a theory of society, of requisite organizing principles, not of specific governmental forms. One task emerging from his essay is to face the issue of just how the individuality he so highly prized is to be protected by the political apparatus. That Rousseau did not work this out in any modern sense is indisputable. He might, however, perhaps have responded that although the protection of the individual is a necessary principle, the precise way in which this is to be accomplished in a modern society is dependent on its general will and the forms of governmental organization it chooses to accept. But is this adequate? The formula of merely generalizing individual obligations, in the alienation of each to the social whole, is not wholly reassuring. If one judges Rousseau's essential orientation to be fundamentally correct, one ensuing obligation is to rethink, in view of it, ways in which the individuality that is essential to a healthy society can be socially protected while at the same time protecting the priority of the community interest.[9]

And yet many of us feel uncomfortable with the concept

9. Ironically, perhaps, the British experience is a case in point. For British thought (with Green and Bosanquet as noted exceptions) has not generally been sympathetic to Rousseau's concept of the general will and his nonhistorical understanding of the social contract—which includes the thesis that what is protected by custom need not necessarily be protected by law. The British tradition of individual liberty (coupled with a majority principle of parliamentary rule and without any written constitution or bill of rights) has, in a real sense, depended more on its functioning social contract and the continuity of its general will as embedded in its tradition than the more explicitly democratic American and French traditions, which have, in contrast, always insisted on a political contract in the form of a written constitution.

of the general will. Perhaps one reason is that our present age has made quantification so synonymous with knowledge that we are not at ease with a reality that cannot be measured. And Rousseau himself is fairly ambiguous on *how* it may be known: if by majority, as he seems to suggest in SC 329, then we may ask how to distinguish this from the "will of all," and why should we assume that the majority necessarily reads the general will correctly? If the general will is to be momentary, without any strong commitments for the future (as suggested in SC 68, but cf. need for "foresight" in SC 105), how could any society plan ahead? And if we take both together with the observation that "public decisions are [not] always equitable" (PE 16; see SC 75), then doesn't the conscientious citizen, other statements to the contrary, have a moral obligation to his society to voice a loud dissent? And yet without some operational notion of a general will, as a "consensus," as "determining the public interest," how could we as citizens, how could our chosen officials, responsively act in divergence from the latest opinion poll? If there is no feel for "the deliberate sense of the community," as Hamilton put it (see 401–08, comment, n. 8), how could it be justly governed? For we do distinguish proper action from votes and voices and we do applaud the courage of statesmen who do not bend to every cry of passionate opinion (see SC 75, 401; PE 32).

One vulnerable aspect of the concept of the general will is the claim that it is authoritative in providing the concept of right or justice for the society. This would seem to be true in fact and can only be challenged perhaps as a proper norm. But what is the viable alternative? If we reject a doctrine of absolutely specific and unexceptionable rights, if we do not believe that a given right must *always* be maintained no matter what the circumstances, then what standard is available? What legitimate source is there for the values and norms of a free society other than that of the people itself? Doesn't any other source involve some kind of paternalistic dictatorship? If all specific rights, to be feasible, must be relative to the current condition of the society, what other source is there except *freely* expressed popular consent (SC 312–14)? If not, what alternative does the critic propose?

There usually are different and conflicting judgments about particular courses of action; these can be resolved by the political procedures a free society has adopted. But the justification in public debate of proposed alternative programs is, within a free society, the value structure of the common good as that society seems to conceive its common good; it is this common conception that frames the policy debates that occur and the public alternatives available.

If a citizen has a moral responsibility for his society, then the general values of his society must be in accord with his will. For we can be morally responsible only for those obligations we have in effect accepted for ourselves (SC 57). But then the presupposition of the authority of the general will is that it is freely formed and expressed in a free society —that public opinion can be debated in the process of resolving disputes, that protection of dissent is requisite for free discussion and free voting (SC 321); that, in short, the citizenry should be freely consulted and that those charged with administrative responsibility of governing should be truly responsive (SC 313, PE 19, 59). The thesis that the general will is authoritative and sovereign is, then, but a restatement of the thesis of popular sovereignty: the only legitimate society is a free society under republican government (see SC 104)—and it thereby carries with it all the open problems any free society must face. (See SC 54, 76 & 329.)

If the political institutions of a society are the prime tools for resolving differences of opinion, protecting the health of the whole, and advancing the common interest—which is, ultimately, the interest of each—then each citizen, by virtue of his citizenship, has a moral responsibility to participate responsibly in those institutions, and to examine how particular political institutions actually do function (in more modern terms than Rousseau could have done in Books Three and Four). Precisely because political institutions epitomize the society (SC 163), they provide a peaceful procedure for reconciling disputes and subloyalties within the society. Political institutions then become the instrument through which the direction of democratic development is democratically determined. As the governing agency of the society (SC 152), government is the one instrument by means of which a society-as-one-whole can determine its own future.

In order to ensure that that future will be developed in accord with the basic values, aspirations, and intentions of the citizenry, the ways the society functions need to be continually examined as to whether operating principles requisite for its development are being maintained. The fundamental constitutional conditions necessarily presupposed in a free society are the Principles of Political Right. Their proper functioning is the prime demand of the general will of a free citizenry. Any proposed reforms, the determination of the need for reform, the specific kinds of reforms needed, can only be evaluated by examining the operative procedural and value agreements we see embodied in the metaphor of a social contract that expresses itself dynamically in the continuing re-formation of the society's general will.

Basic to any such consideration is the point that the ultimate justification of any particular social order is a moral one. For citizenry is requisite for virtue as virtue is for freedom (PE 36). And morality itself arises out of moral conscience, which is the concomitant of, and is founded in, civil society (SC 55–57). Morality and moral obligation are possible only on the thesis that man is a free being. Man's freedom is inherently social and the proper function of a society is the enhancement of the moral freedom of its members.

Given considerations such as these, we still need to re-think what Rousseau has suggested to us in terms of complex political institutions, huge societies, mass communication, and degrees of interdependency engendered by technological developments—none of which he was able to foresee. Our political leaders, to be truly ours, must be called to periodic account for their reading of the general will; yet how shall we ask that they do this, aside from public opinion polls; and how shall we then seek to defend levels of statesmanship which are usually discerned as placing the long-run interests of a society ahead of its momentary passions? If, as Rousseau has recognized, "public decisions are [not] always equitable" (PE 16), how shall we respond to such erroneous decisions without destroying that social continuity upon which any ameliorations or improvements depend? Rousseau lived in an age when the modern nation-state was only beginning to emerge, and he seemed to think that a passionate patriotism was needed as the expression of a community's self-consciousness; yet in our times we have seen some nationalistic passions run rampant: how then shall we cultivate a healthy love of country, which is requisite to that dedication underlying all possible improvements, without permitting it to flow over into that excess which destroys the liberties of its own citizens as well as of those others upon whom they inflict themselves?

These are but some of the questions which should occur to the thoughtful reader as he seeks to bring whatever merit may be seen in Rousseau's suggestions into a contemporary context of concern. However each may develop answers, answers need to be developed. But however developed, it would seem that, within any free society, what universalizes the mutual moral obligations of citizens into a coherent social order is precisely what Rousseau called "principles of political right." It would seem that the only legitimate society is a free society and that freedom demands a sense of responsibility for the good of the whole within which each may find the good for himself. A society cannot legislate individual morality precisely because morality is individual, freely self-imposed obligation. But, as Kant and Green would point out later, the moral responsibility of a society is not to impose a morality but to "hinder the hindrances" to individual moral development, to maintain those operating conditions requisite for meaningful freedoms, requisite for the opportunity for each citizen to develop his own self as a cooperative task of fellow citizenship. This basic function of a free society is the development of a continuing and deepening realization of the dignity of man. As Rousseau insisted, this can be done only among "free peoples" (SC 121; PE 33).

OF THE
SOCIAL CONTRACT
or
Principles of Political Right

Prefatory Note

[1]*This little treatise is extracted from a more extensive work undertaken at an earlier time without consideration of my capacity, and long since abandoned. Of the various fragments that might be selected from what was accomplished, the following is the most considerable, and appears to me the least unworthy of being offered to the public. The rest no longer exists.

BOOK ONE

[2]* I want to inquire whether, taking men as they are and laws as they can be, it is possible to have some legitimate and certain rule of administration in civil affairs. In this investigation I shall always strive to ally what right permits with what interest prescribes, so that justice and utility may not be divided.

[3] I enter upon this inquiry without proving the importance of my subject. I shall be asked whether I am a prince or a legislator that I write on Politics. I reply that I am not, and that it is for this reason that I write on Politics. If I were a prince or a legislator, I should not waste my time in saying what ought to be done; I should do it or remain silent.

*Asterisks (*) follow the numbers of all paragraphs for which explanatory comments are to be found, with regard to either the paragraphs themselves or passages within them; these comments will be found in the Notes, beginning on p.183.

[4] Having been born a citizen of a free State, and a member of the sovereign, however feeble an influence my voice may have in public affairs, the right to vote upon them is sufficient to impose on me the duty of informing myself about them. I feel happy, whenever I meditate on governments, always to find in my researches new reasons for loving that of my own country!

I. Subject of This First Book

[5]* Man is born free, and everywhere he is in chains. One believes himself the master of others, and yet he is a greater slave than they. How has this change come about? I do not know. What can render it legitimate? I believe that I can settle this question.

[6]* If I considered only force and the results that proceed from it, I should say that so long as a People is compelled to obey and does obey, it does well; but that, so soon as it can shake off the yoke and does shake it off, it does better; for, recovering its liberty by the same right by which it was taken away, either it is justified in resuming it, or there was no justification for depriving them of it. But the social order is a sacred right which serves as a basis for all others. Yet this right does not come from nature; it is therefore based on conventions. The question is to know what these conventions are. Before coming to that, I must establish what I have just laid down.

II. Of the First Societies

[7]* The most ancient of all societies, and the only natural one, is the family. Nevertheless children remain bound to their father only as long as they have need of him for their own preservation. As soon as this need ceases, the natural bond is dissolved. The children freed from the obedience which they owe to their father, and the father from the cares

which he owes to his children, become equally independent. If they remain united, it is no longer naturally but voluntarily, and the family itself is kept together only by convention.

[8] This common liberty is a consequence of man's nature. His first law is to attend to his own preservation, his first cares are those which he owes to himself, and as soon as he comes to years of discretion, being sole judge of the means adapted for his own preservation, he becomes thereby his own master.

[9] The family is, then, if you will, the primitive model of political societies; the chief is the image of the father, while the people are the image of the children; and all, being born free and equal, only alienate their liberty for their own advantage. The whole difference is that, in the family, the father's love for his children repays him for the care that he bestows upon them; while, in the State, the pleasure of commanding makes up for the chief's lack of love for his people.

[10] Grotius denies that all human authority is established for the benefit of the governed! He cites slavery as an example. His most invariable mode of reasoning is to establish right by fact.[1] A more rational method could be employed, but none more favorable to Tyrants.

[11] It is then doubtful, according to Grotius, whether the human race belongs to a hundred men, or whether these hundred men belong to the human race; and he appears throughout his book to incline to the former opinion, which is also that of Hobbes. In this way we have mankind divided like herds of cattle, each of which has a master, who looks after it in order to devour it.

[12] Just as a herdsman is of a superior nature to his

1. "Learned researches in public law are often nothing but the history of ancient abuses; and to devote much labor to studying them is misguided pertinacity" (*Treatise on the Interests of France in Relation to Her Neighbors*, by M.L.M.d'A.). That is exactly what Grotius did.

herd, so chiefs, who are the herdsmen of man, are also of a superior nature to their people. Thus, according to Philo's account, the Emperor Caligula reasoned, inferring well enough from this analogy that kings are gods, or that men are brutes.

[13]* The reasoning of Caligula is tantamount to that of Hobbes and Grotius. Aristotle, before them all, had likewise said that men are not naturally equal, but that some are born for slavery and others for domination.

[14] Aristotle was right, but he mistook the effect for the cause. Every man born in slavery is born for slavery; nothing is more certain. Slaves lose everything in their chains, even the desire to escape from them; they love their servitude as the companions of Ulysses loved their brutishness.[2] If, then, there are slaves by nature, it is because there have been slaves contrary to nature. Force made the first slaves; their cowardice perpetuated them.

[15] I have said nothing about King Adam nor about Emperor Noah, the father of three great Monarchs who shared the universe, like the children of Saturn with whom they are supposed to be identical. I hope that my moderation will give satisfaction; for, as I am a direct descendant of one of these Princes, and perhaps of the eldest branch, how do I know whether, by examination of titles, I might not find myself the legitimate king of the human race? Be that as it may, one cannot deny that Adam was Sovereign of the world, as Robinson was of his island, so long as he was its sole inhabitant; and it was a convenient feature of that empire that the monarch, secure on his throne, had nothing to fear from rebellions, or wars, or conspirators.

2. See a small treatise by Plutarch, entitled *That Brutes Employ Reason*.

III. Of the Right of the Strongest

[16]* The strongest man is never strong enough to be always master, unless he transforms his force into right, and obedience into duty. Hence the right of the strongest—a right assumed ironically in appearance, and really established in principle. But will this word never be explained to us? Force is a physical power; I do not see what morality can result from its effects. To yield to force is an act of necessity, not of will; it is at most an act of prudence. In what sense could it be a duty?

[17] Let us suppose for a moment this pretended right. I say that nothing results from it but an inexplicable muddle. For as soon as force constitutes right, the effect changes with the cause; every force which overcomes the first succeeds to its right (privilege). As soon as one can disobey with impunity, he may do so legitimately; and since the strongest is always in the right, it remains merely to act in such a way that one may be the strongest. But what sort of a right perishes when force ceases? If it is necessary to obey by compulsion, there is no need to obey by duty; and if men are no longer forced to obey, obligation is at an end. Obviously, then, this word "right" adds nothing to force; it means nothing here at all.

[18] Obey the powers that be. If that means yield to force, the precept is good but superfluous; I warrant that it will never be violated. All power comes from God, I admit; but every disease does also. Does it follow that we are prohibited from calling in a physician? If a brigand should surprise me in the recesses of a wood: not only am I bound to give up my purse when forced, but am I also in conscience bound to do so when I might conceal it? For after all, the pistol which he holds is also a power.

[19]* Let us agree, then, that might does not make right, and that we are obligated to obey only legitimate powers. Thus my original question ever recurs.

IV. Of Slavery

[20]* Since no man has a natural authority over his fellow men, and since force is not the source of right, conventions remain as the basis of all legitimate authority among men.

[21] If an individual, says Grotius, can alienate his liberty and become the slave of a master, why should a whole people not be able to alienate theirs, and subject themselves to a king? In this there are a good many equivocal words that require explanation; but let us confine ourselves to the word *alienate*. To alienate is to give or sell. Now a man who becomes another's slave does not give himself; he sells himself at the very least for his subsistence; but why does a people sell itself? Far from a king supplying to his subjects their subsistence, he draws his from them; and according to Rabelais, a king does not live on little. Do subjects, then, give up their persons on condition that their goods also shall be taken? I do not see what is left for them to keep.

[22]* It will be said that the despot secures to his subjects civil peace. Just so; but what do they gain by that, if the wars which his ambition brings upon them, together with his insatiable greed and the vexations of his administration, dishearten them more than their own dissensions would? What do they gain if this peace itself is one of their miseries? One lives peacefully also in dungeons; is this enough to find them good? The Greeks confined in the cave of the Cyclops lived peacefully until their turn came to be devoured.

[23] To say that a man gives himself for nothing is to say something absurd and inconceivable; such an act is illegitimate and worthless, for the simple reason that he who performs it is not in his right mind. To say the same thing of a whole people is to suppose a people of madmen; and madness does not make right.

[24] Even if each person could alienate himself, he could not alienate his children; they are born men and free; their liberty belongs to them, and no one has a right to dispose

of it except themselves. Before they have come to an age of discretion, the father can, in their name, stipulate conditions for their preservation and welfare, but not surrender them irrevocably and unconditionally; for such a bequest is contrary to the ends of nature, and exceeds the rights of paternity. It would be necessary, therefore, to ensure that an arbitrary government might be legitimate, that with each generation the people have the option of accepting it or rejecting it; but in that case this government would no longer be arbitrary.

[25]* To renounce one's liberty is to renounce one's quality as a man, the rights of humanity and even its duties. For whoever renounces everything there is no possible compensation. Such renunciation is incompatible with man's nature; and to deprive his actions of all morality is tantamount to depriving his will of all freedom. Finally, a convention which stipulates absolute authority on the one side and unlimited obedience on the other is vain and contradictory. Is it not clear that one is under no obligations whatsoever toward a man from whom one has a right to demand everything? And does not this single condition, without equivalent, without exchange, entail the nullity of the act? For what right would my slave have against me, since all that he has belongs to me? His right being mine, this right of me against myself is a meaningless phrase.

[26]* Grotius and others derive from war another origin for the pretended right of slavery. The victor having, according to them, the right of slaying the vanquished, the latter may purchase his life at the cost of his freedom; a convention so much the more legitimate that it turns to the profit of both.

[27] But it is clear that this pretended right of slaying the vanquished in no way results from the state of war. Men are not naturally enemies, if only for the reason that, living in their primitive independence, they have no mutual relations sufficiently durable to constitute a state of peace or a state

of war. It is the relation of things and not of men which
constitutes war; and the state of war cannot arise from simple personal relations, but only from real relations; private
war—war between man and man—cannot exist either in the
state of nature, where there is no settled ownership, or in
the social state, where everything is under the authority of
the laws.

[28] Private combats, duels, and encounters are acts
which do not at all constitute a state; and with respect to the
private wars authorized by the Establishments of Louis IX,
king of France, and suspended by the Peace of God, they
were abuses of the feudal government, an absurd system if
ever there was one, contrary both to the principles of natural
right and to all good polity.

[29]* War, then, is not a relation between man and man,
but a relation between State and State, in which individuals
are enemies only by accident, not as men, nor even as citizens,[3] but as soldiers; not as members of the fatherland, but
as its defenders. In short, each State can have as enemies
only other States and not individual men, inasmuch as it is
impossible to fix any true relation between things of different natures.

[30] This principle is also conformable to the established

3. The Romans, who understood and respected the rights of war
better than any nation in the world, carried their scruples so far in this
respect that no citizen was allowed to serve as a volunteer without
enlisting expressly against the enemy, and by name against a specific
enemy. A legion in which Cato the Younger made his first campaign
under Popilius having been re-formed, Cato the Elder wrote to
Popilius that, if he consented to his son's continuing to serve under
him, it was necessary that he take a new military oath, because, the first
being annulled, he could no longer bear arms against the enemy. And
Cato also wrote to his son to abstain from appearing in battle until he
had taken this new oath. I know that it will be possible to urge against
me the siege of Clusium and other particular cases; but I cite laws and
customs. No nation has transgressed its laws less frequently than the
Romans, and no nation has had laws so admirable.

maxims of all ages and to the constant practice of all civilized peoples. Declarations of war are not so much warnings to the powers as to their subjects. The foreigner, whether king, or private person, or people, who robs, slays, or detains subjects without declaring war against the prince, is not an enemy, but a brigand. Even in open war, a just prince, while he rightly takes possession of all that belongs to the public in an enemy country, respects the person and property of individuals; he respects the rights on which his own are founded. The aim of war being the destruction of the enemy State, we have a right to slay its defenders so long as they bear arms; but as soon as they lay them down and surrender, ceasing to be enemies or instruments of the enemy, they become again simply men, and one has no further right over their lives. Sometimes it is possible to destroy the State without killing a single one of its members. But war confers no right except what is necessary to its end. These principles are not those of Grotius; they are not based on the authority of poets, but are derived from the nature of things, and are founded on reason.

[31] With regard to the right of conquest, it has no other foundation than the law of the strongest. If war does not confer on the victor the right of slaying vanquished peoples, this right, which he does not possess, cannot be the foundation of a right to enslave them. One has a right to slay an enemy only when it is impossible to enslave him; the right to enslave him is not derived from the right to kill him. It is, therefore, an iniquitous exchange to make him purchase his life, over which the victor has no right, at the cost of his liberty. In establishing the right of life and death upon the right of slavery, and the right of slavery upon the right of life and death—is it not clear that one falls into a vicious circle?

[32]* Even if we suppose this terrible right of killing everybody, I say that a slave made in war, or a conquered people, is under no obligation at all to a master, except to

obey him so far as compelled. In taking an equivalent for his life the victor has conferred no favor on him: instead of killing him unprofitably, the victor has destroyed him for his own advantage. Far, then, from having acquired over him any authority linked to that of force, the state of war subsists between them as before, their relation even is the effect of it; and the exercise of the right of war does not presuppose any treaty of peace. They have made a convention. Be it so; but this convention, far from terminating the state of war, presupposes its continuance.

[33] Thus, in whatever way we view things, the right of slavery is null, not only because it is illegitimate, but because it is absurd and meaningless. These words, *slavery* and *right,* are contradictory; they are mutually exclusive. Whether addressed by a man to a man, or by a man to a people, such a speech as this will always be equally foolish: *I make a convention with you wholly at your expense and wholly for my profit, which I shall observe as long as I please and which you also shall observe as long as I please.*

V. That It Is Always Necessary to Go Back to a First Convention

[34]* Even if I were in accord with all that I have so far refuted, those who favor despotism would be no farther advanced. There will always be a great difference between subduing a multitude and ruling a society. If scattered men, however numerous they may be, are subjected successively to a single person, this seems to me only a case of master and slaves, not of a people and its chief: they form, if you will, an aggregation, but not an association, for they have neither public property nor a body politic. Such a man, had he enslaved half the world, is always only one individual; his interest, separated from that of the rest, is always only a private interest. If he dies, his empire after him is left scat-

tered and disunited, as an oak dissolves and becomes a heap of ashes after the fire has consumed it.

[35]* A people, says Grotius, can give itself to a king. According to Grotius, a people, then, is a people before it gives itself to a king. This gift itself is a civil act, and presupposes a public deliberation. Hence, before examining the act by which a people elects a king, it would be good to examine the act by which a people is a people. For this act, being necessarily anterior to the other, is the real foundation of the society.

[36] In fact, if there were no anterior convention, where, unless the election were unanimous, would be the obligation upon the minority to submit to the decision of the majority? And whence do the hundred who desire a master derive the right to vote on behalf of ten who do not desire one? The law of the plurality of votes is itself established by convention, and presupposes unanimity at least once.

VI. Of the Social Pact

[37]* I suppose that men have reached a point at which the obstacles that endanger their preservation in the state of nature prevail by their resistance over the forces which each individual can exert in order to maintain himself in that state. Then this primitive condition can no longer subsist, and the human race would perish unless it changed its manner of being.

[38] Now as men cannot create any new forces, but only unite and direct those that exist, they have no other means of self-preservation than to form by aggregation a sum of forces which may overcome the resistance, to put them in action by a single motive power, and to make them work in concert.

[39] This sum of forces can be produced only by the combination of many; but the strength and freedom of each man being the primary instruments of his preservation, how

can he pledge them without injuring himself, and without neglecting the care which he owes to himself? This difficulty, applied to my subject, may be stated in these terms:

[40]* "To find a form of association which defends and protects with the whole force of the community the person and goods of every associate, and by means of which each, uniting with all, nevertheless obeys only himself, and remains as free as before." Such is the fundamental problem to which the social contract gives the solution.

[41]* The clauses of this contract are so determined by the nature of the act that the slightest modification would render them vain and ineffectual; so that, although perhaps they have never been formally enunciated, they are everywhere the same, everywhere tacitly admitted and recognized; until, the social pact being violated, each man regains his initial rights and recovers his natural liberty, while losing the conventional liberty for which he renounced it.

[42]* These clauses, rightly understood, are all reducible to one only, namely the total alienation of each associate, with all of his rights, to the whole community: For, in the first place, as each gives himself up entirely, the condition is equal for all, and, the condition being equal for all, no one has any interest in making it burdensome to others.

[43]* Further, the alienation being made without reserve, the union is as perfect as it can be, and no associate has anything more to claim. For if some rights were left to individuals, since there would be no common superior who could judge between them and the public, each, being on some point his own judge, would soon claim to be so on all; the state of nature would still subsist, and the association would necessarily become tyrannical or useless.

[44]* Finally, each, in giving himself to all, gives himself to nobody; and as there is not one associate over whom we do not acquire the same rights which we concede to him over ourselves, we gain the equivalent of all that we lose, and more power to preserve what we have.

[45]* If, then, everything which is not of the essence of

the social pact is set aside, one finds that it reduces itself to the following terms: *Each of us puts in common his person and his whole power under the supreme direction of the general will; and in return we receive in a body every member as an indivisible part of the whole.*

[46]* Forthwith, instead of the particular person of each contracting part, this act of association produces a moral and collective body, which is composed of as many members as the assembly has voices, and which receives from this same act its unity, its common *self* [*moi*], its life, and its will. This public person, which is thus formed by the union of all the individual members, formerly took the name of *City*[4] and now takes that of *Republic* or *body politic,* which is called by its members *State* when it is passive, *Sovereign* when it is active, *Power* when it is compared to similar bodies. With regard to the associates, they take collectively the name of *people,* and are called individually *Citizens,* as participating in the sovereign authority, and *Subjects,* as subjected to the laws of the State. But these terms are often confused and are mistaken one for another; it is sufficient to know how to distinguish them when they are used with complete precision.

4. The real meaning of this word has almost completely disappeared among the moderns; the majority take a town for a City, and a burgher for a Citizen. They do not know that houses make the town, and that citizens make the city. This very mistake once cost the Carthaginians dear. I have never read of the title *Cives* being given to the subjects of a prince, not even in ancient times to the Macedonians, nor, in our days, to the English, although nearer liberty than all the rest. The French alone employ familiarly this name *Citizen,* because they have no true idea of it, as we can see from their dictionaries; but for this fact, they would, by assuming it, commit the crime of contempt. The name, among them, expresses a virtue, not a right. When Bodin wanted to give an account of our Citizens and Burghers he made a gross blunder, mistaking the one for the other. M. d'Alembert has not erred in this, and, in his article *Geneva,* has clearly distinguished the four orders of men (even five, counting mere foreigners) which exist in our town, and of which only two compose the Republic. No other French author I know of has understood the real meaning of the word *Citizen.*

VII. Of the Sovereign

[47]* One sees by this formula that the act of association includes a reciprocal engagement between the public and the individual, and that each individual, contracting so to speak with himself, is engaged in a double relation: namely, as a member of the Sovereign toward individuals, and as a member of the State toward the Sovereign. But we cannot apply here the maxim of civil right that no one is bound by engagements made with himself; for there is a great difference between being obligated to oneself and to a whole of which one forms a part.

[48] It is necessary to note further that the public deliberation which can obligate all subjects to the Sovereign in consequence of the two different relations under which each of them is regarded cannot, for a contrary reason, bind the Sovereign to itself; and that accordingly it is contrary to the nature of the body politic for the Sovereign to impose on itself a law which it cannot transgress. As it can only be considered under one and the same relation, it is in the position of an individual contracting with himself; thus we see that there is not, nor can there be, any kind of fundamental law obligatory for the body of the people, not even the social contract. This does not imply that such a body cannot perfectly well enter into engagements with others in what does not derogate from this contract; for, with regard to foreigners, it becomes a simple being, an individual.

[49] But the body politic or Sovereign, deriving its existence only from the sanctity of the contract, can never bind itself, even to others, in anything that derogates from the original act, such as to alienate some portion of itself, or submission to another Sovereign. To violate the act by which it exists would be to annihilate itself; and what is nothing produces nothing.

[50] As soon as this multitude is thus united into one body, it is impossible to injure one of the members without

attacking the body; still less to injure the body without the members feeling the effects. Thus duty and interest equally obligate the two contracting parties to give mutual assistance; and the same men should seek to combine in this twofold relationship all the advantages which are attendant on it.

[51] Now the Sovereign, being formed only of the individuals who compose it, neither has nor can have any interest contrary to theirs; consequently the Sovereign power needs no guarantee toward its subjects, because it is impossible that the body should wish to injure all its members; and we shall see hereafter that it can injure no one in particular. The Sovereign, for the simple reason that it is, is always everything that it ought to be.

[52] But this is not the case with respect to the relation of subjects to the Sovereign, which, notwithstanding the common interest, would have no security for the performance of their engagements, unless it found means to ensure their fidelity.

[53]* Indeed, each individual may, as a man, have a particular will contrary to, or divergent from, the general will which he has as a Citizen. His private interest may speak to him quite differently from the common interest; his absolute and naturally independent existence may make him regard what he owes to the common cause as a gratuitous contribution, the loss of which will be less harmful to others than will the payment of it be onerous to him; and viewing the moral person that constitutes the State as a being of reason because it is not a man, he would be willing to enjoy the rights of a citizen without being willing to fulfill the duties of a subject: an injustice, the progress of which would bring about the ruin of the body politic.

[54]* In order, then, that the social pact may not be a vain formula, it tacitly includes this engagement, which can alone give force to the others—that whoever refuses to obey the general will shall be constrained to do so by the whole body;

which means nothing else than that he shall be forced to be free; for such is the condition which, giving each Citizen to his Fatherland, guarantees him from all personal dependence, a condition that makes up the spark and interplay of the political mechanism, and alone renders legitimate civil engagements, which, without it, would be absurd and tyrannical, and subject to the most enormous abuse.

VIII. Of the Civil State

[55]* This passage from the state of nature to the civil state produces in man a very remarkable change, by substituting in his conduct justice for instinct, and by giving his actions the morality that they previously lacked. It is only when the voice of duty succeeds physical impulsion, and right succeeds appetite, that man, who till then had only looked after himself, sees that he is forced to act on other principles, and to consult his reason before listening to his inclinations. Although, in this state, he is deprived of many advantages he holds from nature, he gains such great ones in return, that his faculties are exercised and developed; his ideas are expanded; his feelings are ennobled; his whole soul is exalted to such a degree that, if the abuses of this new condition did not often degrade him below that from which he has emerged, he should ceaselessly bless the happy moment that removed him from it forever, and transformed him from a stupid and ignorant animal into an intelligent being and a man.

[56]* Let us reduce this whole balance to terms easy to compare. What man loses by the social contract is his natural liberty and an unlimited right to anything which tempts him and which he is able to attain; what he gains is civil liberty and the ownership of all that he possesses. In order not to be mistaken about these compensations, we must clearly distinguish natural liberty, which is limited only by the force of the individual, from civil liberty, which is limited by the

general will; and possession, which is only the result of force or the right of the first occupant, from ownership, which can only be based on a positive title.

[57]* Besides the preceding, one can add to the acquisitions of the civil state the moral freedom which alone renders man truly master of himself; for the impulsion of mere appetite is slavery, and obedience to the law one prescribes to oneself is freedom. But I have already said too much on this subject, and the philosophical meaning of the term *liberty* does not belong to my subject here.

IX. Of Real Property⁵

[58]* Each member of the community gives himself up to it at the moment of its formation, just as he actually is, himself and all his force, of which the goods he possesses form a part. It is not that by this act possession changes its nature in changing hands and becomes property in those of the Sovereign; but, as the powers of the City are incomparably greater than those of an individual, public possession is also, in fact, more secure and more irrevocable, without being more legitimate, at least for foreigners. For the State, with regard to its members, is master of all their property by the social contract, which in the State serves as the basis of all rights; but with regard to other powers it is master only by right of first occupant which it holds from private individuals.

[59] The right of first occupant, although more real than that of the strongest, becomes a true right only after the establishment of property [ownership]. Every man has by nature a right to all that is necessary to him; but the positive act which makes him owner of certain goods excludes him from the rest. His portion having been allotted, he ought to confine himself to it, and he has no further right against the

5. Cf. PE 42, n.6.—ED.

community. That is why the right of first occupant, so weak in the state of nature, is respected by every member of a civil society. In this right one respects not so much what belongs to others as what does not belong to oneself.

[60]* Generally, in order to authorize the right of first occupant over any land whatsoever, the following conditions are needed. First, the land must not yet be inhabited by anyone; second, a man must occupy only the area required for his subsistence; third, he must take possession of it not by an empty ceremony but by labor and cultivation, the only mark of ownership which, in the absence of legal title, ought to be respected by others.

[61] Indeed, to grant the right of first occupant according to necessity and labor, is it not to extend this right as far as it can go? Can one assign limits to this right? Will the mere setting foot on common ground be sufficient to presume an immediate claim to the ownership of it? Will the power of driving away other men from it for a moment suffice to deprive them of the right of ever returning to it? How can a man or a people take possession of an immense territory and rob the whole human race of it except by a punishable usurpation, since henceforth other men are deprived of the place of residence and sustenance which nature gives to them in common? When Núñez de Balboa on the seashore took possession of the Pacific Ocean and of the whole of South America in the name of the crown of Castile, was this sufficient to dispossess all the inhabitants, and exclude from it all the Princes in the world? On this stand, such ceremonies might have been multiplied vainly enough; and the Catholic King in his cabinet might, by a single stroke, have taken possession of the whole universe; only cutting off afterward from his empire what was previously occupied by other Princes.

[62] It can be understood how the lands of individuals, united and contiguous, become public territory, and how the right of sovereignty, extending itself from the subjects

to the land which they occupy, becomes at once real and personal; this places the possessors in greater dependence, and makes their own powers a guarantee for their fidelity. An advantage which ancient monarchs do not appear to have clearly sensed, for, calling themselves only Kings of the Persians or Scythians or Macedonians, they seem to have viewed themselves as chiefs of men rather than as owners of countries. Those of today call themselves more cleverly Kings of France, Spain, England, etc. In thus holding the land they are quite sure of holding its inhabitants.

[63]* What is remarkable about this alienation is that the community, in receiving the property of individuals, far from robbing them of it, only assures them lawful possession, and changes usurpation into true right, enjoyment into ownership. Then the possessors, being considered as depositaries of the public property, and their rights being respected by all members of the State, and maintained with all its power against the foreign intruder, have, as it were, by a transfer advantageous to the public and still more to themselves, acquired all that they have given up. This is a paradox which is easily explained by distinguishing between the rights which the Sovereign and the owner have over the same property, as shall be seen later.

[64] It may also happen that men begin to unite before they possess anything, and that afterward taking over territory sufficient for all, they enjoy it in common, or share it among themselves, either equally or in proportions fixed by the Sovereign. In whatever manner this acquisition is made, the right which every individual has over his own property is always subordinate to the right which the community has over all; otherwise there would be neither solidity in the social union, nor real force in the exercise of Sovereignty.

[65]* I shall close this chapter and this book with a remark which ought to serve as a basis for the whole social system; it is that instead of destroying natural equality, the fundamental pact, on the contrary, substitutes a moral and

legitimate equality for the physical inequality which nature imposed upon men, so that, although unequal in strength or talent, they all become equal by convention and legal right.[6]

6. Under bad governments this equality is only apparent and illusory; it serves only to keep the poor man in his misery and the rich in his usurpations. In fact, laws are always useful to those who possess and injurious to those who have nothing; whence it follows that the social state is advantageous to men only so far as they all have something, and none of them has too much.

BOOK TWO

I. That Sovereignty Is Inalienable

[66]* The first and most important consequence of the principles established above is that the general will can only direct the forces of the State in keeping with the end for which it was instituted, which is the common good; for if the opposition of private interests has made the establishment of societies necessary, the harmony of these same interests has made it possible. That which is common to these different interests forms the social bond; and if there were not some point in which all interests agree, no society could exist. Now it is only on this common interest that the society should be governed.

[67]* I say, then, that sovereignty, being only the exercise of the general will, can never be alienated, and that the Sovereign, which is only a collective being, can be represented only by itself; power can well be transmitted, but will cannot.

[68] In fact, if it is not impossible that a private will agree on some point with the general will, it is at least impossible that this agreement should be lasting and constant; for the private will naturally tends to preferences, and the general will to equality. It is still more impossible to have a guarantee for this agreement; even though it should always exist, it would be an effect not of art but of chance. The Sovereign may indeed say: I now will what a certain man wills, or at least what he says that he wills; but it cannot say: what that man wills tomorrow, I shall also will; since it is absurd that the will should bind itself for the future and since it is not incumbent on any will to consent to anything contrary to the good of the being that wills. If, then, the people promises simply to obey, it dissolves itself by that act, it loses its quality as a people; at the instant that there is a master, there

is no longer a Sovereign, and forthwith the body politic is destroyed.

[69] This is not to say that the orders of the chiefs cannot pass for expressions of the general will, so long as the Sovereign, free to oppose them, does not do so. In such case, from the universal silence one should presume the consent of the people. This will be explained at greater length.

II. That Sovereignty Is Indivisible

[70] For the same reason that sovereignty is inalienable, it is indivisible. For either the will is general[1] or it is not; it is the will either of the body of the people, or only of a part. In the first case, this declared will is an act of sovereignty and constitutes law. In the second case, it is only a private will, or an act of magistracy; it is at most a decree.

[71]* But our political men, not being able to divide sovereignty in its principles, divide it in its object: they divide it into force and will, into legislative power and executive power; into rights of taxation, of justice, and of war; into internal administration and power of treating with foreigners: sometimes they confound all these parts and sometimes separate them. They make the Sovereign to be a fantastic being formed of borrowed pieces; it is as if they composed a man from several bodies, one having eyes, another having arms, another having feet, and nothing more. Charlatans of Japan, it is said, cut up a child before the eyes of the spectators; then, throwing all its limbs, one after another, into the air, they make the child come back down alive and whole. Such almost are the juggler's tricks of our politicians; after dismembering the social body by a

---

1. For a will to be general, it is not always necessary that it be unanimous, but it is necessary for all the voices to be counted; any formal exclusion destroys the generality.

deception worthy of a carnival, they recombine the parts, one knows not how.

[72]* This error comes from not having formed exact notions of sovereign authority, and from having taken as parts of this authority what are only emanations from it. Thus, for example, the act of declaring war and that of making peace have been looked at as acts of sovereignty; this is not the case, since each of these acts is not a law, but only an application of the law, a particular act which determines the case of the law, as will be clearly seen when the idea attached to the word *law* will be fixed.

[73] In following out the other divisions in the same way, one would find that whenever sovereignty appears divided, a mistake has been made; that the rights which are taken as parts of that sovereignty are all subordinate to it, and always suppose supreme wills of which these rights are merely the execution.

[74]* One could not say to what extent this lack of exactitude has made obscure the conclusions of authors in matters of political right, when they wished to judge the respective rights of kings and peoples along the principles they had established. Anyone can see, in Chapters III and IV of the first book of Grotius, how this learned man and his translator, Barbeyrac, became entangled and embarrassed in their sophisms, fearful of saying too much or not saying enough according to their views, and of offending the interests they needed to conciliate. Grotius, having taken refuge in France through discontent with his own fatherland, and wishing to pay court to Louis XIII, to whom his book is dedicated, spares nothing to despoil the people of all their rights and, in the most artful manner, to bestow them on kings. This also would clearly have been the wish of Barbeyrac, who dedicated his translation to the king of England, George I. But unfortunately, the expulsion of James II, which he calls abdication, forced him to be guarded, to equivocate, to

evade, in order not to make William appear a usurper. If these two writers had adopted true principles, all their difficulties would have been lifted, and they would have always been coherent; but they would have regretfully spoken the truth and would have paid court only to the people. For truth hardly leads to fortune, and the people confer no ambassadorships, university chairs, or pensions.

III. Whether the General Will Can Err

[75]* It follows from what precedes that the general will is always upright and always tends toward the public utility; but it does not follow that the deliberations of the people always have the same rectitude. One wishes always his own good, but does not always discern it. The people is never corrupted, though often deceived, and then only does it seem to will that which is bad.

[76]* There is often a great difference between the will of all and the general will; the latter regards only the common interest, the other regards private interests and is only the sum of particular wills: but remove from these wills the pluses and minuses which cancel each other out² and the general will remains as the sum of the differences.

[77]* If, when an adequately informed people deliberates, the Citizens having no communication among themselves, from the large number of small differences the general will would always result, and the deliberation would always be good. But when factions are formed, partial associations at the expense of the whole, the will of each of

---

2. "Every interest," says M. d'A., "has different principles. The accord of two private interests is formed by opposition to that of a third." He might have added that the accord of all interests is formed by opposition of it to each. Unless there were different interests, the common interest would scarcely be felt and would never meet with any obstacles; everything would go of itself, and politics would cease to be an art.

these associations becomes general with regard to its members, and particular with regard to the State: one is then able to say that there are no longer as many voters as there are men, but only as many as there are associations. The differences become less numerous and yield a less general result. Finally, when one of these associations is so large that it overcomes the rest, you no longer have a sum of small differences as the result, but a unique difference; then there no longer is a general will, and the opinion which dominates is only a private opinion.

[78]* It matters, then, in order to have the general will expressed well, that there be no partial societies in the State, and that each Citizen speak only his own opinions.[3] Such was the unique and sublime institution of the great Lycurgus. But if there are partial associations, it is necessary to multiply their number and so prevent inequality, as was done by Solon, Numa, and Servius. These precautions are the only valid ones, in order that the general will always be enlightened and that the people are not deceived.

IV. Of the Limits of the Sovereign Power

[79]* If the State or the City is only a moral person whose life consists in the union of its members, and if the most important of its cares is that of its own conservation, it needs a universal and compulsive force to move and dispose every part in the manner most appropriate for the whole. As nature gives each man an absolute power over all his limbs, the social pact gives the body politic an absolute power over all its members, and it is the same power which, directed by the

3. "It is true," says Machiavelli, "that some divisions harm the republic while others are beneficial to it; those that are injurious are accompanied by cabals and factions; those that assist it are maintained without cabals and factions. No founder of a republic can provide against enmities within it, and so he therefore ought to provide at least that there shall be cabals" (*History of Florence*, Book VII).

general will, bears, as I have said, the name of sovereignty.

[80]* But beyond the public person, we have to consider the private persons who compose it, and whose life and liberty are naturally independent of it. It is then necessary to distinguish clearly the respective rights of the Citizens and of the Sovereign[4] as well as between the duties which the former have to fulfill as subjects and the natural right which they ought to enjoy in their quality as men.

[81]* Granted that whatever part of his power, his goods, and his liberty each alienates by the social pact is only that part whose use is important to the community; we must also agree that the Sovereign alone is judge of that importance.

[82]* All the services that a citizen can render to the State, he owes to it as soon as the Sovereign demands them; but the Sovereign, on its side, cannot impose any burden on its subjects that is useless to the community; it cannot even wish to do so; because under the law of reason nothing happens without cause, just as under the law of nature.

[83]* The engagements which bind us to the social body are obligatory only because they are mutual, and their nature is such that in fulfilling them one cannot work for others without also working for oneself. Why is the general will always upright,[5] and why do all constantly desire the well-being of each, if not because no one appropriates this word *each* to himself without thinking of himself as voting on behalf of all? This proves that equality of right and the notion of justice it produces derive from the preference which each gives to himself, and consequently from the nature of man; that the general will, to be truly such, must be just in its object as in its essence; that it ought to proceed from all in order to be applicable to all; and that it loses its

---

4. Attentive readers, I beg you, do not hasten to accuse me here of contradiction. I have not been able to avoid it in these terms, owing to the poverty of the language; but wait.

5. In this context, *droite* could be construed as "righteous."—Ed.

natural rectitude when it is directed to some individual and determinate object, because in that case, judging from what is foreign to us, we have no true principle of equity to guide us.

[84]* In effect, so soon as a matter of fact or particular right is in question on a point which has not been regulated by a previous general convention, the affair becomes contentious. It is a lawsuit in which the interested individuals are one of the parties and the public the other, but in which I perceive neither the law which must be followed, nor the judge who should decide. It would be ridiculous to wish to refer the matter for an express decision of the general will, which can only be the decision of one of the parties, and which, consequently, is for the other party only a will that is foreign, partial, and inclined on such an occasion to injustice as well as it is subject to error. Thus, just as a particular will cannot represent the general will, the general will in turn changes its nature when it has a particular object and cannot, as general, decide about either a man or a fact. When the people of Athens, for example, named or deposed their chiefs, decreed honor to one, imposed penalties on another, and by multitudes of particular decrees exercised indiscriminately all the functions of government, the people no longer had any general will properly so called; it no longer acted as Sovereign but as Magistrate. This will appear contrary to common ideas, but I must be allowed time to set forth my own.

[85] What generalizes the will, one must see from this, is not so much the number of voices as the common interest that unites them; for, in this institution, each necessarily submits to the conditions that he imposes on others: an admirable accord of interest and justice which gives to common deliberations a spirit of equity that seems to disappear in the discussion of any particular affair, for want of a common interest to unite and identify the ruling principle of the judge with that of the party.

[86]* By whatever path we return to our principle, we always arrive at the same conclusion: the social pact establishes among citizens such an equality that they all engage themselves under the same conditions and ought to enjoy the same rights. Thus, by the nature of the pact, every act of sovereignty, that is to say every authentic act of the general will, obligates or favors all the citizens equally; so that the Sovereign knows only the body of the nation, and distinguishes none of those who compose it. What then is properly an act of sovereignty? It is not a convention of the superior with the inferior, but a convention of the body with each of its members. A legitimate convention, because it has the social contract for its base; equitable, because it is common to all; useful, because it can have no object other than the general welfare; and firm, because it has for its guarantee the public force and supreme power. So long as the subjects submit only to such conventions, they obey no one, but only their own will; and to ask how far the respective rights of the Sovereign and the Citizens extend is to ask up to which point the latter can engage themselves, each toward all and all toward each.

[87] One sees thereby that the Sovereign power, wholly absolute, wholly sacred, wholly inviolable as it is, neither passes nor can pass the limits of general conventions, and that every man can fully dispose of what is left to him of his goods and his liberty by these conventions; so that the Sovereign never has a right to burden one subject more than another, because then the matter becomes individual, and its power is no longer competent.

[88]* These distinctions once admitted, it is so false that in the social contract there is, on the part of individuals, any real renunciation, that their situation, as a result of this contract, is in reality preferable to what it was before: instead of an alienation they have only made an advantageous exchange of an uncertain and precarious mode of existence for a better and more assured one, of natural independence

for liberty, of the power to injure others for their own safety, and of their strength, which others might overcome, for a right [6] which the social union renders invincible. Their life itself, which they have dedicated to the State, is continually protected by it; and when they expose their lives for its defense, what do they do but restore what they have received from it? What do they do but what they would do more frequently and with more risk in the state of nature, when, engaging in inevitable struggles, they would defend at the peril of their lives their means of preserving it? All have to fight, if need be, for the fatherland, it is true; but then no one ever has to fight for himself. Do we not gain, still, to run this risk for that which assures our safety, a part of the risks we would have to run for ourselves as soon as our security was taken away?

V. Of the Right of Life and Death

[89]* One asks how individuals having no right to dispose of their own lives can transmit to the Sovereign this right which they do not possess? This question appears difficult to resolve only because it is poorly posed. Every man has a right to risk his own life in order to preserve it. Has it ever been said that one who throws himself out of a window to escape from a fire is guilty of suicide? Has this crime, indeed, ever been imputed to a man who perishes in a storm although, on embarking, he was not ignorant of the danger?

[90]* The social treaty has as its end the conservation of the contracting parties. He who desires the end desires also the means, and these means are inseparable from some risks, even from some losses. He who desires to preserve his life at the expense of others ought also to give it up for them when necessary. Still, the Citizen is no longer judge of the

6. In this context, *droit* might be construable as "protection."—ED.

peril to which the law requires that he expose himself; and when the Prince has said to him: "It is expedient for the State that you die," he should die; because it is only on this condition that he has lived in security until then, and his life is no longer only a benefit of nature, but a conditional gift of the State.

[91]* The penalty of death inflicted on criminals can be seen almost from the same viewpoint: it is in order not to be the victim of a murderer that a person consents to die if he becomes one. In this treaty, far from disposing of his own life, one only thinks of guaranteeing it, and it is not to be presumed that any of the contracting members plans at that time to be hanged.

[92] Besides, every malefactor, attacking the social right, becomes by his crimes a rebel and traitor to his fatherland; he ceases to be a member of it by violating its laws, and even makes war against it. The conservation of the State then is incompatible with his own, so one of the two must perish, and when the guilty one is executed, it is less as a Citizen than as an enemy. The proceedings, the judgment, are the proofs and declaration that he has broken the social treaty, and consequently is no longer a member of the State. Yet as he is acknowledged to be such, at least by his residence, he ought to be removed from it by exile as a violator of the pact, or by death as a public enemy; for one such enemy is not a moral person, but a man, and it is then that the right of war is to slay the vanquished.

[93] But, one will say, the condemnation of a Criminal is a particular act. Agreed: likewise, this condemnation does not concern the Sovereign; it is a right which it can confer though it is itself unable to exercise. All my ideas hold together, but I do not know how to explain them all at once.

[94]* Besides, the frequency of physical punishment is always a sign of weakness or indolence in the Government. There is no one so wicked who could not be made good for

something. One has a right to execute, even as an example, only someone who cannot be preserved with danger.

[95] As regards the right to pardon or to exempt a guilty person from the penalty imposed by the law and pronounced by the judge, it belongs only to that which is above both the judge and the law, that is to say to the Sovereign; still, its right in this is not very distinct, and the cases of using it are very rare. In a well-governed State there are few punishments, not because many pardons are given, but because there are few criminals; the multitude of crimes assures their impunity when the State declines. Under the Roman Republic neither the senate nor the consuls attempted to grant pardons; the people themselves did not grant any, although they sometimes revoked their own judgments. Frequent pardons announce that crimes will soon need them no longer, and each sees to where that leads. But I feel my heart murmur and hold back my pen: let us leave these questions for discussion to the just man who has never done wrong and who never has had need of pardon himself.

VI. Of the Law

[96] By the social pact we have given existence and life to the body politic; it is now a matter of giving it movement and will through legislation. For the original act by which this body is formed and united still determines nothing with respect to what it should do to preserve itself.

[97]* What is good and conforming to order is such by the nature of things and independent of human conventions. All justice comes from God, he alone is the source; but if we knew how to receive it from so high, we would need neither government nor laws. Without doubt there is a universal justice emanating from reason alone; but this justice, in order to be admitted among us, must be recipro-

cal. Considering things from a human viewpoint, the laws of justice, lacking a natural sanction, are ineffectual among men; they only bring good to the wicked and evil to the just man when he observes them with everyone else and no one observes them with him. Conventions and laws are then needed in order to unite rights with duties and to bring justice to its object. In the state of nature, where everything is common, I owe nothing to those to whom I have promised nothing, and I recognize as belonging to others only what is useless to me. It is not so in the civil state, where all the rights are fixed by the law.

[98] But what then is a law? As long as one continues to attach to this word only metaphysical ideas, one will continue to reason without understanding, and when one will have said what a law of nature is, one will not have a better idea of what is a law of the State.

[99] I have already said that there is no general will concerning a particular object. In effect, this particular object is either in the State or outside the State. If it is outside the State, a will that is foreign to it is not general in relation to it; and if within the State, that object is part of it; then there is formed between the whole and its part a relation which makes the whole two separate entities, of which the part is one, and the whole less this same part is the other. But the whole less one part is not the whole, and so long as the relation subsists, there is no longer any whole but two unequal parts: from which it follows that the will of one of them is no longer general in relation to the other.

[100] But when the whole people decrees for the whole people, it considers only itself; and if a relation is then formed, it is between the entire object from one point of view and the whole object from another point of view, without any division of the whole. It is this act that I call a law.

[101] When I say that the object of the laws is always general, I mean that the law considers the subjects in a body

and the actions as abstract, never a man as an individual nor
a particular action. Thus the law can very well decree that
there will be privileges, but it cannot confer them on anyone
by name; the law can create several Classes of Citizens, even
assign the characteristics that confer a right to membership
in these Classes, but it cannot name specific persons to be
admitted to them; it can establish a royal Government and
a hereditary succession, but it cannot elect a king or appoint
a royal family; in a word, no function that relates to an
individual object belongs to the legislative power.

[102]* On this idea one sees instantly that it is no longer
necessary to ask who is responsible for making the laws,
since they are acts of the general will; nor whether the
Prince is above the laws, since he is a member of the State;
nor if the law can be unjust, since no one is unjust to himself;
nor how one is free and subject to the laws, since they are
only registers of our wills.

[103] One sees further that the law uniting the universality of the will with that of the object, what any man, whoever
he may be, orders on his own, is not a law; what is ordered
even by the Sovereign regarding a particular object is not
a law, but a decree, not an act of sovereignty, but of magistracy.

[104]* I therefore call every State ruled by laws a Republic, under whatever form of administration it could have: for
then only the public interest governs and the public entity
[Latin: *res publica*] is real. Every legitimate Government is
republican;[7] I will explain later what Government is.

[105]* Laws are properly only the conditions of the civil
association. The People, submitting to the laws, ought to be
their author; it concerns only those who are associating

---

7. I do not understand by this word only an Aristocracy or a Democracy, but in general any government directed by the general will, which
is the law. In order to be legitimate, the Government must not confound itself with the Sovereign, but should be its minister; then monarchy itself is a republic. This will be clarified in the next book.

together to regulate the conditions of the society. But how will they regulate them? Will it be in a common accord by sudden inspiration? Does the body politic have an organ to announce its will? Who will give it the foresight necessary to frame its acts and publish them in advance, or how will it pronounce them at the moment of need? How will a blind multitude, which often does not know what it wants because it rarely knows what is good for it, carry out an enterprise so great and also difficult as a system of legislation? By itself the people always wants the good, but by itself does not always discern it. The general will is always upright,[8] but the judgment which guides it is not always enlightened. It is necessary to make it see objects as they are, sometimes as they ought to appear, to point out the good road it seeks, to guard it from the seduction of private wills, to bring before its eyes considerations of places and times, to balance the attraction of present and tangible advantages against the danger of distant and hidden evils. Private individuals see the good they reject; the public wants the good it does not see. All have equal need of guides. It is necessary to obligate the former to conform their wishes to their reason; it is necessary to teach the latter to know what it wants. Then from public enlightenment results the union of the understanding and the will in the social body, hence the precise concourse of the parts, and finally the maximum force of the whole. From this arises the necessity of a Legislator.

VII. Of the Legislator

[106]* In order to discover the best rules of society which are suitable to nations, there would be needed a superior intelligence who saw all the passions of men and who had not experienced any of them; who would have no relation

---

8. Rousseau's word *droite* can be construed here as meaning "righteous."—ED.

to our nature and yet knew it thoroughly; whose happiness would not depend on us and who would be quite willing to occupy himself with ours; finally, one who, preparing for himself a distant glory in the progress of time, could work in one age and find satisfaction in another.[9] Gods would be needed to give laws to men.

[107] The same reasoning that Caligula used as to fact, Plato used with regard to right in order to define the civil or royal person whom he seeks in his book on ruling [i.e., the *Statesman*]. But if it is true that a great Prince is a rare man, what will a great Legislator be? The first has only to follow the model which the other has to propose. The latter is the engineer who invents the machine, the former is only the workman who puts it in readiness and makes it work. In the birth of societies, says Montesquieu, it is the chiefs of republics who make the institutions, and afterward it is the institutions which form the chiefs of republics.

[108]* He who dares to undertake the instituting of a people ought to feel himself capable, as it were, of changing human nature; of transforming each individual, who in himself is a perfect and solitary whole, into part of a greater whole from which this individual receives in some way his life and his being; of altering the constitution of man so as to reinforce it; of substituting a partial and moral existence for the physical and independent existence we have all received from nature. It is necessary, in a word, to remove man's own forces in order to give him some that are strange and which he is not able to use without the help of others. The more these natural forces are dead and annihilated, the greater and more durable are those acquired, the more too is the institution solid and perfect: so that if each Citizen is

9. A people only becomes famous when its legislation begins to decline. One does not know for how many centuries the institutions of Lycurgus conferred happiness on the Spartans before they came to be known by the rest of Greece.

nothing, and can be nothing, except in combination with all others, and if the force acquired by the whole be equal or superior to the sum of the natural forces of all individuals, one can say that legislation has attained the highest possible point of perfection.

[109] The Legislator is in all respects an extraordinary man in the State. If he ought to be so by his genius, he is not less so by his function. It is not magistracy, it is not sovereignty. This office, which constitutes the republic, does not enter into its constitution; it is a particular and superior function which has nothing in common with human dominion; for if he who controls men should not have control over the laws, he who has control over the laws should not control men; otherwise, the laws, as ministers of his passions, would often serve only to perpetuate his acts of injustice; he would never be able to prevent his private views from corrupting the sacredness of his work.

[110] When Lycurgus gave laws to his fatherland, he began by abdicating the throne. It was the custom of most Greek towns to entrust the establishment of their laws to foreigners. The modern republics of Italy have often imitated this practice; the republic of Geneva also found it worked well.[10] Rome, in its finest age, saw all the crimes of Tyranny reborn in its bosom, and itself on the verge of peril, because of having united legislative authority and sovereign power in the same hands.

[111] Yet the Decemvirs themselves never arrogated the right to pass any law on their sole authority. "Nothing that we propose to you," they said to the people, "can pass into

10. Those who consider Calvin only as a theologian poorly understand the extent of his genius. The drafting of our wise Edicts, in which he played a large part, does him as much honor as his *Institutes*. Whatever revolution time may bring about in our cult, so long as the love of fatherland and of liberty will not be extinguished among us, the memory of that great man will not cease to be blessed.

law without your consent. Romans, be yourselves the authors of the laws that ought to secure your happiness.''

[112] He who drafts the laws, then, does not have or should not have any legislative right, and even the people cannot, if it wishes, divest itself of this incommunicable right, because according to the fundamental pact, only the general will obligates individuals and one cannot be assured that a particular will has conformed to the general will until after it has been submitted to the free votes of the people; I have already said that, but it is not useless to repeat it.

[113] Thus one finds at the same time in the work of legislation two things which seem incompatible: an enterprise above human force, and to execute it an authority that is nothing.

[114] Another difficulty merits attention. Wise men who wish to speak their own language to the people instead of using the common speech will not be understood. Besides, there are a thousand kinds of ideas that it is impossible to translate into the language of the people. Very general views and very remote objects are equally beyond their grasp: each individual, appreciating no other plan of government than that which relates to his private interest, appreciates with difficulty the advantages he should receive from the continual privations which good laws impose. For a newly formed people to be able to appreciate the sane maxims of politics and to follow the fundamental rules of statecraft, it would be necessary that the effect could become the cause; that the social spirit, which ought to be the accomplishment of the institution, would preside over the institution itself; and that men be already, prior to the laws, that which they should become by means of them. Since the Legislator is able to employ neither force nor reasoning, he must have recourse to an authority of a different order, which can win without violence and persuade with convincing.

[115] This is what in all times has forced the fathers of

nations to have recourse to the intervention of heaven, and to give the Gods credit for their own wisdom, to the end that the peoples, brought under the laws of the State as to those of nature, and recognizing the same power in the formation of man and in that of the city, obey with liberty and bear with docility the yoke of public felicity.

[116] This sublime reason which rises above the reach of common men the Legislator places in the mouth of the immortals in order to win over by divine authority those unable to be moved by human prudence.[11] But not every man can make the Gods speak or be believed when he announces himself as their interpreter. The great soul of the Legislator is the true miracle which should prove his mission. Any man can engrave stone tablets, or buy an oracle, or feign a secret relationship with some divinity, or train a bird to speak in his ear, or find some other crude means of imposing on the people. He who knows only this could even assemble by chance a crowd of madmen, but he will never found an empire and his extravagant work will soon perish with him. Vain delusions form a transient bond; only wisdom renders it durable. The Judaic law which still subsists, and that of the child of Ishmael, which has ruled half the world for ten centuries, still proclaim today the great men who enunciated them; and while proud philosophy or blind party spirit sees in them only lucky impostors, the true student of politics admires in their institutions this great and powerful genius who presides over durable institutions.

[117] It is not necessary to conclude from this with Warburton that politics and religions have among us a common object, but rather that in the origin of nations, one serves as instrument of the other.

---

11. "And truly," says Machiavelli, "there never was any lawgiver among any people who did not have recourse to God, for otherwise his laws would not have been accepted, for many benefits are known to a prudent man who does not have reasons evident enough to enable him to persuade others" (*Discourses on Titus Livy*, I, 11).

VIII. Of the People

[118]* Just as an architect, before raising a large building, observes and tests the soil in order to see if it is able to sustain the weight, the wise instructor does not begin by drawing up laws that are good in themselves, but first examines whether the people for whom he intends them are fitted to support them. This is why Plato refused to provide laws to the Arcadians and Cyrenians, knowing that these two peoples were rich and could not tolerate equality; it is for this reason that one witnessed good laws and wicked men in Crete, because Minos had only disciplined a people steeped in vice.

[119] A thousand nations have flourished on earth which never could have borne good laws; and even those which could have done so, for as long as they lasted, had only a short time to do so. Most Peoples, as most men, are docile only in their youth; they become incorrigible as they age. Once customs are established and prejudices have taken root, it is a dangerous and vain enterprise to want to reform them; the people are not able to tolerate their evils being touched even in order to destroy them, like those stupid and cowardly patients who quiver at the sight of a doctor.

[120] To be sure, just as some diseases unhinge men's minds and remove the memory of the past, it is sometimes found during the lifetime of States violent epochs in which revolutions do to the people what certain crises do to individuals, in which the horror of the past takes the place of forgetfulness, and in which the State, inflamed by civil wars, is reborn, so to speak, from its ashes and regains the vigor of youth in springing from the arms of death. Such was Sparta at the time of Lycurgus, such was Rome after the Tarquins, and such among us were Holland and Switzerland after the expulsion of the Tyrants.

[121] But these events are rare; they are exceptions, the reason for which is always found in the particular constitu-

tion of the excepted State. They could not even happen twice with the same people, for it can make itself free when it is still barbarous, but it cannot do so when the civil strength is exhausted. Then troubles can destroy it without revolutions being able to reestablish it, and as soon as its chains are broken, it falls apart and ceases to exist. It then needs a master, not a liberator. Free Peoples, remember this maxim: "One can acquire liberty, but one can never recover it."

[122] Youth is not infancy. For Nations as for men there is a time of youth, or, if one prefers, of maturity, that must elapse before subjecting them to laws; but the maturity of a people is not always easy to discern, and if it is anticipated, the work is ruined. One people is capable of discipline on its birth, another is not after ten centuries. The Russians will never be truly civilized, because they were too early. Peter had an imitative genius; he did not have the true genius which creates and makes everything out of nothing. A few of the things he did were good, the majority were ill-timed. He saw that his people was barbarous, he did not see that it was not ready for a lawful order; he wished to civilize it when it was only needed to discipline it. He wished at first to make Germans, Englishmen, when he should have begun by making Russians: he prevented his subjects from ever becoming what they might have been, by persuading them that they were what they were not. It is in this way that a French Tutor trains his pupil to shine for a moment in childhood, and then never to be anything. The Russian Empire will want to subjugate Europe and will itself be subjugated. The Tartars, its subjects or its neighbors, will become its masters and ours. This revolution seems to me inevitable. All the Kings of Europe are working in concert to accelerate it.

IX. *(Continued)*

[123]* As nature has set limits to the stature of a well-formed man, beyond which there are only Giants and Dwarfs, so too, with regard to the best constitution of a State, there are limits to the possible extent it may have so that it should be neither too large to be well governed, nor too small to maintain itself. There is in every body politic a *maximum* of force that should not be exceeded, and which is often distended as it grows larger. The more the social bond is extended, the more it is loosened; and generally a small State is proportionally stronger than a large one.

[124] A thousand reasons demonstrate this maxim. In the first place, administration becomes more difficult at great distances, as a weight becomes heavier at the end of a longer lever. It also becomes more burdensome in proportion as its levels are multiplied: for each town has first its own administration, for which the people pay, each district its own, still paid for by the people, then each province, then the large governments, the Satrapies, the Viceroyalties, which need always to be funded more lavishly as one goes higher, and always at the expense of the unfortunate people; finally comes the supreme administration which overwhelms everyone. So many surcharges continually exhaust the subjects: far from being well governed by all these different orders, they are less well governed than if they had only one above them. Meanwhile, hardly any resources remain for emergencies; and when it is necessary to have recourse to them, the State is always on the brink of ruin.

[125] This is not all; not only does the Government have less vigor and speed to enforce observation of the laws, prevent harassments, correct abuses, prevent seditious enterprises which are undertaken in remote places; but the people have less affection for their chiefs, who are never seen, for the fatherland, which to their eyes is like the world, and for their fellow citizens, most of whom are strangers.

The same laws cannot be suitable for so many diverse provinces which have different customs, who live under contrasting climates, and cannot tolerate the same form of government. Different laws only engender trouble and confusion among peoples who, living under the same chiefs and in continual communication, mingle or intermarry in different areas, and submitting to different customs, never know if their patrimony is really theirs. Talents are hidden, virtues ignored, vices unpunished, in that multitude of men, unknown to each other, whom the seat of the supreme administration brings together in one place. The Chiefs, overwhelmed with work, see nothing for themselves; clerks govern the State. Finally, the measures necessary to maintain the general authority, which so many distant Officers wish to evade or impose, absorb all public attention; there remains none for the welfare of the people, and barely any for its defense if needed; and thus a body too large for its constitution collapses and perishes under its own weight.

[126] On the other side, the State ought to provide itself a certain base for its solidity, to resist the shocks it will not fail to experience and the efforts which it will be constrained to make in order to sustain itself: for all peoples have a kind of centrifugal force, by which they continually act against one another, tending to aggrandize themselves at the expense of their neighbors, like the vortices of Descartes. Thus weak men risk being quickly swallowed up and none can preserve himself except by placing himself in a kind of equilibrium with all, which renders the pressure almost equal.

[127] One sees that there are reasons for expansion and reasons for contraction, and it is not the least talent of the student of politics to find between the two the most advantageous proportion to the conservation of the State. One can say in general that the former, being only external and relative, ought to be subordinated to the others, which are internal and absolute; a strong and wholesome constitution

is the first thing to be sought, and one should count more on the vigor born out of a good government than on the resources provided by a large territory.

[128] Besides, one has seen States so constituted that the necessity of conquest entered into their constitution itself, and that, in order to maintain themselves, they were forced to expand ceaselessly. Perhaps they prided themselves greatly on this happy necessity, which nevertheless showed them, with the limit of their greatness, the inevitable moment of their fall.

X. (Continued)

[129]* One can measure a body politic in two ways: namely, by the extent of its territory and by the number of its people; and there is between them a suitable ratio according to which the State can be given its true dimension. Men make the State and it is the terrain that nourishes the men: the relation is then that the land should suffice for the maintenance of its inhabitants, and that there be as many inhabitants as the land can nourish. It is in this proportion that is found the *maximum* power of a given number of people; for if the terrain is too large, guarding it is onerous, its cultivation insufficient, its products superfluous; this is the proximate cause of defensive wars. If there is not enough land, the State finds it necessary to supplement its produce at the discretion of its neighbors; this is the proximate cause of offensive wars. Every people which has by its position no alternative between commerce or war is inherently weak; it depends on its environment, it depends on its neighbors, it depends on events; it has nothing but an uncertain and brief existence. It subjugates and changes situations or it is subjugated and is nothing. It is able to conserve itself as free only through being petty or grand.

[130] One is not able to provide an arithmetically fixed ratio between the extent of land and the number of men, a

relation that is reciprocally sufficient, because of the differences which are found in the qualities of terrain, in degrees of fertility, in the nature of produce, in the influence of climate, as much as in the temperaments of the men who inhabit it, some of whom consume little in a fertile country, others much from a barren soil. It is also necessary to have regard to the greater or lesser fecundity of the women, to what the country is able to have that is more or less favorable to the population, to the number of men the legislator is able to bring together by his institutions; so the legislator ought to found his judgment not on what he does see but on what he can foresee, not focus his vision on the actual condition of the population but on what it should naturally become. Finally, there are a thousand occasions where the particular contingencies of place require or permit that more territory be embraced than seems necessary. Thus men will spread out in a mountainous country, where the natural products, the woods, the pastures, require less labor, where experience teaches that women are more fecund than in the plains, and where a great amount of sloping land can provide only a small horizontal base, the only one that can be counted on for vegetation. Or, on the other hand, people can restrict themselves to the seashore, even among nearly sterile rocks and sand; because fishing there can supplement in large part the products of the earth, because men ought to be more concentrated in order to repel pirates, and besides, it is much easier to relieve the country, by colonies, of too many inhabitants.

[131] To these conditions for the institution of a people it is necessary to add one which cannot replace the others, but without which they are all useless: it is that they enjoy abundance and peace; for the time in which the State is organized, as that when a battalion is formed, is the instant when the body is least capable of resistance and most easily destroyed. One would resist better in absolute disorder than in a moment of ferment, when each is occupied with his own

status and not the common danger. Should a war, a famine, a sedition arise in this time of crisis, the State is inevitably overturned.

[132] Many governments have indeed been established during such storms; but then it is those governments themselves that destroy the State. Usurpers always bring about or choose disjointed times, in order to pass, under the cover of public terror, destructive laws which the people would never adopt when calm. The choice of the moment of instituting a government is one of the surest signs by which one can distinguish the work of the Legislator from that of the Tyrant.

[133] What people is then suitable for legislation? That which finds itself already bound by some union of origin, interest, or convention, but still has never carried the true yoke of the laws; that which has neither customs nor superstitions deeply rooted; that which does not fear being set upon by a sudden invasion, which, without entering into the quarrels of its neighbors, can alone resist each of them, or is able to use the aid of one to repulse the other; that whose every member can be known by all, and where no man is charged with a greater burden than he can bear; that which is able to get along without other peoples and which all other peoples are able to get along without;[12] that which is neither rich nor poor, and can be self-sufficient; finally, that which unites the steadfastness of an ancient people with the docility of a new one. What renders the work of legislation

---

12. If, of two neighboring peoples, one is not able to get along without the other, this would be a very difficult situation for the first, and very dangerous for the second. Every wise nation, in such case, would be forced to quickly deliver the other from this dependence. The Republic of Thlascala, an enclave in the Mexican Empire, preferred to deny itself salt rather than buy it from Mexicans or even accept it gratuitously. The wise Thlascalans saw the trap hidden under that liberality. They kept themselves free; and this small State, enclosed within that great Empire, finally was the instrument of its ruin.

arduous is less what it must establish than that which it must destroy; and that which renders success so rare is the impossibility of finding the simplicity of nature joined to the needs of society. All these conditions, it is true, are difficult to bring together. Thus one sees few well-constituted States.

[134]* There is still in Europe one country capable of legislation; it is the Isle of Corsica. The valor and constancy with which this brave people have known how to recover and defend their liberty well deserves that some wise man should teach them how to save it. I have a feeling that one day this small Isle will astound Europe.

XI. Of the Diverse Systems of Legislation

[135]* If one seeks to find precisely what constitutes the greatest good of all, which ought to be the goal of every system of legislation, one will find that it reduces itself to two principal objects, *liberty* and *equality.* Liberty, because all self-dependence is so much force taken away from the body of the State; equality because liberty cannot subsist without it.

[136] I have already said what civil liberty is; with regard to equality, it is necessary not to understand by this word that every degree of power and of wealth should be absolutely the same, but that, as to power, it should be above all violence and never exercised except in virtue of position and the laws; and as to wealth, no citizen should be so opulent as to be able to buy another, and none so poor as to be constrained to sell himself.[13] This presumes on the side of the mighty moderation, of goods and influence, and

---

13. Do you wish, then, to give stability to the State? Bring the two extremes together as much as possible: allow neither excess opulence nor beggars. These two conditions, naturally inseparable, are equally fatal to the common good; from one springs the fomenters of tyranny, from the other the tyrants: it is always between them that the trading of public liberty transpires: one buys it, the other sells it.

on the side of the lowly, moderation of avarice and of covetousness.

[137]* This equality is said to be a chimerical fantasy
which cannot exist in practice. But if abuse is inevitable,
does it follow that abuse should not be at least regulated?
It is precisely because the force of things always tends to
destroy equality that the force of legislation should always
tend to maintain it.

[138]* But these general objects of every good institution ought to be modified in each country by the relations
that arise, as much from the local situation as from the
character of the inhabitants, and it is upon these relations
that it is necessary to assign to each people a particular
institutional system, which should be the best, not perhaps
in itself, but for the State for which it is designed. For
example, is the soil barren and sterile; or the country too
densely populated? Turn your care to industry and the arts,
whose products you will exchange for the provisions you
lack. On the other hand, do you occupy rich plains and
fertile hillsides? On a good terrain, do you lack inhabitants?
Give your care to agriculture, which multiplies the population, and drive away the arts, which only further depopulate
the country by gathering the few inhabitants in a few
places.[14] Do you occupy extended and convenient shores?
Cover the sea with vessels, cultivate commerce and navigation; you will have a brief and brilliant existence. Does the
sea bathe nearly inaccessible rocks on your beaches? Remain
barbarians and fish-eaters; you will live more tranquilly,
perhaps better, and surely more happily. In a word, beyond
the maxims common to all, each People contains within
itself some cause which orders them in a particular manner

14. Any branch of foreign commerce, says M. d'Argenson, diffuses
a deceptive utility through the kingdom generally; it can only enrich
a few individuals, even some towns, but the nation as a whole gains
nothing, and the people are none the better for it.

and renders its legislation appropriate to itself alone. Thus, in ancient times the Hebrews and recently the Arabs had made religion their principal object, the Athenians letters, Carthage and Tyre commerce, Rhodes navigation, Sparta war, and Rome virtue. The author of *The Spirit of the Laws* has shown us many examples of the art by which the legislator directs the institution toward each of these objects.

[139]* What renders the constitution of a State truly solid and durable is when the proper means are so observed that natural relations and the laws always fall into concert on the same points, and that the latter, so to speak, only assure, accompany, and rectify the former. But if the Legislator, mistaking his object, takes a principle different from that which arises from the nature of things, the one tending to servitude and the other to liberty, the one to wealth and the other to increasing population, the one to peace and the other to conquest, one will see the imperceptible enfeeblement of the laws, the impairment of the constitution, and the State will not cease to be agitated until destroyed or changed, and invincible nature will have retaken her empire.

XII. Division of the Laws

[140] To organize the whole, to give the best possible form to the public entity, there are diverse relations to consider. First of all, the action of the entire body operating on itself, that is, the relation of all to all, or of the Sovereign to the State, this relation being composed, as we shall see later, of the relations of the intermediate terms.

[141]* The laws which govern this relationship carry the name of political laws, and are also called fundamental laws, not without some reason if these laws are wise. For if there is in each State only one good way of ordering it, the people who have found it ought to adhere to it: but if the established order is bad, why should one take as fundamental

laws which prevent it from being good? Besides, in every situation, a people is always the master of changing its laws, even the best; for if it pleases a people to do itself harm, who has the right to prevent it?

[142] The second relation is that of the members among themselves or with the entire body, and this relation ought to be in the first case as little as in the second case it is as great as possible: so that each Citizen should be in a perfect independence of all the others, and in an excessive dependence on the City; which is always achieved by the same means; because only the force of the State secures the liberty of its members. It is from this second relation that the civil laws arise.

[143] One can consider a third kind of relation between man and the law, namely that of punishable disobedience, and it is this which gives rise to the establishment of the criminal laws, which are basically less a particular species of law than the sanction of all the others.

[144]* To these three types of law is joined a fourth, the most important of all; it is engraved neither in marble nor in bronze, but in the hearts of the citizens; it is the true constitution of the State; every day it takes on new force; when the other laws age or wither away, it revives or supplements them, and conserves a people in the spirit of its institution, imperceptibly substituting the force of habit for that of authority. I speak of habitual conduct, of customs, and especially of opinion; a part of the laws unknown to our political thinkers, but on which the success of everything else depends; something with which the great Legislator secretly occupies himself while he seems to concern himself with particular regulations that are only the frame of the vault, of which moral customs, slower to arise, finally form the immovable Keystone.

[145]*Among these diverse Classes, the political laws, which constitute the form of Government, are alone relevant to my subject.

BOOK THREE

[146]* Before speaking of the diverse forms of Government, let us try to fix the precise meaning of that word, which has not yet been very well explained.

I. Of Government in General

[147]* I warn the reader that this chapter should be read with care, and that I do not know the art of being clear to those who do not wish to be attentive.

[148] Every free action has two causes which concur to produce it, the one moral, namely the will that determines the act; the other physical, namely the power that executes it. When I walk toward an object, it is first necessary that I want to go there; in the second place, that my feet carry me there. Should a paralytic wish to run, should an agile man not wish to do so, both will remain where they are. The body politic has the same motive power: in it one likewise distinguishes force and will. The latter is under the name of *legislative power,* the former under the name of *executive power.* Nothing is or should be done there [in the body politic] without their concurrence.

[149]* We have seen that the legislative power belongs to the people, and can belong to it alone. It is easy to see, on the contrary, by the principles already established, that the executive power cannot belong to the general public as Legislative or Sovereign; because this power consists only in particular acts which are not the province of the law, nor consequently of the Sovereign, all of whose acts can only be laws.

[150] It is then necessary for the public force to have an appropriate agent that unifies it and puts it to work according to the directions of the general will, which serves as the means of communication between the State and the Sover-

eign, which in some way accomplishes in the public person what the union of soul and body does in man. This is in the State the reason for Government, improperly confused with the Sovereign, of which it is only the Minister.

[151]* What then is the Government? An intermediate body established between the subjects and the Sovereign for their mutual correspondence, charged with the execution of the laws, and to the maintenance of liberty, both civil and political.

[152]* The members of this body are called Magistrates or *Kings,* that is to say *Governors;* and the body as a whole bears the name of *Prince.* [1] Thus those who claim that the act by which a people submits to its chiefs is not a contract are quite correct. It is absolutely only a commission, an employment in which simple officers of the Sovereign exercise in its name the power which it has entrusted to them, and which it can limit, modify, and take back when it pleases to do so, since the alienation of such a right is incompatible with the nature of the social body, and contrary to the goal of the association.

[153] I then call *Government* or supreme administration the legitimate exercise of the executive power, and Prince or Magistrate, the man or the body charged with that administration.

[154]* In the Government are found the intermediary forces, whose relationship composes the relation of the whole to the whole or of the Sovereign to the State. One can represent this last relation by that of the extremes of a continuous proportion, of which the proportional mean is the Government. The Government receives from the Sovereign the orders it gives to the people, and so that the State may be in good equilibrium it is necessary, all things considered, that there be equality between the product or power

---

1. It is for this reason that in Venice the name of *most serene Prince* is given to the college, even when the Doge does not attend it.

of the Government taken in itself and the product or power of the citizens, who are sovereigns on one side and subjects on the other.

[155]* Further, one could not alter any of these three terms without instantly destroying the proportion. If the Sovereign wishes to govern, or if the Magistrate wishes to provide laws, or if the subjects refuse to obey, disorder takes the place of regularity, force and will no longer act in concert, and the State falls into despotism or anarchy. Finally, as there is only one proportional mean in each relationship, only one good government is possible in a State. But, as a thousand events can change the relationships of a people, different Governments are able to be good not only for diverse peoples, but for the same people at different times.

[156] To try to give an idea of the diverse relations which reign between the two extremes, I will take as an example the number of people, as an easy relationship to express.

[157] Suppose the State is composed of ten thousand citizens. The Sovereign can only be considered collectively and as a body. But each private person in his quality as subject is considered as an individual. Thus the Sovereign is to the subject as ten thousand to one; this is to say that each member of the State is only one ten thousandth of the sovereign authority, even he is entirely subjected to it. Should the people be composed of one hundred thousand men, the condition of the subjects does not change, and each bears equally the entire dominion of the laws, while his vote, reduced to one hundred thousandth, has ten times less influence in their forming. The subject, then, always remains one, the ratio of the Sovereign to the subject always increases in proportion to the number of Citizens. Whence it follows that the larger the State grows, the more liberty diminishes.

[158] When I say that the ratio increases, I understand that it is farther removed from equality. Thus the larger the ratio in the geometric sense, the lesser the relation in the

everyday sense; in the first, the relation is considered according to the quantity measured by the quotient, and in the latter, considered according to identity, estimated by similarity.

[159] Now the less the individual wills relate to the general will, that is to say customary conduct to the laws, the more repressive force has to be increased. The Government, then, in order to be good, should be relatively stronger as the people becomes more numerous.

[160] On the other hand, the growth of the State giving the trustees of public authority more temptations and means to abuse their power, the more the Government has to have force to contain the people, the more force the Sovereign should have in turn in order to contain the Government. I speak here not of an absolute force, but of the relative force of the diverse parts of the State.

[161] It follows from this double ratio that the continued proportion between the Sovereign, the Prince, and the people is hardly an arbitrary idea, but a necessary consequence of the nature of the political body. It follows further that one of the extremes, namely the people as subject, being fixed and represented by unity, whenever the double ratio increases or diminishes, the single ratio increases or diminishes similarly, and consequently the middle term is changed. This serves to show that there is no one constitution of Government unique and absolute, but that it is possible to have as many Governments of different natures as there are States of different sizes.

[162] If, in reducing this system to ridicule, one would say that in order to find this proportional mean, and form the body of Government, it is only necessary, according to me, to take the square root of the number of the people, I would respond that I take that number here only as an example, that the relations of which I speak are measured not solely by the number of men, but in general by the amount of action, which results from combining a multitude

of causes; that, moreover, if to express myself in fewer words I borrow geometric terms for a moment, I am aware of the fact that geometric precision has no place in moral quantities.

[163]* The Government is on a small scale what the body politic which contains it is on the large scale. It is a moral person endowed with certain faculties, active as the Sovereign, passive as the State, and one can break it down into other, similar relations, from which consequently arise a new proportion, and still another within this, similar to the order of tribunals, until one arrives at an indivisible middle term, that is to say one sole chief or supreme magistrate, who is able to be represented, in the middle of this progression, much as the unifying element between the series of fractions and that of whole numbers.

[164] Without embarrassing ourselves with this multiplication of terms, let us be content to consider the Government as a new body within the State, distinct from the people and the Sovereign, and intermediate between the two.

[165] The essential difference between these two bodies is that the State exists by itself, and the Government exists only through the Sovereign. Thus only the dominant will of the Prince is or ought to be the general will or the law; its force is only the public force concentrated in itself: as soon as it wishes to derive from itself some absolute and independent act, the bond tying the whole together begins to loosen. Finally, if it should happen that the Prince have a particular will more active than that of the Sovereign, and if, in order to obey this private will, he use some of the public force which is in its hands, so that there would be, so to speak, two Sovereigns, one of right and the other of fact: at that instant the social union would vanish and the body politic be dissolved.

[166]* However, for the body of the Government to have an existence, a real life that distinguishes it from the

body of the State, for all its members to be able to act in concert and fulfill the purpose for which it has been instituted, it needs a particular *self,* a sensibility common to its members, a force, a will of its own that tends toward its own conservation. This particular existence presumes assemblies, councils, a power to deliberate, to resolve, rights, titles, privileges which belong exclusively to the Prince, and which render the condition of the magistrate more honorable, in proportion to which it is more arduous. The difficulties lie in the method of disposing, within the whole, this subordinate whole, in such a way that it may not weaken the general constitution while strengthening its own; that it always distinguish its particular force directed to its own conservation from the public force directed to the conservation of the State, and that, in a word, it always be ready to sacrifice the Government to the people and not the people to the Government.

[167] Besides, although the artificial body of the Government is the product of another artificial body, and has in some respects only a borrowed and subordinate life, that does not prevent it from being able to act with more or less vigor or speed, to enjoy, so to speak, more or less robust health. Finally, without directly departing from the goal for which it was instituted, it can deviate more or less from it according to the manner in which it is constituted.

[168] From all these differences arise the diverse relations that the Government ought to have with the body of the State, according to the accidental and particular relationships by which that same State is modified. For often the Government that is best in itself will become the most vicious, if its relations are not altered according to the defects of the body politic to which it belongs.

II. Of the Principle Which Constitutes the Diverse Forms of Government

[169]* In order to expose the general cause of these differences, it is necessary to distinguish here the Prince and the Government, as I have already distinguished the State from the Sovereign.

[170] The body of the magistracy can be composed of a greater or lesser number of members. We have said that the relation of the Sovereign to the subjects was greater as the number of people was greater, and by an evident analogy we can say the same of the Government with regard to the Magistrates.

[171] Now the total force of the Government, being always that of the State, does not vary: from which it follows that the more of that force it uses on its own members, the less remains for it to act on the whole people.

[172] Thus the more numerous are the Magistrates, the weaker the Government. As that maxim is fundamental, let us apply it to clarify it better.

[173]* We can distinguish in the person of the magistrate three essentially different wills. First, the individual's own will, which tends only to his private advantage; second, the common will of the magistrates, which relates itself uniquely to the advantage of the Prince, and which can be called the corporate will, being general in relation to the Government, and particular in relation to the State, of which the Government is a part; third, the will of the people, or the sovereign will, which is general as much in relation to the State considered as the whole, as in relation to the Government considered as part of the whole.

[174] In a perfect system of legislation, the particular or individual will ought to be null, the corporate will proper to the Government very subordinate, and consequently the general or sovereign will always dominant and the sole rule of all the others.

[175]* According to the natural order, on the contrary, these different wills become more active as they become more concentrated. Thus the general will is always the weakest, the corporate will has the second rank, and the private will is first of all; so that in the Government each member is first himself, then Magistrate, and then citizen, a gradation directly opposed to what the social order requires.

[176]* Granting this, suppose that the whole Government is in the hands of one man. The particular will and the corporate will are then perfectly united, and consequently the latter is in the highest possible degree of intensity. Further, as it is the degree of will on which the use of force depends, and the absolute force of the Government does not vary, it follows that the most active of Governments is that of one man.

[177] On the contrary, suppose we unite the Government with the legislative authority; let us make the Sovereign into the Prince and all of the Citizens into as many Magistrates. Then the corporate will, confounded with the general will, will be no more active than it and will leave to the particular will its full force. Thus the Government, always with the same absolute force, will have attained its *minimum* relative force or activity.

[178] These relations are incontestable, and other considerations also serve to confirm them. One sees, for example, that each magistrate is more active in his group than each citizen is in his, and consequently the particular will has much more influence in the acts of the Government than in those of the Sovereign; for each magistrate is nearly always charged with some function of Government, while each citizen, taken separately, exercises no function of sovereignty. Besides, the more a State is extended, the more its real force is increased even though not by reason of its size: but if the State remains the same, the magistrates may well be multiplied without the Government acquiring any more

real force, because that force is the force of the State, whose measure remains unchanged. Thus the relative force or activity of the Government diminishes, without its absolute or real force being able to increase.

[179] It is also certain that public matters are expedited more slowly as more people are charged with them, that in giving too much importance to prudence one does not give enough to fortune, that one lets opportunity escape, and that owing to excessive deliberation the fruits of deliberation are often lost.

[180]* I have just proved that the Government is weakened as the magistrates are multiplied, and I have already proved that the larger the population, the more the repressive force should be increased. From this it follows that the ratio of the magistrates to the Government ought to be the inverse ratio of subjects to Sovereign; this is to say that the more the State grows, the more the Government should shrink; so that the number of chiefs diminishes as the number of people is increased.

[181] But I speak here only of the relative force of Government, not of its rectitude: for, on the contrary, the more numerous the magistracy, the more the corporate will approaches the general will; whereas under a single magistrate, this same corporate will is, I have said, only a particular will. Thus one loses on one side what one gains on the other, and the art of the Legislator is to know how to fix the point where the force and the will of the Government are always combined in the reciprocal proportion most advantageous to the State.

III. Division of Governments

[182]* We have seen in the preceding chapter why one distinguishes the diverse species or forms of Governments by the number of members who compose them; it remains to see here how this division is made.

[183] The Sovereign can, in the first place, commit the charge of Government to all the people or the majority of the people, in such a way that more citizens are magistrates than simply individual citizens. One gives to this form of government the name of *Democracy*.

[184] Or it can confine the Government to the hands of a small number, so that there are more simple Citizens than magistrates; this form bears the name of *Aristocracy*.

[185] Finally, it can concentrate the whole Government in the hands of one sole magistrate from whom all the others derive their power. This third form is the most common and is called *Monarchy* or royal Government.

[186]* One should note that all these forms or at least the first two are more or less variable and may indeed have a considerable range; for Democracy can embrace all the people or be restricted to half. Aristocracy, in its turn, can confine itself to half the number down to the smallest, indeterminately. Royalty itself is susceptible to some division. Sparta always had two Kings by its constitution; and one has seen in the Roman Empire as many as eight Emperors at one time without being able to say that the Empire was divided. Thus there is a point where each form of Government blends with the next, and one sees that, under three sole types, Government can really be divided into as many diverse forms as the State has Citizens.

[187] There is more: this same Government being in some respects able to subdivide itself into other parts, one part administered in one manner and the other part in another, from these three combined forms there can emerge a multitude of mixed forms, each of which is multipliable by all the simple forms.

[188] In all times, there has been much dispute about the best form of Government, without considering that each of them is the best in certain cases, and the worst in others.

[189] If in different States the number of supreme magistrates should be in an inverse ratio to that of the Citizens,

it follows that generally Democratic Government suits small states, Aristocratic medium-sized, and Monarchical large ones. This rule is immediately derived from the principle, but how count the multitude of circumstances which can furnish exceptions?

IV. Of Democracy

[190]* He who makes the law knows better than anyone how it ought to be executed and interpreted. It seems then that there could be no better constitution than the one in which the executive power is joined to the legislative. But it is just that which renders this Government insufficient in certain regards, because things that ought to be distinguished are not, and the prince and the Sovereign, being the same person, only form as it were a Government without a Government.

[191]* It is not good that he who makes the laws execute them, nor that the body of the people turn their attention away from general considerations in order to give it to particular objects. Nothing is more dangerous than the influence of private interests in public affairs, and the abuse of laws by the Government is a lesser evil than the corruption of the Legislator, the inevitable result of private considerations. Then, the State having been corrupted in its substance, all reform becomes impossible. A people who would never abuse the Government would not abuse independence either; a people who would always govern well would have no need of being governed.

[192] To take the term in a rigorous sense, there has never existed a true Democracy, and it will never exist. It is contrary to the natural order that the greater number should govern and that the lesser number should be governed. One cannot imagine the people remaining constantly assembled in order to attend to public affairs, and one readily sees that it would not know how to establish commissions

for this purpose without the form of the administration changing.

[193] In fact, I think it possible to lay down as a principle that when the functions of the government are divided among several tribunals, sooner or later those with the fewest members acquire the greatest authority, if only because of the facility in expediting the public business which naturally brings this about.

[194] Besides, how many things difficult to unite does this Government presume! First, a very small State where the people are easily assembled and where each citizen can easily know all the others; second, a great simplicity of moral customs, which prevents a multitude of public matters and thorny discussions; next, a great equality of rank and fortune, without which equality in rights and authority would not long subsist; finally, little or no luxury because luxury either is the result of wealth or renders it necessary: it corrupts both the rich and the poor, the one by possession, the other by covetousness; it sells the fatherland to indolence and vanity; it deprives the State of all its citizens in order to enslave some to others, and all to opinion.

[195] That is why a celebrated author[2] has named virtue as the principle of the Republic, for all these conditions could not subsist without virtue; but failing to make the necessary distinctions, this great genius often lacked accuracy and sometimes clarity, and did not see that the Sovereign authority being everywhere the same, the same principle ought to function in every well-constituted State, more or less, it is true, according to the form of Government.

[196] Let us add that there is no Government so subject to civil wars and internal agitations as the Democratic or popular, because there is none which tends so strongly and continually to change its form, nor demands more vigilance and courage in order to be maintained in its own form. It

2. I.e., Montesquieu; see *The Spirit of the Laws,* III, 3—ED.

is especially in this constitution that the Citizen ought to arm himself with force and steadfastness, and to say each day of his life from his heart what a virtuous Palatine[3] said in the Diet of Poland: *"Malo periculosam libertatem quam quietum servitium."* [I prefer liberty with danger to peace with slavery.]

[197] If there were a people of Gods, it would govern itself democratically. A Government so perfect is not suited to men.

V. Of Aristocracy

[198] We have here two very distinct moral persons, namely the Government and the Sovereign, and consequently two general wills, the one in relation to all the citizens, the other solely for the members of the administration. Thus, although the Government is able to regulate its internal policy as it pleases, it is never able to speak to the people in the name of the Sovereign, that is to say in the name of the people itself; this must never be forgotten.

[199] The first societies governed themselves aristocratically. The family heads deliberated among themselves about public affairs. The young people deferred without distress to the authority of experience. Hence the names of *Priests, Ancients,*[4] *Senate, Elders.* The savages of North America still govern themselves this way in our day, and are very well governed.

[200] But, as the inequality due to institutions prevailed over natural inequality, wealth or power[5] was preferred to

3. The Palatine of Posen, father of the king of Poland, duke of Lorraine.

4. The French word is *Gerontes,* a traditional name of the French stage for the father who is both miserly and duped; it generally indicates a self-important old man without any practical wisdom.—ED.

5. It is clear that the word *optimates,* among the ancients, meant not the best, but the most powerful.

age, and Aristocracy became elective. Finally, the power transmitted with the father's goods to the children created patrician families, rendering the Government hereditary, and one witnessed Senators twenty years of age.

[201]* There are then three kinds of Aristocracy: natural, elective, hereditary. The first is suited only for simple peoples; the third is the worst of all governments. The second is the best: it is Aristocracy properly named.

[202] Beyond the advantage of the distinction between the two powers, aristocracy has that of the choice of its members; for in popular Government all the Citizens are born magistrates; but this one limits them to a small number, and they only become so by election:[6] a means by which probity, insight, experience, and all the other reasons for public preference and esteem are so many new guarantees of being wisely governed.

[203] Additionally, assemblies are more conveniently held, public affairs are better discussed, expedited with more order and diligence, the repute of the State is better sustained abroad by venerable Senators than by an unknown or scorned multitude.

[204]* In a word, it is the best and most natural order that the wisest should govern the multitude, when it is certain that they will govern it for its profit and not for their own; there being no need to uselessly multiply devices, nor to do with twenty thousand men what one hundred well-chosen men can do still better. But it need be remarked that the corporate interest begins here to direct the public force less under the rule of the general will, and that another inevita-

6. It is very important to regulate by laws the form of the election of the magistrates, because leaving it to the will of the prince, one could not escape falling into hereditary Aristocracy, as happened in the Republics of *Venice* and *Berne.* Also, the first has long been a dissolved State; but the second maintains itself by the extreme wisdom of its Senate: it is a very honorable and very dangerous exception.

ble propensity removes from the laws a part of the executive power.

[205] With regard to particular proprieties, a State should not be so small, nor a people so simple and righteous, that the execution of the laws immediately ensues from the public will, as in a good Democracy. Nor again must a nation be so large that the chiefs, dispersed in order to govern, are able to determine the Sovereign each in his own department, and begin by making themselves independent in order to finally become the masters.

[206] But if Aristocracy requires some fewer virtues than popular Government, it requires others which are properly its own; as moderation among the wealthy and contentment among the poor; for it seems that a rigorous equality would be out of place there; it was not even observed in Sparta.

[207]* Further, if this form permits a certain inequality of fortune, it is indeed so that generally the administration of public affairs should be entrusted to those who are better able to give their time to it, but not, as Aristotle claims, so that the wealthy always be preferred. On the contrary, it is important that an opposite choice should sometimes inform the people that there are more important reasons for preference in the merits of men than in their wealth.

VI. Of Monarchy

[208]* Up to this point we have considered the Prince as a moral and collective person, united by the force of the laws, and entrusted with the executive power in the State. We now have to consider this power united in the hands of one natural person, a real man, who alone has the right to dispose of it according to the laws. He is what one calls a Monarch or a King.

[209] Completely contrary to other administrations where a collective entity represents an individual, in this one an individual represents a collective entity; so that the moral

unity which constitutes the Prince is at the same time a physical unity, in which all the faculties which the law combines in the other with such effort are found naturally combined.

[210] Thus the will of the people, and the will of the Prince, and the public force of the State, and the private force of the Government, all respond to the same motive, all the mechanisms of the machine are in the same hand, everything works to the same end; there are no opposing movements that cancel each other, and one can imagine no kind of constitution in which a lesser effort produces more notable an action. Archimedes tranquilly seated on the shore and effortlessly pulling along a large Vessel represents to me a skillful monarch governing his vast States from his private study, and making everything move while appearing to be motionless.

[211] But if there is no Government that has more vigor, there is none where the private will has greater sway and more easily dominates others; everything works to the same end, it is true, but this end is not the goal of public happiness, and the very force of the Administration ceaselessly operates to the detriment of the State.

[212]* Kings want to be absolute, and from afar one calls out to them that the best means for being so is to make themselves loved by their peoples. This maxim is very fine and even very true in some respects. Unfortunately, it will always be jeered at in the Courts. Power which comes from the love of the peoples is without doubt the greater; but it is precarious and conditional, and never will satisfy Princes. The best Kings wish to be able to be wicked if it pleases them, without ceasing to be the masters. A political sermonizer will tell them in vain that the power of the people being their own, their greatest interest is that the people should be flourishing, numerous, formidable. They know very well that is not true. Their personal interest is first that the People be weak, miserable, and never able to resist

them. I admit that, supposing the subjects always perfectly submissive, the interest of the Prince should then be that the people are powerful, to the end that this power, being his own, would make him formidable to his neighbors; but this interest is only secondary and subordinate, and as the two suppositions are incompatible, it is natural that Princes always give preference to the maxim which is most immediately useful to them. It is this that Samuel strongly represented to the Hebrews; it is this that Machiavelli made evident. While feigning to give lessons to the Kings he has given great ones to the peoples. *The Prince* of Machiavelli is the book of republicans.[7]

[213] We have found, by general relationships, that monarchy is suitable only to large States, and we find this again by examining it itself. The more numerous the public administration, the more the ratio of the Prince to the subjects diminishes and approaches equality, so that this relation is one of equality even as in Democracy. This same ratio increases as the Government shrinks, and it is at its *maximum* when the Government is in the hands of a single man. Then there is found too great a distance between the Prince and the People, and the State lacks cohesiveness. In order to create this, intermediary orders are needed. Princes, Grandees, and the nobility are necessary to fill them. Now none of this is suited to a small State, which is ruined by all these distinctions.

[214] But if it is difficult that a large State be well gov-

---

7. Machiavelli was an honest man and a good citizen; but, attached to the house of Medici, he was forced, during the oppression of his fatherland, to disguise his love for liberty. The mere choice of his execrable hero sufficiently manifests his secret intention; and the opposition of the maxims of his book *The Prince* and those of his *Discourses on Titus Livy* and his *History of Florence* shows that this profound political thinker has had until now only superficial or corrupt readers. The court of Rome has sternly prohibited his book; I certainly believe it: it is that court which he most clearly depicts.

erned, it is much more difficult that it be well governed by one man alone, and everyone knows what happens when the King appoints deputies.

[215] An essential and inevitable defect which will always place monarchical government beneath the republican is that in the latter the public voice hardly ever raises to the highest positions any but enlightened and capable men, who fill them with honor; whereas those who attain rank in monarchies are most often merely petty bunglers, petty rascals, petty intriguers, whose petty talents, which enable them to attain high posts in the Courts, only serve to show the public their ineptitude as soon as they have attained these posts. The people is mistaken in its choice much less than the Prince, and a man of true merit is almost as rare in the ministry as a fool at the head of a republican government. Also, when by some lucky chance one of those men born to govern takes control of public business in a monarchy almost wrecked by this crowd of fine managers, one is totally surprised by the resources that he finds, and it is an epoch-making event in a country.

[216] For a monarchical State to be well governed, it would be necessary that its size or extent be proportionate to the capabilities of he who governs. It is easier to conquer than to rule. With a sufficient lever, the world can be moved by a finger, but to sustain it requires the shoulders of Hercules. Should the State be the least bit large, the Prince is nearly always too small for it. When on the contrary it happens that the State is too small for its chief, which is very rare, it is still badly governed, because the chief, always following the grandeur of his views, forgets the people's interest, and makes them no less discontent by the abuse of his overabundant talents than does a chief limited by those which he lacks. It would require, so to speak, that a kingdom enlarge or contract itself in every reign according to the capacity of the Prince; rather, as the talents of a Senate are

more stable, the State is able to have permanent boundaries and the administration would not go on any less well.

[217] The most perceptible inconvenience of the Government of a single person is the lack of that continual succession which forms in the other two an uninterrupted bond. One King dies, another is needed; elections leave dangerous intervals, they are stormy, and unless the Citizens have a disinterestedness and integrity which this Government hardly manages to permit, intrigue and corruption intermingle throughout. It is difficult for one to whom the State has been sold not to sell it in turn, and recoup for himself from the helpless the money that the powerful have extorted from him. Sooner or later everything becomes venal under such an administration, and the peace which is enjoyed under kings is worse than the disorder of these interregnums.

[218] What has been done to prevent these ills? Crowns have been made hereditary in certain families, and an order of succession has been established which prevents any dispute at the death of Kings. That is to say, substituting the inconvenience of regencies for that of elections, an apparent tranquillity has been preferred to a wise administration, and it is preferred to risk having infants, monsters, or imbeciles for chiefs than having to argue over the choice of good Kings; it has not been considered that in thus exposing oneself to the risk of this alternative, one sets nearly all the odds against himself. It was a very sensible reply that Dionysius the Younger gave to his father, who, reproaching him for a dishonorable action, said: "Have I given you such an example?" "Ah," replied the son, "your father was not king."

[219] Everything conspires to deprive a man elevated to command others of justice and reason. Much trouble is taken, it is said, to teach young Princes the art of ruling: it does not seem that this education profits them. One would do better to begin by teaching them the art of obeying. The

greatest kings celebrated by history were not brought up to rule; it is a science that one has never mastered less than after having studied it too much, and that one acquires better by obeying than by commanding. *Nam ultissimus idem ac brevissimus bonarum malarumque rerum delectus, cogitare quid aut nolueris sub alio principe, aut volueris.* [Because the best and shortest way to discover what is good and what is bad is to ask what you would have wished to happen or not to happen, if another than you had been king.][8]

[220] One consequence of this lack of coherence is the instability of royal government, which, being regulated alternatively on one level and then on another, according to the character of the ruling Prince or of the people ruling for him, cannot long maintain a fixed aim or a consistent course of conduct: this variation, which always makes the state drift from maxim to maxim, from project to project, does not take place in other Governments, where the prince is always the same. Thus one sees that in general if there is more cunning in a Court, there is more wisdom in a Senate, and that Republics go to their goals by more constant and better-followed policies; whereas each revolution in the [royal] Ministry produces one in the State; the maxim common to all Ministers, and nearly all Kings, being to take up the reverse of their predecessors in everything.

[221] From this same incoherence is found the solution of a sophism very familiar to all defenders of royalty: not only is civil Government compared to the Government of the household and the prince to the father of the family, an error already refuted, but all the virtues of which he will have need are liberally ascribed to this magistrate, while always supposing that the Prince is what he ought to be; with the aid of this supposition royal Government is evidently preferable to any other, because it is incontestably

8. Tacitus, *Histories* [I, 16].

the strongest, and in order to also be the best, it lacks only a corporate will more conformable to the general will.

[222] But if, according to Plato,[9] the king by nature is such a rare person, how many times will nature and fortune converge to crown him? And if royal education necessarily corrupts those who receive it, what should one hope from a succession of men trained to rule? It is surely deliberate self-deception to confound royal Government with that of a good King. To see what this Government is in itself, it is necessary to consider it under stupid or wicked Princes; for they will come to the Throne as such, or the Throne will make them such.

[223] These difficulties have not escaped our Authors, but they are not embarrassed by them. The remedy is, they say, to obey without a murmur. God gives bad Kings in his anger, and one must endure them as chastisements from Heaven. This discourse is edifying, without doubt; but I do not know if it is not more appropriate to the pulpit than in a book about politics. What is to be said of a doctor who promises miracles and whose entire art is to exhort his sick charge to have patience? One knows well that it is necessary to suffer a bad Government when one has one: the question should be how to find a good one.

VII. Of Mixed Governments

[224]* Properly speaking, there is no simple Government. A single Chief must have subordinate magistrates; a popular Government must have a Chief. Thus, in the partition of the executive power, there is always a gradation from the greater number to the less, with this difference, that sometimes the greater number depends on the lesser number, and sometimes the lesser number on the greater number.

9. The *Statesman.*

[225] Sometimes there is an equal division, either when the constituent parts are in mutual dependence, as in the Government of England; or when the authority of each part is independent but imperfect, as in Poland. This latter form is bad, because there is no unity in the government, and the State lacks cohesion.

[226] Which is better, a simple Government or a mixed Government? This question is much debated among political thinkers, and it requires the same response I have already given concerning every form of Government.

[227] Simple Government is best in itself, solely because it is simple. But when the executive power does not depend enough on the legislative, that is to say when there is a greater ratio between the Prince and the Sovereign than between the people and the Prince, this defect of proportion must be remedied by dividing the Government; for then all its parts have no less authority over the subjects, and their division renders them all of them together less strong against the Sovereign.

[228] The same disadvantage is also prevented by establishing intermediate magistrates who, leaving the Government in its entirety, only serve to balance the two powers and to maintain their respective rights. Then the Government is not mixed, it is tempered.

[229] One can remedy the opposite disadvantage by similar means, and when the Government is too loose, Tribunals can be established to concentrate it: this is practiced in all Democracies. In the first case one divides the Government to weaken it, and in the second, in order to reinforce it; for the *maximum* force and weakness are found equally in simple Governments, whereas the mixed forms provide a medium force.

VIII. That Every Form of Government Is Not Appropriate for Every Country

[230]* Liberty, not being a fruit of all climates, is not within the reach of all peoples. The more one contemplates this principle established by Montesquieu, the more one senses its truth. The more one contests it, the more one is given occasion to establish it by new proofs.

[231]* In all the Governments of the world the public person consumes, yet produces nothing. From where, then, comes the substance it consumes? From the labor of its members. It is the surplus of private individuals that produces what is needed by the public. Hence it follows that the civil State can subsist only as long as the labor of men produces more than their own needs.

[232] Now this excess is not the same in all countries of the world. In several it is considerable, in others it is moderate, in others null, in others negative. This ratio depends on the fertility of the climate, the kind of labor which the soil requires, the nature of its products, the physical strength of its inhabitants, the greater or lesser consumption necessary for them, and on several other similar ratios of which it is composed.

[233] On the other hand, all Governments are not of the same nature; some are more or less ravenous, and the differences are based on this other principle, that the further public contributions are removed from their source, the more burdensome they are. This burden is not to be measured by the amount of taxes but by the path they must take in order to return to the hands from which they came; when this circulation is prompt and well established, it is unimportant whether little or much is paid; the people is always rich and finances always thrive. On the contrary, however little the People gives, when this small sum does not revert to it, by always giving it soon exhausts itself; the State is never wealthy, and the people is always destitute.

[234] It follows that the greater the distance from the people to the Government increases, the more burdensome do the tributes become: thus in a Democracy the people is least encumbered, in Aristocracy more so, and in Monarchy, it carries the greatest weight. Monarchy then is suited only to wealthy nations; Aristocracy, to States of moderate wealth and size; Democracy, to small and poor States.

[235] In effect, the more one reflects on it, the more one finds in this the difference between free States and monarchies: in the first, everything is used for the common utility; in the others, the public and private forces are reciprocal, and the former are augmented by the weakening of the latter. Finally, in place of governing the subjects in order to render them happy, despotism makes them miserable in order to govern them.

[236]* There are then in each climate natural causes by which we can assign the form of Government toward which the force of the climate leads it, and we can even say what kind of inhabitants it should have. Unproductive and sterile places where the produce does not repay the labor ought to remain uncultivated and deserted, or should only be inhabited by Savage peoples. The places where human labor yields only bare necessities should be inhabited by barbarous peoples, all polity being an impossibility there; places where the excess of the produce over the labor is moderate are suitable for free peoples; those where abundant and fertile soil yields much produce for little labor want to be governed monarchically, so that the excess of the subjects' surplus may be consumed by the luxury of the Prince; for it is better that this excess should be absorbed by the government than dissipated by private individuals. There are exceptions, I know: but these exceptions themselves confirm the rule, in that sooner or later they produce revolutions which restore things to the order of nature.

[237] Let us always distinguish general laws from the particular causes which can modify their effect. Even if the

whole south were covered with Republics and the entire north with despotic States, it would not be less true that, through the effect of climate, despotism is suited to warm countries, barbarism to cold countries, and a good polity to the intermediate regions. I see, however, that one can agree with the principle and still be able to dispute its application; one could say that there are very fertile cold countries and some very unproductive southern ones. But this difficulty is only one for those who do not examine the thing in all its relationships. It is necessary, as I have already said, to consider those of work, labor, consumption, etc.

[238] Let us suppose that of two pieces of land equal in size, one produces five units and the other ten. If the inhabitants of the former consume four and those of the latter nine, the excess of the first product will be $\frac{1}{5}$ and that of the second $\frac{1}{10}$. The ratio between these two surpluses being then the inverse of the produce of each, the piece of land which yields only five will provide a surplus double that of the piece of land which produces ten.

[239] But it is not a question of a doubled product, and I do not believe that any person dares in general to claim the fertility of the cold countries to be even equal to that of the warm countries. At any rate, let us suppose this equality; let us, if one wishes, put England in balance with Sicily, and Poland with Egypt. More to the south we will have Africa and the Indies; farther north we will have nothing more. For this equality of produce, what difference is there in cultivation? In Sicily it is only necessary to scratch the soil; in England what effort is demanded to work it! Now where more hands are needed to obtain the same product, the surplus should necessarily be less.

[240] Consider, beyond this, that the same quantity of men consume much less in the warm countries. The climate requires only that people should be sober in order to be in good health: Europeans who want to live as at home all perish from dysentery and indigestion. "We are," says Char-

din, "carnivorous beasts, wolves, in comparison with Asians. Some attribute the sobriety of the Persians to the fact that their country is scantily cultivated, but I believe on the contrary that their country is less abundant in food because the inhabitants need less. If their frugality," he continues, "resulted from the scarcity of the country, it would only be the poor who ate little, whereas it is so of the people generally; and one would eat more or less in each province according to the fertility of the country, whereas the same sobriety is found everywhere in the kingdom. They pride themselves greatly on their manner of living, saying that one need only look at their complexion to see that it is much better than those of the Christians. Indeed, the complexion of the Persians is smooth; while that of their subjects, the Armenians, who live in European fashion, is coarse and blotchy, and their bodies are fat and heavy."

[241] The more one approaches the equator, the less do people live on. They eat nearly no meat; rice, maize, couscous, millet, cassava are their ordinary foods. There are in the Indies millions of men whose nutrition costs less than a penny a day. We see in Europe itself noticeable differences in appetite between northern and southern peoples. A Spaniard will live eight days on a German's dinner. In the countries where men are most voracious, luxury itself is directed toward matters of consumption. In England it is displayed on a table loaded with meats; in Italy you are regaled with sugar and flowers.

[242] Luxury in clothing again offers similar differences. In climates where seasonal changes are sudden and violent, one has clothes that are better and simpler; in those where one dresses only for ornament, splendor is more sought than utility, for clothes themselves are a luxury. In Naples you will see men every day promenade along the Posillipo with gold-embroidered coats but no stockings. It is the same with regard to buildings: one gives everything for magnificence when one fears no damage from the weather. In Paris, in

London, one wishes to be warmly and comfortably housed. In Madrid one has superb salons, but no windows that shut, and one sleeps in mere rat holes.

[243] The foods are much more substantial and succulent in warm countries; this is a third difference which cannot fail to influence the second. Why does one eat so many vegetables in Italy? Because they are good, nourishing, of excellent flavor. In France, where they are grown only with water, they are not nourishing and scarcely count for anything on the tables. They do not, however, take up less ground and cost at least as much effort to cultivate. Experience shows that the wheat of Barbary, inferior in other respects to that of France, yields much more flour, and that French wheat in turn yields more than the wheat of the north. From this one can infer that a similar gradation is generally observable in the same direction from the equator to the pole. Now is it not a clear disadvantage to have an equal quantity of product with a lesser quantity of nourishment?

[244]* To all these different considerations I can add one which springs from and strengthens them: warm countries have less need of inhabitants than cold countries, and would be able to nourish a greater number; hence a double surplus is produced, always to the advantage of despotism. The greater the area inhabited by the same number of inhabitants, the more difficult rebellions become; because concerted action cannot be taken promptly and secretly, and because it is always easy for the Government to discover projects and to cut communications; but the closer together a numerous people is packed, the less is the Government able to usurp from the Sovereign: the chiefs deliberate as safely in their rooms as the Prince in his council, and the crowd is assembled as quickly in the squares as the troops in their quarters. The advantage of a tyrannical Government in this regard is then to act over great distances. With the aid of the points of support which it establishes, its power

increases with distance like that of levers.[10] The power of the people, on the contrary, acts only when concentrated; it evaporates and disappears when spread out, like the effect of gunpowder scattered on the ground, which only takes fire grain by grain. The least populous countries are thus the best adapted for tyranny: ferocious beasts reign only in deserts.

IX. Of the Signs of a Good Government

[245]* When one then asks what is absolutely the best Government, one poses a question as insoluble as indeterminate; or, if you wish, it has as many correct solutions as there are possible combinations in the absolute and relative positions of peoples.

[246] But if one asked by what sign one can know that a given people is well or badly governed, this would be another thing, and the question of fact could be resolved.

[247] However, it is not resolved, because each wants to do so in his own way. The subjects extol public tranquillity, the Citizens the liberty of private individuals; the one prefers the security of possessions, the other that of persons; one holds that the best Government is the most severe, the other maintains that it is the mildest; one believes that crimes should be punished, and the other that they should be prevented; one finds it good to be feared by neighbors, the other prefers to be ignored by them; one is satisfied when money circulates, the other demands that the people have bread. Even though agreement should be had on these and similar points, would we have advanced? Moral quanti-

---

10. This does not contradict what I said before (Book Two, IX) on the inconveniences of large States; for if it were there a matter of the authority of the government over its members, it is here that of its power against the subjects. Its scattered members serve as points of support to it for acting upon the people at a distance, but it has no point of support for acting on its members themselves. Thus, in one case, the length of the lever in fact is weakness, and in the other case it is power.

ties lacking any precise measure, if there were agreement on the sign, how could there be about its evaluation?

[248] For my part, I am always astounded that such a simple sign is overlooked, or that one has the bad faith not to admit it. What is the end of political association? It is the preservation and the prosperity of its members. And what is the surest sign that they are preserved and prospering? It is their number and population. Do not go then to look elsewhere for this much-disputed sign. All other things being equal, the Government under which, without external aids, without naturalizations, without colonies, the Citizens become populous and multiply most is infallibly the best; that under which a people diminish and wither away is the worst. Calculators, it is now your concern; count, measure, compare.[11]

11. One should judge on the same principle the centuries which merit preference regarding the prosperity of the human race. Those in which literature and art were seen to flourish have been too much admired, without the secret object of their cultivation being penetrated, without their fatal consequences being considered. *"Idque apud imperitos humanitas vocabatur, quum pars servitutis esset"* (Tacitus, *Agricola,* XXI). [Fools bestowed the word "humanity" on what was already the beginning of slavery.] Shall we never detect in the maxims of books the gross self-interest which makes the Authors speak? No, whatever they may say, when, despite its brilliancy, a country is being depopulated, it is untrue that all goes well, and it is not enough that a poet should have an income of one hundred thousand livres for his epoch to be the best of all. The apparent repose and tranquillity of the chiefs must be regarded less than the welfare of entire nations and especially of the most populous states. Hail lays waste a few cantons, but it rarely causes scarcity. Riots and civil wars greatly startle the chiefs, but they do not produce the real misfortunes of peoples, who may even relax while it is being disputed who shall tyrannize over them. It is from their permanent condition that their real prosperity or calamities arise; when all remains crushed under the yoke, it is then that everything withers; it is then that the chiefs destroy them at their leisure: *"ubi solitudinem faciunt, pacem appellant"* (Tacitus, *Agricola,* XXXI). ["where they create solitude (when they have made the country into a desert), they say that peace reigns"]. When the quarrels of the great agitated the kingdom

X. Of the Abuse of the Government, and of Its Tendency to Degenerate

[249] As the private will incessantly acts against the general will, so the Government makes a continual effort against the Sovereignty. The more this effort increases, the more the constitution deteriorates, and as there is here no other corporate will which, by resisting that of the Prince, would balance it, sooner or later there must come a time when the Prince finally oppresses the Sovereign and breaks the social treaty. It is this inherent and inevitable vice that, from the birth of the body politic, tends without respite to destroy it, just as old age and death finally destroy the body of a man.

[250] There are two general ways by which a Government degenerates: namely, when it shrinks, or when the State dissolves.

[251]* The government shrinks when it passes from a large to a small number, that is from Democracy to Aristocracy, and from Aristocracy to Royalty. That is its natural inclination.[12] If it were to go backward from a small number

---

of France, and the coadjutor of Paris carried a dagger in his pocket to the *Parlement*, that did not prevent the French people from living happily and in large numbers in free and honorable ease. Ancient Greece flourished in the midst of the most cruel wars; blood flowed there in streams, and the whole country was covered with men. It seemed, said Machiavelli, that amid murders, proscriptions, and civil wars our republic became more powerful; the virtue of its citizens, their customary conduct, their independence, were more effective in strengthening it than all its dissensions had been in weakening it. A little agitation gives strength to men's souls, and what truly makes the species prosper is not so much peace as liberty.

12. The slow formation and the progress of the republic of Venice in its lagoons offers a notable example of this succession; and it is indeed astounding that, after more than twelve hundred years, the Venetians seems to be still in only the second stage, which began with the *Serrar di Consiglio* [Closing of the Council] in 1198. As for the ancient Dukes, for whom they are reproached, whatever the *Squittinio*

to a large one, it could be said that it slackens, but this inverse progress is impossible.

[252] In effect, the government only changes its form when its exhausted mainspring leaves it too weakened to be able to preserve itself. Now if it would slacken more as it

---

della libertà veneta may say, it is proved that they were not their sovereigns.

One will not fail to cite as an objection the Roman Republic as having pursued a completely opposite development, passing from Monarchy to Aristocracy, and from Aristocracy to Democracy. I am far from thinking about it in this way.

The first establishment of Romulus was a mixed Government, which promptly degenerated into Despotism. For some particular reasons, the State perished before its time, as we see a newly born baby die before reaching manhood. The expulsion of the Tarquins was the true epoch of the birth of the Republic. But it did not assume a stable form at first, because it only completed half of the work by not abolishing the patriciate. For in this manner, the hereditary Aristocracy, which is the worst of the legitimate administrations, remaining in conflict with the Democracy, always an uncertain and fluctuating form of government, was not settled until the establishment of the Tribunes, as Machiavelli has proved; only then was there a true Government and a true Democracy. In fact, the people were at the time not only Sovereign, but also magistrate and judge; the Senate was only a subordinate tribunal to temper or concentrate the Government; and the consuls themselves, although patricians as well as first magistrates and absolute generals in war, were in Rome only the presidents of the people.

From that time on, the Government was also seen to follow its natural propensity and tend strongly to Aristocracy. The Patriciate abolishing itself, as it were, the Aristocracy was no longer in the body of Patricians as it was in Venice and Genoa, but in the body of the Senate, composed of patricians and plebeians, and also in the body of the Tribunes when they began to usurp active power; for words make no difference to things, and when the people has chiefs who govern for it, it is always an Aristocracy.

From the abuses of the Aristocracy were born the civil wars and the triumvirate. Sulla, Julius Caesar, Augustus, became in fact true Monarchs; and finally, under the despotism of Tiberius, the State was dissolved. Roman history does not then refute my principle: it confirms it.

extends itself, its force would become completely null, and it would subsist still less. It is then necessary to wind and adjust the spring as it unravels; otherwise the State which it sustains will fall into ruin.

[253] The dissolution of the State can occur in two ways.

[254]* First, when the Prince no longer administers the State in accordance with laws and usurps the sovereign power. Then a remarkable change occurs; it is not the Government but the State that shrinks: I mean to say that the large State dissolves and another is formed within it, composed solely of the members of the Government, and it is for the rest of the People only its master and tyrant. So that at the instant that the Government usurps sovereignty, the social pact is broken; and all ordinary Citizens, returning by right to their natural liberty, are forced but no longer obligated to obey.

[255] The same situation also occurs when the members of the Government separately usurp the power which they only ought to exercise as a body; this is no less a violation of the laws, and produces a still greater disorder. Then one has, so to say, as many Princes as Magistrates; and the State, no less divided than the Government, perishes or changes its form.

[256]* When the State dissolves, the abuse of Government, whatever it might be, takes the common name of *anarchy.* To distinguish, Democracy degenerates into *Ochlocracy,* Aristocracy into *Oligarchy;* I should add that Royalty degenerates into *Tyranny,* but this last word is equivocal and requires explanation.

[257] In the ordinary sense, a Tyrant is a King who governs with violence and without regard to justice and to the laws. In the precise sense, a Tyrant is a private individual who arrogates royal authority to himself without having a right to it. It is thus that the Greeks understood this word

Tyrant: they gave it indifferently to good and bad Princes whose authority was not legitimate. Hence *Tyrant* and *usurper* are two perfectly synonymous words.[13]

[258] To give different names to different things, I call the usurper of royal authority a *Tyrant,* and the usurper of the Sovereign power a *Despot.* The Tyrant is he who intrudes himself contrary to the laws in order to govern according to the law; the Despot is he who places himself above the laws themselves. Thus the Tyrant may not be a Despot but the Despot is always a Tyrant.

XI. Of the Death of the Body Politic

[259]* Such is the natural and inevitable inclination of the best-constituted Governments. If Sparta and Rome have perished, what State can hope to last forever? If we wish to form a durable establishment, let us then not seek to make it eternal. In order to succeed, one should neither attempt the impossible, nor flatter oneself with giving to the work of men a solidity that human things do not admit of.

[260] The body politic, just as the human body, begins to die at its moment of birth and carries within itself the causes of its destruction. But each can have a constitution more or less robust and suited to preserve it for a longer or shorter time. The constitution of man is the work of nature; that of the State is the work of art. It does not rest with men

13. *"Omnes enim et habentur et dicuntur tyranni, qui potestate utuntur perpetua in ea civitate quae libertate usa est"* (Cornelius Nepos, *Life of Militades,* VIII). [All are considered and called tyrants, who hold perpetual power in a State that has had liberty.] It is true that Aristotle (*Nicomachean Ethics,* VIII, 10) distinguishes the tyrant from the king, in that the first governs for his own benefit and the latter solely for the benefit of his subjects; but beyond the fact that generally all the Greek authors have taken the word *Tyrant* in another sense, as appears most clearly in Xenophon's *Hiero,* it would seem to follow from Aristotle's distinction that since the beginning of the world not a single King has yet existed.

to prolong their lives; it is the responsibility of men to prolong that of the State as far as possible, by giving it the best constitution that it can have. The best-constituted will come to an end, but later than another, if no unforeseen accident brings about its premature destruction.

[261] The principle of political life is in the Sovereign authority. The legislative power is the heart of the State, the executive power is its brain, which gives movement to all the parts. The brain can fall into paralysis and the individual still lives. A man remains an imbecile and lives; but as soon as the heart has ceased its functions, the animal is dead.

[262] It is not by the laws that the State subsists, but by the legislative power. The law of yesterday does not obligate today, but tacit consent is presumed from silence, and the sovereign is deemed to confirm continually the laws which it does not abrogate while being able to do so. Whatever it has once declared it wills it wills always, until the declaration is revoked.

[263] Why then is so much respect paid to ancient laws? It is for that very reason. One must believe that it is only the excellence of ancient wills which has enabled them to be so long preserved: if the Sovereign had not constantly recognized them as salutary, it would have revoked them a thousand times. That is why, far from being weakened, the laws unceasingly acquire new strength in every well-constituted State; the prejudice in favor of antiquity renders them more venerable each day; in contrast, wherever the laws weaken as they grow older, it is proof that there is no longer legislative power, and that the State no longer lives.

XII. How the Sovereign Authority Is Maintained

[264] The Sovereign, having no other force than the legislative power, acts only by the laws; and the laws being only authentic acts of the general will, the Sovereign can only act when the people is assembled. The people assem-

bled, it will be said, what a chimera! It is a chimera today, but it was not two thousand years ago. Have men changed their nature?

[265]* The limits of the possible in moral things are less narrow than we think. It is our weaknesses, our vices, our prejudices which shrink them. Sordid souls do not believe in great men: vile slaves smile with a mocking air at the word *liberty*.

[266]* From what has been done let us consider what can be done. I will not speak of the ancient republics of Greece; but the Roman Republic was, it seems to me, a large State, and the town of Rome a large town. The last census in Rome showed four hundred thousand citizens bearing arms, and the last enumeration of the Empire more than four million Citizens without counting subjects, foreigners, women, infants, slaves.

[267] What unimaginable difficulty in assembling frequently the immense population of this capital and its environs! However, few weeks passed without the Roman people being assembled, even several times. And it exercised not only the rights of sovereignty, but part of those of Government. It handled certain matters, it judged certain causes, and in the public assembly the whole people were also often magistrate as Citizen.

[268] By going back to the earliest times of Nations, one would find that most of the ancient governments, even monarchies such as those of the Macedonians and the Franks, had similar Councils. Be it as it may, this single incontestable fact answers all difficulties. To argue from the existent to the possible produces a consequence that seems good to me.

XIII. (Continued)

[269] It is not sufficient that the assembled people should have once fixed the constitution of the State giving sanction to a body of laws; it is not sufficient that it should have

established a perpetual Government, or that it should have once and for all provided for the election of magistrates. Beyond the extraordinary assemblies which unforeseen events can require, there is need for fixed and periodical ones which nothing can abolish or postpone, so that on the appointed day the people be legitimately convoked by the law, without need for any other formal convocation.

[270] But excepting these assemblies lawful solely by their date, every assembly of the People that has not been convoked by the magistrates charged with that purpose and according to prescribed forms ought to be regarded as illegitimate, and all that is done in it as null; because the order to be assembled itself should emanate from the law.

[271]* As for the more or less frequent resumption of legitimate assemblies, they depend on so many considerations that one could not know how to give them precise rules. Still, one can say in general that the more force the Government has, the more frequently should the Sovereign show itself.

[272] This, I will be told, may be good for a single town; but what is to be done when the State comprises several towns? Will the Sovereign authority be divided? or should it be concentrated in a single town and subjugate all the rest?

[273] I reply that one should do neither one nor the other. First, the sovereign authority is simple and one, and cannot be divided without being destroyed. In the second place, a town, no more than a Nation, can be legitimately subject to another, because the essence of the body politic is first the harmony of obedience and liberty, and these words *subject* and *sovereign* are identical correlatives whose idea is united under the single word Citizen.

[274] I reply again that it is always an evil to combine several towns into a single city, and that, wishing to create this union, one should not flatter oneself in expecting that the natural drawbacks can be avoided. One cannot object that the abuse of large States cannot be brought against

someone who only wants small ones; but how give to small States enough force to resist the large ones? Just as each of the Greek towns resisted the great King, and as more recently Holland and Switzerland resisted the house of Austria.

[275]* In any case, if one cannot reduce the State to just boundaries, there is one expedient: it is to not allow a capital, to make the Government sit alternatively in each town, and to assemble in it, each in turn the Estates of the country.

[276] Populate the territory equally, extend the same rights everywhere, carry abundance and life everywhere; thus the State will become at once the strongest and best governed possible. Remember that the walls of the towns are formed only from the debris of rural houses. For each Palace I see rising in the capital, I believe I see an entire rural country laid in ruins.

XIV. (Continued)

[277]* The moment the People is legitimately assembled in Sovereign body, all jurisdiction of the Government ceases; the executive power is suspended, and the person of the humblest Citizen is as sacred and inviolable as that of the first Magistrate, because where the Represented part is found, there is no longer a Representative. Most of the tumults that arose in Rome in the *comitia* came from having ignored or neglected this rule. The Consuls then were only the Presidents of the People, the Tribunes simple Speakers,[14] the Senate was nothing at all.

[278] These intervals of suspension, when the Prince recognizes or ought to recognize an actual superior, have

14. Nearly in the sense that one gives this name in the Parliament of England. The resemblance of these offices would have placed the Consuls and the Tribunes in conflict, even if all jurisdiction had been suspended.

always been fearful for him; and these assemblies of the people, who are the shield of the body politic and the curb of the Government, have been in all times the horror of the chiefs: hence such men never lack concerns, objections, obstacles, promises, in order to discourage citizens from assemblies. When the latter are avaricious, cowardly, fainthearted, and more loving of repose than of liberty, they do not long hold out against the redoubled efforts of the Government: it is thus that, as the resisting force is ceaselessly augmented, the Sovereign authority evaporates at the end, and most cities fall and perish before their time.

[279] But between Sovereign authority and arbitrary Government there is sometimes introduced an intermediate power of which one must speak.

XV. Of Deputies or Representatives

[280]* As soon as public service ceases to be the principal concern of the Citizens, and they prefer to serve with their purses instead of their persons, the State is already nearly in ruin. Is it necessary to march to combat? they pay for troops and remain at home; is it necessary to go to the Council? they name deputies and remain at home. By dint of laziness and money, they finally have soldiers to enslave the fatherland and representatives to sell it.

[281] It is the worry over commerce and the arts, the greedy pursuit of gain, indolence, and the love of comforts, which exchange personal services for money. One gives part of his profit in order to augment it at his convenience. Give money and soon enough you will have chains. This word *finance* is a slave's word; it is unknown in the City. In a truly free State the citizens do everything with their arms and nothing with money. Far from paying to exempt themselves from their duties, they will pay to perform them Themselves. I am certainly far from commonly held ideas; I believe that forced labor is less contrary to liberty than taxes.

[282] The better the State is constituted, the more do public affairs outweigh private ones in the minds of the Citizens. There is even a much smaller number of private affairs, because as the sum of general well-being provides considerably more to that of each individual, less remains to be sought by individual exertions. In a well-conducted city each hastens to the assemblies; under a bad Government nobody wants to take a step to attend them, because no one takes an interest in what is done there, as it is foreseen that the general will does not prevail; and so in the end domestic concerns absorb everything. Good laws lead to better laws; bad laws bring on worse ones. As soon as someone says of the affairs of the State *Why is it important to me?* one should count the State as lost.

[283]* The cooling of the love of the fatherland, the activity of private interest, the immensity of States, conquests, the abuse of Government, have suggested the procedure of using Deputies or Representatives of the people in the assemblies of the Nation. This is what in certain countries one dares to call the Third Estate. Thus the particular interest of two orders is placed at first and second rank; the public interest is only at the third.

[284]* Sovereignty cannot be represented for the same reason that it cannot be alienated; it consists essentially in the general will, and the will cannot be represented: it is itself, or it is something other; there is no middle ground. The deputies of the people then are not and cannot be its representatives, they are only its commissioners; they can conclude nothing definitively. Every law that the People in person has not ratified is null; it is not a law. The English people thinks itself free, but is greatly mistaken; it is only free during the election of the members of Parliament: as soon as they are elected, it is enslaved, it is nothing. In the short moments of its liberty, the use made of it well merits its loss.

[285] The idea of Representatives is modern: it comes to us from feudal Government, from that iniquitous and absurd Government in which the human species is degraded, and where the name of man is dishonored. In the ancient Republics and even in the Monarchies, the people never had representatives; they did not know this word. It is very noteworthy that in Rome, where the Tribunes were so sacred, one could not even imagine that they might usurp the functions of the people, and in the midst of such a large multitude, they never tried to pass a single Plebiscite on their own authority. One can, however, imagine the embarrassment sometimes caused by the crowd by what occurred in the times of the Gracchi, when a part of the Citizens gave their vote from the rooftops.

[286] Where right and liberty are everything, inconveniences are nothing. Among this wise people, everything was estimated in its just measure; it allowed the Lictors to do what the Tribunes would not have dared to do; it did not fear that the Lictors would wish to represent it.

[287]* To explain, however, how the Tribunes sometimes represented it, it suffices to understand how the Government represents the Sovereign. The Law being only the declaration of the general will, it is clear that, in the legislative power, the people cannot be represented; but it can and ought to be in the executive power, which is only force applied to the Law. This shows on close examination that very few Nations have laws. Be that as it may, it is certain that the Tribunes, not having any part of the executive power, were never able to represent the Roman people by right of their office, but only by usurping those of the Senate.

[288] Among the Greeks, everything the people had to do it did by itself: it was unceasingly assembled in the public square. It lived in a mild climate; it was not avaricious; slaves did its work; its prime business was its liberty. Not having

the same advantages, how conserve the same rights? Your more rigorous climate gives you more needs,[15] six months of the year the public square is not usable, your indistinct tongues cannot be understood in the open air; you give more for your own gain than for your liberty, and you fear slavery far less than misery.

[289] What! is liberty only maintained with the support of servitude? Perhaps. The two extremes meet. Everything not in nature has its inconveniences, and civil society more than all the rest. There are such unfortunate circumstances where one can save his liberty only at the expense of another, and where the citizen can only be perfectly free when the slave is completely enslaved. Such was the position of Sparta. As for you, modern peoples, you have no slaves, but you are slaves; you pay for their liberty with your own. You boast of your preference in vain; I find in it more of cowardice than of humanity.

[290] I do mean by all this neither that slaves are necessary nor that the right of slavery is legitimate, since I have proved the contrary: I only state the reasons why modern peoples who believe themselves free have Representatives, and why ancient peoples did not. Be that as it may, the instant that a People gives itself Representatives, it is no longer free; it is no more.

[291] All things considered, I do not see that it should henceforth be possible for the Sovereign to preserve among us the exercise of its rights unless the City is very small. But if it is very small, will it be subjugated? No. I will show later[16] how the external power of a great People can be

15. To adopt in cold countries the luxury and indolence of the Orientals is to wish to be given their chains; it is to submit to them more necessarily than they do.

16. It is this which I intended to do in a sequel to this work, when in considering foreign relations I would come to confederations. This is a wholly new matter and one where the principles have still to be established.

united with the convenient polity and good order of a small
State.

XVI. That the Institution of the Government Is Not a Contract

[292] The Legislative power once well established, it is
a matter of establishing the executive power as well; for this
latter, only operating by particular acts, not being of the
essence of the other, is naturally separate from it. If it were
possible for the Sovereign, considered as such, to have executive power, right and fact would be so confounded that one
would no longer know what is law and what is not, and the
body politic thus denatured would soon fall prey to the
violence against which it was instituted.

[293] The Citizens being all equal by the social contract,
all can prescribe what all ought to do, whereas no one has
a right to make another do what he does not do himself.
Now it is properly this right, indispensable to make the
body politic live and move, that the Sovereign gives to the
Prince in instituting the Government.

[294]* Several have held that the act of this establishment
was a contract between the People and the chiefs it gives
itself; a contract by which is stipulated between the two
parties the conditions under which the latter obligates itself
to command and the former to obey. One will agree, I am
sure, that this is a strange manner of contracting. But let us
see if this opinion is tenable.

[295]* First, the supreme authority can no more be
modified than alienated; to limit it is to destroy it. It is
absurd and contradictory that the Sovereign give itself a
superior; to obligate oneself to obey a master is to go back
to one's full liberty.

[296] Further, it is evident that this contract of the people
with such or such persons would be a particular act. Whence

it follows that this contract would be neither a law nor an act of sovereignty, and consequently it would be illegitimate.

[297] One sees also that the contracting parties would be under the law of nature alone and without any guarantee of their reciprocal engagements, which is repugnant in every way to the civil state. He who has force in hand being always the master of its use, we might as well give the name of contract to the act of a man who would say to another: "I give you all my goods, on the condition that you will return to me whatever pleases you."

[298] There is only one contract in the State; it is that of association, and that alone excludes all others. No public Contract can be imagined which would not be a violation of the first.

XVII. Of the Institution of the Government

[299]* Under what idea, then, must we conceive the act by which the Government is instituted? I will first note that this act is complex or composed of two others: namely, the establishment of the law and the execution of the law.

[300] By the first, the Sovereign resolves that there will be a body of Government established under such form; and it is clear that this act is a law.

[301] By the second, the People name the chiefs who will be entrusted with the established Government. Now this naming, being a particular act, is not a second law, but only a consequence of the first and a function of Government.

[302] The difficulty is to understand how one can have an act of Government before the Government exists, and how the People, who is only Sovereign or subject, can become Prince or Magistrate in certain circumstances.

[303]* It is here that is uncovered one of those astounding properties of the body politic, by which it reconciles seemingly contradictory operations. For here occurs a sud-

den conversion of Sovereignty into Democracy; so that, without any perceivable change, and solely by a new relation of all to all, the Citizens having become Magistrates pass from general acts to particular acts, and from the law to its execution.

[304]* This changing of relation is not a subtlety of speculation without example in practice: it occurs every day in the Parliament of England, where the lower Chamber on certain occasions turns itself into a Committee of the Whole, in order to better discuss its business, and thus becomes a simple commission, from the Sovereign Court that it was the preceding moment; as such it then reports to itself, as the House of Commons, what it decided in the Committee of the Whole, and deliberates again under one title about what it has already resolved under another.

[305] Such is the advantage proper to Democratic Government, that it can be established in fact by a simple act of the general will. After this, that provisional Government remains in office, if such form is adopted, or establishes in the name of the Sovereign the Government prescribed by the law, and thus all is according to rule. It is not possible to institute the Government in any other legitimate manner without renouncing the principles heretofore established.

XVIII. Means of Preventing Usurpation of the Government

[306] From these clarifications it follows, in confirmation of Chapter XVI [par. 292–98], that the act which institutes the Government is not a contract but a Law, that those entrusted with the executive power are not the masters of the people but its officers, whom it can establish and depose when it pleases, that there is no question for them of contracting but of obeying, and that in undertaking the functions which the State imposes on them, they are only fulfill-

ing their duty as Citizens, without having any sort of right
to dispute about the conditions.

[307] When it happens that the People institutes a hereditary Government, be it monarchical in one family, or aristocratic in an order of Citizens, it is not an engagement that
it undertakes: it is a provisional form which it gives to the
administration, until it pleases it to put in order another.

[308]* It is true that these changes are always dangerous,
and that the established Government must only be touched
if it becomes incompatible with the public good; but this
circumspection is a maxim of politics and not a rule of right,
and the State is no more bound to leave civil authority to
its chiefs than military authority to its Generals.

[309] It is also true that in such a case one should observe
with greatest care all the requisite formalities in order to
distinguish a regular and legitimate act from a seditious
tumult, and the will of a whole people from the clamors of
a faction. Especially in this odious case one should only
concede in full rigor of what is right what cannot be refused,
and it is also from this obligation that the Prince draws a
great advantage in preserving its power despite the people,
without anyone being able to say that it has usurped the
power. For in seeming to exercise only its rights, it could
very easily extend them, and under the pretext of maintaining the public peace obstruct the assemblies destined to
reestablish good order; so that it takes advantage of a silence
it prevents from being broken, or of irregularities it has had
committed, in order to suppose in its favor the consent of
those whom fear silences and to punish those who dare to
speak. It is thus that the Decemvirs, having first been elected
for one year, then continued for another, tried to retain
their power perpetually by not permitting the *comitia* to
assemble; and it is by this easy means that all governments
in the world, when once invested with public force, sooner
or later usurp the Sovereign authority.

[310]* The periodical assemblies of which I have already

spoken are suited to prevent or defer this evil, especially when they have no need of formal convocation; for then the Prince would not be able to prevent them without openly declaring himself violator of the laws and enemy of the State.

[311] The opening of these assemblies, which have for their only object the maintenance of the social treaty, should always be done with two propositions that cannot be suppressed, and which pass separately by vote.

[312]* The first: "Whether it pleases the Sovereign to preserve the present form of Government."

[313] The second: "Whether it please the People to leave the administration to those presently charged with it."

[314]* I presume here what I believe I have demonstrated: namely, that there is in the State no fundamental law which cannot be revoked, not even the social pact; for if all the Citizens assemble in order to break this pact by common accord, one cannot doubt that it would be very legitimately broken. Grotius even thinks that each person can renounce the State of which he is a member, and regain his natural liberty and his goods on leaving the country.[17] Now it would be absurd that all the Citizens together cannot do what each of them can do separately.

---

17. It being well understood that one does not leave in order to evade his duty and avoid serving the fatherland at the moment it has need of us. Flight then would be criminal and punishable; it would no longer be withdrawal, but desertion.

BOOK FOUR

-◆◆◆-

I. That the General Will Is
Indestructible

[315]* As long as several men together consider themselves as a single body, they have only one will which relates
to the common preservation and to the general well-being.
Then all the activities of the State are vigorous and simple,
its maxims are clear and luminous, it has no entangled and
conflicting interests, the common good is clearly apparent
everywhere and only good sense is needed to perceive it.
Peace, union, equality, are enemies of political subtleties.
Upright and simple men are hard to deceive because of their
simplicity; snares and refined pretexts do not impose upon
them; they are not even clever enough to be duped. When
one sees among the happiest people in the world groups of
peasants regulating the affairs of State under an oak tree and
always conducting themselves wisely, can one keep from
scorning the refinement of other nations, who render themselves illustrious and miserable with so much art and mystery?

[316] A State thus governed has need of very few Laws,
and to the extent that it becomes necessary to promulgate
new ones, this necessity is universally seen. The first man
who proposes them does no more than say what all have
already felt, and there is no question of intrigues or eloquence in order to pass into law what each has already
resolved to do, as soon as he is sure that the others will do
likewise.

[317] What deceives those who reason is that seeing only
States badly constituted from their origin, they are im-
pressed by the impossibility of maintaining a similar polity
in such States. They laugh on imagining all the follies to
which a cunning knave, an insinuating speaker, could per-

suade the people of Paris or London. They do not know that Cromwell would have been put to hard labor by the people of Berne, and the Duke of Beaufort imprisoned by the Genevans.

[318]* But when the social bond begins to loosen and the State to weaken; when private interests begin to make themselves felt and the small societies to influence the great one, the common interest degenerates and finds opponents: unanimity reigns no more in the votes, the general will is no longer the will of all, contradictions, debates arise, and the best advice does not pass without disputes.

[319] Finally, when the State, near its ruin, subsists only as a vain and illusory form, when the social bond is broken in all hearts, when the vilest interest impudently takes on the sacred name of the public good, then the general will becomes mute; all, guided by secret motives, no longer express their opinions as Citizens, as if the State had never existed; and they falsely pass under the name of Laws iniquitous decrees which have only private interest as their goal.

[320] Does it follow from this that the general will is annihilated or corrupted? No, it is always constant, unalterable, and pure; but it is subordinated to others that prevail over it. Each, detaching his own interest from the common interest, sees clearly that he cannot completely separate himself from it, but his part in the public evil does not seem anything to him compared with the exclusive good he intends to appropriate. This private good excepted, he wishes the general good for his own interest as strongly as anyone else. Even in selling his vote for money he does not extinguish the general will in himself; he eludes it. The fault he commits is to change the status of the question and to answer another than what he has been asked; so that instead of saying by his vote, "It is advantageous to the State," he says, "It is advantageous to a certain man or a certain party that such or such a motion passes." Thus the law of public order in the assemblies is not so much to maintain the general will

as to make sure that it always is questioned and that it always responds.

[321] I could here present many reflections on the simple right of voting in every act of sovereignty; a right which nothing is able to take away from the Citizens; and on the right to state opinions, to propose, divide, to discuss, that the Government has always great care to leave only to its members; but this important matter would require a separate treatise, and I cannot say everything in this one.

II. Of Voting

[322] From the preceding chapter one sees that the manner in which general affairs are managed gives a sufficiently accurate indication of the actual state of the habitual conduct, and the health of the body politic. The more harmony reigns in the assemblies, that is to say the closer opinions approach unanimity, the more dominant is the general will; but long debates, dissensions, tumult, indicate the ascendancy of private interests and the decline of the State.

[323]* This seems less evident when two or more orders enter into its constitution, as in Rome the Patricians and the Plebeians, whose quarrels often troubled the *comitia,* even in the finest times of the republic; but this exception is more apparent than real, for then, by the vice inherent in the body politic, there are, so to speak, two States in one: what is not true of the two together is true of each separately. And in fact, even in the stormiest times the plebiscites of the people, when the Senate did not interfere with them, always passed tranquilly and by a large majority of votes: the Citizens having only one interest, the people only one will.

[324] At the other extremity of the circle unanimity returns. It is when the citizens, having fallen into slavery, no longer have either liberty or will. Then fright and flattery change votes into acclamations; one no longer deliberates, but adores or curses. Such was the vile manner of expressing

opinions in the Senate under the Emperors. Sometimes it was done with ridiculous precautions. Tacitus observed that under Otho, the Senators, in overwhelming Vitellius with execrations, arranged to make a frightening noise at the same time so that if, by chance, he became the master, he would not know what each of them had said.

[325] From these diverse considerations arise the maxims by which one ought to regulate the manner of counting the votes and comparing opinions, according to whether the general will is more or less easy to know, and the State more or less declining.

[326]* There is only one single law which by its nature requires unanimous consent. It is the social pact: for civil association is the most voluntary act in the world; every man being born free and master of himself, no one can, under any pretext whatever, subjugate him without his assent. To decide that the son of a slave is born a slave is to decide that he is not born a man.

[327]* If, then, at the time of the social pact, there are found some opponents of it, their opposition does not invalidate the contract, it only prevents them from being included in it: they are foreigners among citizens. When the State is instituted, consent is in residence; to live in a territory is to submit oneself to sovereignty.[1]

[328]* Outside of this basic contract, the voice of the greater number always obliges all the others; it is a consequence of the contract itself. But one asks how a man can be free and forced to conform to wills that are not his own. How are opponents free and yet subject to laws to which they have not consented?

[329]* I respond that the question is poorly posed. The

1. This should always be understood for a free State; for otherwise family, goods, need for asylum, necessity, or violence can detain an inhabitant in the country despite himself; and then his residence alone no longer supposes his consent to the contract or to the violation of the contract.

citizen consents to all the laws, even those which are passed despite him, and even to those that punish him when he dares to violate any of them. The constant will of all the members of the State is the general will: by it they are citizens and free.[2] When a law is proposed in the assembly of the People, what is asked of them is not precisely whether they approve the proposition or reject it, but whether or not it conforms to the general will which is their own: each in giving his vote states his opinion on that question, and from the counting of the votes is taken the declaration of the general will. When the opinion contrary to mine prevails, that only proves that I was mistaken, and that what I had considered to be the general will was not. If my private opinion had prevailed, I would have done something other than I had wanted to do, and then I would not have been free.

[330] This supposes, it is true, that all the characteristics of the general will are still in the majority; when they cease to be there, whichever side one takes, there is no longer any liberty.

[331]* In showing earlier how private wills have been substituted for the general will in public deliberations, I have sufficiently indicated the practicable means for preventing this abuse; I will speak of it again later on. With regard to the proportional number of the votes required to declare this will, I have also stated the principles by which one can determine it. The difference of a single vote breaks a tie, only one opposed breaks unanimity; but between unanimity and a tie vote there are many unequal divisions, at each of which one can fix this number according to the condition and needs of the body politic.

2. In Genoa, one reads in front of the prisons and on the chains of those condemned to the galleys the word *Libertas.* This application of the motto is fine and just. It is only the malefactors in all states who prevent the Citizen from being free. In a country where all such people would be in the Galleys, one would enjoy the most perfect liberty.

[332] Two general maxims can serve to regulate these ratios: the one, that the more important and serious the deliberations, the closer the prevailing opinion should approach unanimity; the other, that the more the matter requires speed of decision, the more one can reduce the prescribed difference in the division of opinions: in deliberations that must be resolved immediately, a majority by one vote should suffice. The first of these maxims seems more suitable to laws, and the second to business matters. Be that as it may, it is by their combination that the best ratios are established by which a majority can decide.

III. Of Elections

[333] With regard to the elections of the Prince and the Magistrates, which are, as I have said, complex acts, there are two routes by which to proceed: namely, by choice and by lot. Both have been employed in diverse Republics, and a very complicated mixture of the two is still seen in the election of the Doge of Venice.

[334] "Voting by lot," says Montesquieu, "is of the nature of democracy." I agree, but how is that? "Drawing lots," he continues, "is a mode of election that afflicts no one: it leaves to each citizen a reasonable hope of serving the fatherland." These are not the reasons.

[335]* If we note that the election of the chiefs is a function of Government and not of Sovereignty, one will see why the way of drawing lots is in the nature of Democracy, where the administration is so much better as its acts are less multiplied.

[336] In every true Democracy, the magistracy is not an advantage, but an onerous responsibility which cannot be justly imposed on one individual rather than on another. The law alone can impose this responsibility on the one whose lot is drawn. For then, the condition being equal for all, and the choice dependent on no human will, there is no

private application that alters the universality of the law.

[337]* In an Aristocracy, the Prince chooses the Prince, the Government is preserved by itself, and it is there that voting is appropriate.

[338]* The example of the election of the Doge of Venice far from destroying this distinction confirms it; this combined form is suitable to a mixed government. For it is an error to take the Government of Venice as a true Aristocracy. If the People there have no part in the Government, the nobility there is the people itself. A multitude of poor poverty-stricken noblemen[3] never approach any magistracy, and have for their nobility only the empty title of Excellency and the right to attend the grand Council. This grand Council being as numerous as our general Council in Geneva, its illustrious members have no more privileges than our simple Citizens. It is certain that, setting aside the extreme disparity of the two Republics, the burghers of Geneva exactly correspond to the Venetian patricians; our natives and inhabitants correspond to the Townsmen and people of Venice; our peasants correspond to the subjects on the mainland: finally, in whatever manner we consider this Republic, apart from its size, its Government is no more aristocratic than ours. The whole difference is that, not having any chief for life, we do not have the same need to draw lots.

[339] Elections by lot would have few disadvantages in a true Democracy, where, all being equal in moral conduct and talents as in maxims and fortune, the choice would become almost indifferent. But I have already said that there is no true Democracy.

[340] When choice and lot are combined, the first should be used in positions that require special talents, such as military offices; the other is suitable for those in which good sense, justice, and integrity suffice, such as judicial respon-

---

3.The French phrase is *pauvres Barnabotes.*—ED.

sibilities; because in a well-constituted State these qualities are common to all citizens.

[341] Neither lot nor voting has any place in a monarchical Government. The Monarch being by right the sole Prince and the one Magistrate, the choice of his lieutenants belongs only to him. When the Abbé de Saint-Pierre proposed to multiply the Councils of the king of France, and to elect the members by ballot, he did not see that he was proposing to change the form of the Government.

[342]* It would remain for me to speak of the manner of casting and collecting the votes in the assembly of the people; but perhaps the account of the Roman practice in that respect will explain more clearly all the maxims which I might be able to establish. It is not unworthy of a judicious reader to see in some detail how public and private affairs were treated in a Council of two hundred thousand men.

IV. Of the Roman Comitia

[343]* We have no trustworthy records of the early times of Rome; there is even a great probability that most things which have been reported are fables;[4] and in general the most instructive part of the annals of peoples, which is the history of their founding, is the most defective. Experience teaches us every day of the causes giving rise to the revolutions of empires: but as peoples are no longer being formed, we hardly have anything but conjectures to explain how they were formed.

[344] The practices one finds established at least testify that these practices had an origin. Of the traditions that

4. The name *Rome,* which presumably comes from *Romulus,* is Greek and means *force;* the name *Numa* is also Greek, and means *law.* What is the likelihood that the first two Kings of that town bore in advance names so well related to what they did?

reach back to these origins, those which the greatest authorities support and which the strongest reasons confirm ought to be accepted as most certain. These are the maxims that I have tried to follow in inquiring how the freest and most powerful people on earth exercised its supreme power.

[345]* After the foundation of Rome, the nascent Republic, that is to say the army of the founder, composed of Albans, Sabines, and foreigners, was divided into three classes, which took from this division the names of *Tribes.* Each of these Tribes was subdivided into ten *Curiae* [sections], and each *Curia* into *Decuriae* [ten subsections], at the head of which were placed chiefs called *Curiones* and *Decuriones.*

[346]* Beyond this, a body of one hundred Horsemen or Knights, called *Centuria,* was drawn from each Tribe, by which one sees that these divisions, not very necessary in a market town, were at first only military. But it seems that an instinct for greatness induced the little town of Rome from the first to organize itself in a manner suitable to the capital of the world.

[347] From this first division, one disadvantage soon resulted. The tribe of the Albans[5] and that of the Sabines[6] remained always in the same condition, while that of the foreigners[7] increased continually through perpetual influx of new members and soon surpassed the other two. The remedy Servius found for this dangerous abuse was to change the division, and in place of the one based on races, which he abolished, he substituted another, drawn from the districts of the city occupied by each Tribe. In place of the three Tribes he made four, each of which occupied one of the hills of Rome and bore its name. Thus, by remedying the current inequality, he also prevented it for the future;

5. Ramnenses.
6. Tatienses.
7. Luceres.

and in order that this might be a division not only of places but of men, he forbade the inhabitants of one quarter to move to another; which prevented the races from blending together.

[348] He also doubled the three old centuries of Cavalry, and added twelve others to them, but always under the old names; a simple and judicious means by which he effected a distinction between the body of Knights and that of the People, without making the latter murmur.

[349] To these four urban Tribes Servius added fifteen others, called rustic Tribes, because they were formed of inhabitants of the countryside, divided into the same number of cantons. Subsequently the same number of new ones was formed, and the Roman People finally found itself divided into thirty-five Tribes, a number which remained fixed until the end of the Republic.

[350] From this distinction between the urban Tribes and the rural Tribes resulted an effect worthy of note, because there is no other instance of it, and because Rome owed to it both the preservation of her moral customs and the growth of her empire. It might be supposed that the urban Tribes soon arrogated to themselves the power and the honors, and were ready to debase the rustic Tribes: it was quite the reverse. One knows the taste of the early Romans for life in the countryside. This taste derived from their wise founder, who united to liberty rustic and military labor, and relegated so to speak to the town the arts, crafts, intrigue, fortune, and slavery.

[351] Thus, as all the illustrious men of Rome lived in the country and cultivated their land, it was customary to seek only there the supporters of the Republic. This condition, being that of the worthiest Patricians, was honored by everyone; the simple and laborious life of the Villagers was preferred to the idle and slack life of the Burghers of Rome, and someone who would have been only an unhappy proletarian in the town, by working in the fields, became a

respected Citizen. It is not without reason, said Varro, that our magnanimous ancestors established in the Village the nurseries of those robust and valiant men who defended them in times of war and nourished them in times of peace. Pliny says positively that the Tribes of the fields were honored because of the men who composed them; whereas the cowards whom one wanted to disgrace were transferred as a mark of ignominy into the urban Tribes. The Sabine Appius Claudius, having come to settle in Rome, was overwhelmed there with honors and enrolled in a rustic Tribe which took the name of his family. Finally, freedmen all entered the urban Tribes, never the rural; and during the whole of the Republic there is not a single example of any of these freedmen attaining any seat in the magistracy even though he had become a citizen.

[352] This maxim was excellent; but it was pushed so far that finally a change and certainly an abuse of policy resulted from it.

[353] First, the Censors, after having long arrogated the right of arbitrarily transferring citizens from one Tribe to another, permitted most of them to be enrolled in whichever pleased them; this permission, which surely served no use, removed one of the great strengths of the censorship. Additionally, as the Great and the powerful all enrolled themselves in the Tribes of the countryside, and the freedmen became citizens remaining with the population in the urban ones, the Tribes in general no longer had any particular place or territory; but all found themselves so intermingled that it was impossible to distinguish the members of each except by the registers, so that the idea of the word *Tribe* thus passed from the real to the personal, or rather became nearly chimerical.

[354] It also happened that the urban Tribes, being nearer at hand, were often found to be the strongest in the *comitia,* and sold the State to those who deigned to buy the votes of the rabble which composed them.

[355] With regard to the *Curiae,* the founder having formed ten in each tribe, the entire Roman people then enclosed in the walls of the town consisted of thirty *Curiae,* each of which had its temples, its gods, its officers, its priests, and its festivals, called *compitalia,* resembling the *paganalia* which the rural tribes later had.

[356] In Servius's new apportionment, the number thirty being incapable of equal distribution into four Tribes, he was unwilling to touch them; and the *Curiae,* independent of the tribes, became another division of the inhabitants of Rome. But there was no question of *Curiae* either in the rural tribes or in the people who composed them, because the Tribes having become a purely civil establishment, and another policy to levy troops having been introduced, the military divisions of Romulus were found superfluous. Thus, although every Citizen was enrolled in a Tribe, there were many who were not enrolled in a *Curia.*

[357] Servius made yet a third division, which had no relation to the two preceding ones, but became by its effects the most important of all. He distributed the whole Roman people into six classes, which he distinguished neither by residence nor by individual attributes, but by property. So that the first classes were filled by the rich, the last by the poor, and the middle by those who enjoyed a moderate fortune. These six classes were subdivided into one hundred and ninety-three other bodies, called centuries; and these bodies were so distributed that the first class alone comprised more than half, and the last counted for only one subdivision, even though it alone contained more than half of the inhabitants of Rome.

[358] In order that the people would not so clearly discern the consequences of this last form, Servius pretended to give it a military aspect; he introduced into the second class two centuries of armorers, and two centuries of war instruments into the fourth. In each class, except the last, he distinguished the young and the old, that is to say those who

were obligated to bear arms and those whose age exempted them by law; this distinction, more than that of property, produced the necessity of frequently redoing the census or enumeration. Finally, he wished the assembly to be held in the Campus Martius, and that all who were of age to serve gather there with their arms.

[359] The reason he did not follow in the last class this same division of young and old is that the populace of which it was composed was not accorded the honor of bearing Arms for the fatherland: it was necessary to have hearths in order to obtain the right of defending them; and out of those innumerable troops of beggars with which the armies of Kings today glitter, there is no one perhaps who would not have been chased with disdain from a Roman cohort, when soldiers were the defenders of liberty.

[360] One further distinguished, however, in the last class, the *proletarians* from those one called the *capite censi*. The first, not completely destitute, at least sometimes gave Citizens to the State, sometimes even soldiers when the need was pressing. As for those who had nothing at all, and could only be tallied by a head count, they were regarded as wholly worthless, and Marius was the first who deigned to enroll them.

[361] Without deciding here if this third enumeration was good or bad in itself, I think I can affirm that it was made practicable only by the simple habits of the early Romans, their disinterestedness, their taste for agriculture, their dislike of commerce and the ardent pursuit of gain. Where is the modern people among whom rapacious greed, restlessness of spirit, intrigue, continual changes of residence, and perpetual revolutions of fortunes would have let such an institution endure for twenty years without overturning the whole State? It is even well to note that customary conduct and the censorship[8] were stronger than this institution in

8. It is well to note that although Rousseau is speaking of a Roman institution, the French word *censure* has a wider meaning than its En-

correcting the vices in Rome, and that many a rich man was relegated to the class of the poor for having made too great a display of his wealth.

[362] From all this one can easily understand why mention is scarcely ever made of more than five classes, although there were really six. The sixth, providing neither soldiers to the army nor voters to the Campus Martius,[9] and being of almost no use to the Republic, rarely counted for anything.

[363] Such were the different divisions of the Roman people. Let us now see the effect they produced in the assemblies. These assemblies, when legitimately convoked, were called *Comitia:* ordinarily they were held in the Roman Forum or in the *Campus Martius,* and were distinguished as *comitia* by *Curiae,* by Centuries, and by Tribes, according to which of these three forms they were organized: the *comitia* by *Curiae* was instituted by Romulus; those by Centuries by Servius; those by tribes by the Tribunes of the people. No law received sanction, no magistrate was elected, except in the *comitia;* and as no Citizen was not enrolled in a *Curia,* in a Century, or in a Tribe, it follows that no citizen was excluded from the right of voting, and that the Roman people was truly Sovereign by right and in fact.

[364] In order that the *Comitia* be legitimately assembled and that what was done there have the force of law, three conditions were necessary: the first that the body or the Magistrate who convoked them be invested with the necessary authority; the second that the assembly be held on one of the days permitted by the law; the third that the auguries be favorable.

---

glish translation, viz., that of social approbation as well, and in some contexts this broader meaning seems to be what he really has in mind. Cf. 401–8. —ED.

9. I say to the *Campus Martius* because it was there that the *comitia* were assembled by *centuriae:* in the two other forms, the people were assembled in the *Forum* or elsewhere; and then the *capite censi* had as much influence and authority as the first Citizens.

[365] The reason for the first regulation need not be explained. The second is a matter of policy: thus it was not permitted to hold the *Comitia* on feast and market days, when country people coming to Rome on business did not have time to spend the day in the Forum. By the third, the Senate bridled a proud and restless people, and appropriately tempered the ardor of seditious Tribunes; but these found more than one way to elude this hindrance.

[366] Laws and the election of chiefs were not the only points submitted to the judgment of the *Comitia;* the Roman people having usurped the most important functions of Government, it can be said that the destiny of Europe was settled in its assemblies. This variety of objects gave rise to the various forms these assemblies took according to the matters which had to be decided.

[367]* In order to judge these diverse forms, it suffices to compare them. Romulus, in instituting the *Curiae,* sought to contain the Senate by means of the people and the people by means of the Senate, while dominating both equally. He thus gave the people by this form all the authority of numbers in order to balance that of power and of riches left to the patricians. But, according to the spirit of Monarchy, he left more advantage to the patricians through the influence of their Clients upon the majority of votes. This admirable institution of Patrons and Clients was a masterpiece of politics and humanity without which the Patriciate, so contrary to the spirit of the Republic, would not have been able to subsist. Rome alone has had the honor of giving to the world such a fine example from which no abuse ever resulted and which nevertheless has never been followed.

[368] This same form of *Curiae* having subsisted under the Kings down to Servius, and the region of the last Tarquin not having been considered legitimate, the royal laws came to be generally designated by the name of *leges curiatae.*

[369] Under the Republic the *Curiae,* always limited to the four urban tribes, and containing only the populace of

Rome, could suit neither the Senate, which was at the head of the Patricians, nor the Tribunes, who, although plebeians, were at the head of the comfortably situated citizens. They fell then into disrepute, and their degradation was such that their thirty assembled Lictors did what the *comitiae* by *Curiae* should have done.

[370] The division by Centuries was so favorable to the Aristocracy that one does see at first how the Senate did not always prevail in the *Comitia* of that name, and by which the consuls, Censors, and other curial Magistrates were elected. In effect, of the one hundred and ninety-three centuries which formed the six classes of the whole Roman people, the first Class comprising ninety-eight, and the votes being counted only by Centuries, this first class alone outnumbered all the others in votes. When all these Centuries were in accord, one did not even continue to count the votes; what the smallest number had decided passed for a decision of the multitude; and one can say that in the *comitia* by centuries, business was more regulated by the majority of money than by votes.

[371] But this extreme authority was moderated by two means: first, the Tribunes usually, and a great number of Plebeians always, being in the class of the rich, balanced the influence of the Patricians in this first class.

[372] The second means consisted in this, that instead of making the Centuries begin to vote according to their order, which would have always begun with the first, one century was drawn by lot and that one[10] proceeded alone to the election; after that all the Centuries, called another day according to their rank, repeated the same election and ordinarily confirmed it. One thus took the authority of example away from rank to give it to lot, according to the principle of Democracy.

---

10. This *Centuria,* thus chosen by lot, was called *prœrogativa,* because its suffrage was demanded first; hence came the word *prerogative.*

[373] From this practice another advantage resulted; the Citizens from the countryside had the time between the two elections to inform themselves of the merit of the candidate provisionally named, so that they could vote knowledgeably. But, under the pretext of haste, this practice came to be abolished, and the two elections took place on the same day.

[374] The *Comitia* by Tribes were properly the Council of the Roman people. They were only convoked by the Tribunes; in them the Tribunes were elected and passed their plebiscites. Not only did the Senate have no rank in them, it did not have even the right to attend; and, forced to obey laws on which they were not able to vote, the Senators, in this regard, were less free than the lowest Citizens. This injustice was altogether mistaken, and alone sufficed to invalidate the decrees of a body to which all members were not admitted. Should all the patricians have attended these *comitia* according to the right they had as Citizens, becoming then simple private individuals, they would hardly have had influence in a formal vote that relied on a head count, and in which the least proletarian had as much power as the Prince of the Senate.

[375] One sees then that besides the order which resulted from these diverse divisions for the counting of the votes of such a great People, the divisions were not reduced to forms indifferent in themselves, but each had effects relative to the purposes for which it was preferred.

[376] Without entering into this in greater detail, it follows from the preceding explanations that the *comitia* by Tribes was more favorable to popular Government, and the *comitia* by Centuries to Aristocracy. With regard to the *comitia* by *Curiae,* where only the populace of Rome formed the majority, as they were only good for favoring tyranny and evil designs, they deserved to fall into discredit, the seditious themselves abstaining from a means which only too plainly would reveal their projects. It is certain that the entire majesty of the Roman People was found only in the *Comitia* by Centuries, which were alone complete; seeing

that the rural tribes were absent from the *Comitia* by *Curiae* and the Senate and the Patricians from the *Comitia* by Tribes.

[377] As to the manner of collecting the votes, it was among the early Romans as simple as their customary conduct, although still less simple than in Sparta. Each gave his vote with a loud voice, and a registrar wrote them down accordingly; a majority of votes in each tribe determined the vote of the tribe, a majority of votes among the tribes determined the vote of the people, and so with the *Curiae* and Centuries. This usage was good as long as honesty reigned among the Citizens, and each was ashamed to vote publicly for an unjust opinion or on an unworthy subject; but when the people became corrupted and votes were bought, it was preferred that votes be given in secret in order to contain purchasers by distrust, and to furnish scoundrels the means of not being traitors.

[378] I know that Cicero blames this change and attributes to it in part the ruin of the republic. But although I feel the weight that one should have for Cicero's authority here, I cannot share his opinion. I think, on the contrary, that because not enough similar changes were made, the fall of the State was accelerated. As the diet of healthy persons is unfit for the sick, so we should not wish to govern a corrupt people by the same Laws appropriate to a good people. Nothing proves this maxim better than the duration of the republic of Venice, the semblance of which still exists uniquely because its laws are only suited for wicked men.

[379] To each Citizen, then, tablets were distributed for each to vote without others knowing his opinion. New formalities were also established for the collecting of the tablets, the counting of the votes, the comparison of the numbers, etc. This did not prevent the Officers in charge of these functions[11] from being suspect. Finally, in order to prevent

---

11. *Custodes, distributores, rogatores suffragiorum.* [Inspectors, canvassers, clerks of the voting.]

intrigue and traffic in votes, edicts were passed, the multitude of which demonstrates their uselessness.

[380] Toward the closing years it was often found necessary to resort to extraordinary expedients in order to compensate for the insufficiency of the laws. Sometimes miracles were alleged; but this means, which could deceive the people, could not deceive those who governed them: sometimes one suddenly convoked an assembly before the Candidates had had the time to conduct their intrigues; sometimes one used a whole meeting for speaking when the people were seen ready to take the bad side. But at last ambition eluded everything; and it is incredible that in the midst of such abuses, this immense people, by favor of its ancient regulations, did not fail to elect Magistrates, to pass laws, to judge cases, to expedite its public and private business, with almost as much facility as the Senate itself could have done.

V. Of the Tribunate

[381] When an exact proportion between the constitutive parts of the State cannot be established, or when indestructible causes incessantly alter their relations, then a special magistracy is instituted, which is not incorporated into the others, but which places each term back into its true relation with the others, and serves as a liaison or a middle term, either between the Prince and the People, or between the Prince and the Sovereign, or if necessary between the two sides at the same time.

[382] This body, which I will call the *Tribunate*, is the preserver of the laws and of the legislative power. Sometimes it serves to protect the Sovereign against the Government, as the Tribunes of the people did in Rome; sometimes to sustain the government against the people, as the Council of Ten now does in Venice; and sometimes to maintain the balance on either side, as the Ephors did in Sparta.

[383] The Tribunate is not a constitutive part of the City,

and should have no share of the legislative or executive power, but it is in this that its power is greater: for, able to do nothing, it can prevent everything. It is more sacred and revered, as defender of the laws, than the Prince who executes them and the Sovereign who gives them. This was very clearly seen in Rome when the proud patricians, who always despised the entire people, were forced to flinch before a simple officer of the people, who had neither auspices nor jurisdiction.

[384] The Tribunate wisely tempered is the strongest buttress of a good constitution; but if it has even a little too much force it dislocates everything: weakness is not in its nature; and provided that it is something, it is never less than it should be.

[385] It degenerates into tyranny when it usurps the executive power of which it is only the moderator, and when it wishes to dispense laws which it should only protect. The enormous power of the Ephors, which was without danger as long as Sparta preserved its moral customs, accelerated the corruption once it had begun. The blood of Agis, slain by these tyrants, was avenged by his successor: the crime and the punishment of the Ephors equally hastened the fall of the Republic; and after Cleomenes, Sparta was no longer anything. Again, Rome perished in the same way and the excessive power of the tribunes, usurped by degree, finally served, with the aid of laws made for liberty, as a safeguard of the emperors who destroyed it. As for the Council of Ten in Venice, it is a Tribunal of blood, equally horrible to the Patricians and to the People, and far from resolutely defending the laws, it only serves, after their degradation, to strike secret blows which no one dares to notice.

[386] The Tribunate is weakened, like the Government, by multiplication of its members. When the Tribunes of the Roman people, originally two in number, later five, wanted to double this number, the Senate let them do so, being

quite sure of controlling some by the others; this did not fail to happen.

[387] The best means of preventing the usurpations of such a formidable body, a means which until now no Government has deemed expedient, would be not to render this body permanent, but to set intervals during which it would remain suppressed. These intervals, which should not be long enough to let abuses have time to become established, can be fixed by law, in such a manner that they can easily be abridged in case of need by extraordinary commissions.

[388] This means seems to me without inconvenience, because, as I have said, the Tribunate, forming no part of the constitution, can be removed without the constitution suffering; and it seems to be efficacious, because a newly established magistrate begins not with the power his predecessor had but only with that which the law gives him.

VI. Of the Dictatorship

[389]* The inflexibility of laws, which prevents them from adapting to events, can in certain cases render them pernicious and cause the ruin of the State in a crisis. The order and slowness of formalities demand a space of time which circumstances sometimes refuse. A thousand cases can present themselves for which the legislator has not provided, and it is a very necessary foresight to sense that everything cannot be foreseen.

[390] It is then not necessary to want to strengthen political institutions so much that the power to suspend their effect is removed. Even Sparta let her laws lie dormant.

[391] But only the greatest dangers can outweigh the danger of altering the public order, and the sacred power of the laws should never be arrested unless it is a matter of the safety of the fatherland. In these rare and obvious cases, public security is provided for by a special act which entrusts its responsibility to the most worthy. This commission can

be conferred in two ways, according to the kind of danger.

[392] If, in order to remedy it, it suffices to augment the activity of the government, one may concentrate this activity in one or two of its members. Thus it is not the authority of the laws that is changed but only the form of their administration. But if the danger is such that the formal process of the law is an obstacle to guaranteeing them, then a supreme chief is named who silences all the laws and suspends for a moment the Sovereign authority; in such case, the general will is not doubted, and it is evident that the first intention of the people is that the State should not perish. In this way the suspension of the legislative authority does not abolish it: the magistrate who silences it cannot make it speak; he dominates it without power to represent it; he can do everything except make laws.

[393] The first means was employed by the Roman Senate when it charged the Consuls by a consecrated formula to provide for the safety of the republic. The second was employed when one of the two consuls named a Dictator,[12] a usage of which Alba had given the example to Rome.

[394] In the early days of the Republic, recourse had often been had to the Dictatorship, because the State still was not firmly enough set to be able to maintain itself solely by the force of its constitution.

[395] Moral customs rendering superfluous at that time many precautions which would have been necessary in another time, one did not fear either that a Dictator would abuse his authority or that he would try to retain it beyond his term. On the contrary, it seemed that such great power was a burden to him in whom it was vested, so that he hastened to divest himself of it; as if it were too painful and perilous a position to take the place of the laws!

[396] Thus it is not the danger of abuse, but that of

12. This nomination was made at night and in secret, as if it were shameful to place a man above the laws.

degradation, that makes me blame the indiscreet use of this supreme magistracy in early times. For as long as it was wasted on elections, dedications, and pure formalities, it was feared that it would become less formidable when needed, and that one would accustom oneself to regard it as an empty title which was employed only in empty ceremonies.

[397] Toward the end of the Republic, the Romans, having become more circumspect, were as unreasonably sparing in the use of the Dictatorship as they had formerly been unreasonably wasteful of it. It was easy to see that their fear was ill-founded, that the very weakness of the capital then formed its security against the magistrates in its own core, that a Dictator would be able in certain cases to defend public liberty without being able to assail it, and that the chains of Rome would not be forged in Rome itself, but in its armies: the slight resistance of Marius against Sulla, of Pompey against Caesar, plainly demonstrated what could be expected from the authority within against the force from without.

[398] This error made them commit great mistakes. Such, for example, was not naming a Dictator in the Catiline affair: for as it was only a question of the interior of the town and, at most, some province of Italy, a Dictator, with the unlimited authority that the laws gave him, would have easily dissipated the conspiracy, which was stifled only by a combination of happy accidents which human prudence would never have anticipated.

[399] Instead of that, the senate contented itself to hand all its power over to the Consuls; whence it happened that Cicero in order to act efficaciously was constrained to exceed this power on an important point, and although the first transports of joy gave approval to his conduct, later he was justly called to account for the blood of Citizens shed contrary to the laws; a reproach which one could not have made against a Dictator. But the eloquence of the Consul carried all; and he himself, although a Roman, preferring his

glory more than his fatherland, sought not so much the most legitimate and the surest means of saving the State, but to have all the honor from this affair.[13] Thus he was justly honored as liberator of Rome, and justly punished as violator of the laws. However brilliant his recall, it is certain that it was a pardon.

[400] Additionally, in whatever manner this important commission may be conferred, it is important to fix its duration to a very short term which can never be prolonged. In the crises that call for its being established, the State is soon destroyed or saved, and after the current need is passed, the Dictatorship becomes tyrannical or useless. In Rome the Dictators held office for only six months, the majority abdicated before this term. If the term had been longer, perhaps they would have been tempted to prolong it still further, as the Decemvirs did theirs of one year. The Dictator had only the time to deal with the need which had led to his election; he did not have time to come up with other projects.

VII. Of the Censorship

[401]* Just as the declaration of the general will is done by the law, the declaration of public judgment is done by the censorship; public opinion is the kind of law of which the Censor is the Minister, and which he applies only to particular cases, as does the Prince.

[402] Far from being the arbiter of the opinion of the people, then, the censorial tribunal only declares it, and as soon as it deviates from that opinion, its decisions are vain and ineffectual.

[403] It is useless to distinguish the moral customs of a

13. He could not satisfy himself in this by proposing a dictator, not being able to name himself and not being sure that his colleague would nominate him.

nation from the objects of its esteem; for all these things come from the same principle and are necessarily confounded. Among all the peoples of the world, it is not nature but general opinion that decides the choice of their pleasures. Reform the opinions of men and their customs and manners will themselves be purified. One always likes what is good or what one finds to be so, but it is on this judgment that one deceives oneself: it is therefore this judgment which needs adjusting. He who judges customs judges honor, and he who judges honor takes his law from opinion.

[404]* The opinions of a people arise from its constitution; although the law does not regulate customs, it is legislation that gives them birth: when legislation is impaired customs degenerate, but then the judgment of the Censors will not do what the force of the laws has not done.

[405] It follows from this that the Censorship can be useful to conserve customs, but never to reestablish them. Establish Censors while the laws are vigorous; as soon as they have lost vigor, everything is desperate; nothing that is legitimate has any force when the laws no longer have any.

[406]* The Censorship maintains moral customs by preventing opinions from being corrupted, by conserving their rectitude[14] through wise applications, sometimes even in fixing them when they are still uncertain. The use of seconds in duels, carried to madness in the kingdom of France, was abolished there by these few words in an edict of the king: "As for those who have the cowardice to name seconds." This judgment, anticipating that of the public, decided it immediately. But when the same edicts wished to proclaim that it was also cowardice to fight duels, which is very true, but contrary to the common opinion, the public mocked this decision, on which its judgment was already formed.

14. The French word is *droiture*.—ED.

[407] I have already said elsewhere[15] that public opinion not being subject to constraint, there should be no vestige of this in the tribunal established to represent it. One cannot admire too much that art with which this resource, wholly lost among moderns, was put to work among the Romans and better still among the Lacedaemonians [Spartans].

[408] A man of bad moral conduct having proposed a good recommendation in the council of Sparta, the Ephors, without taking notice, arranged for a virtuous citizen to offer the same advice. What honor for the one, what shame for the other, without having to give either praise or blame to either of the two! Certain drunkards of Samos[16] defiled the tribunal of the Ephors; the next day by public Edict the Samians were permitted to be filthy. A true punishment would have been less severe than such impunity. When Sparta declared what was or was not decent, Greece did not appeal from its judgments.

VIII. Of Civil Religion

[409]* Men had at first no other Kings than the Gods, no other Government than the Theocratic. They reasoned like Caligula; and at that time they reasoned aptly. It requires a long change of sentiments and ideas in order for one to resolve to take one's peer for a master, and to flatter oneself that this would be good.

[410] From the sole fact that one placed God at the head of each political society, it followed that there were as many Gods as peoples. Two peoples foreign to each other, and nearly always enemies, could not recognize the same master

15. I only indicate in this chapter that which I have treated in much greater length in the *Letter to M. d'Alembert.*

16. They were from another island, but the delicacy of our language prohibits naming it on this occasion.

for very long. Two armies engaged in battle with each other could not obey the same chief. Thus from national divisions polytheism resulted, and from this came theological and civil intolerance, which are naturally the same, as will be stated later.

[411] The fantasy the Greeks had of rediscovering their Gods among barbarous peoples came from that other notion they had of regarding themselves as the natural Sovereigns of those peoples. But it is a ridiculous erudition of our own day that revolves around the notion that the Gods of diverse nations are identical: as if Moloch, Saturn, and Chronos could be the same God; as if the Baal of the Phoenicians, the Zeus of the Greeks, and the Jupiter of the Latins could be the same; as if something could remain common among different chimerical Beings bearing different names!

[412] Should one ask how under paganism, when each State had its own cult and its Gods, there were no wars of religion? I respond that it was for the very reason that each State, having its own cult as well as its own Government, did not distinguish between its Gods and its laws. Political war was also Theological; the districts of the Gods were so to speak fixed by the borders of the Nations. The God of one people had no right over other peoples. The Gods of the pagans were not jealous Gods; they partitioned among themselves the empire of the world: Moses himself and the Hebrew people sometimes countenanced this idea by speaking of the God of Israel. It is true they regarded the Gods of the Canaanites, a proscribed people devoted to destruction and whose place they were to occupy, as nothing; but see how they spoke of the divinities of neighboring peoples whom they were forbidden to attack: "The possession of that which belongs to Chamos, your god," said Jephthah to the Ammonites, "is it not legitimately yours? We possess by the same title the lands that our victorious God has ac-

quired."[17] In that, it seems to me, there was a well-recognized parity between the rights of Chamos and those of the God of Israel.

[413] But when the Jews, subjected to the Kings of Babylon and later to the Kings of Syria, wished to persist in not recognizing any other God than their own, this refusal, regarded as a rebellion against the victor, brought on them the persecutions we read of in their history, and of which no other example is seen before Christianity.[18]

[414] Each Religion having then been uniquely attached to the laws of the State which prescribed it, there was no other manner of converting a people than to subjugate it, no other missionaries than conquerors, and as the obligation to change cults became the law of the conquered, it was necessary to conquer before speaking of it. Far from men combating for the Gods, it was, as in Homer, the Gods who combated for men; each asked his own god for victory, and paid for it with new altars. The Romans, before taking a place, summoned its Gods to abandon it, and when they left to the Tarrantines their angered Gods, they then regarded those Gods as subject to their own and forced to pay them homage. To the vanquished they left their own Gods just as they left them their own laws. A crown for Jupiter in the Capitol was often the only tribute they imposed.

[415] Finally, the Romans having extended with their

17. "*Nonne ea quae possidet Chamos deus tuus, tibi jure debentur?*" Such is the text of the Vulgate. Father de Carriéres has translated it: "Do you not believe you have a right to possess what belongs to Chamos your God?" I am ignorant of the force of the Hebrew text; but I see that, in the Vulgate, Jephthah positively recognized the right of the god Chamos, and that the French translator weakens this acknowledgment by an "according to you" which is not in the Latin.

18. There is strongest evidence that the war of the Phoenicians, called a sacred war, was not a war of religion. Its object was to punish sacrileges, not to subdue nonbelievers.

empire their cult and their Gods, and having often themselves adopted those of the conquered by granting to them
the right of the City, the peoples of this vast empire imperceptibly found themselves having multitudes of Gods and
cults, nearly everywhere the same: and that is how paganism
was finally known in the world as only one and the same
Religion.

[416] It was in these circumstances that Jesus came to
establish upon the earth a Spiritual kingdom; this, separating
the theological from the political system, ended the unity of
the State, and caused the internal divisions which have never
ceased to agitate christian peoples. For as this new idea of
a kingdom in another world was unable to enter into the
heads of pagans, they always regarded the Christians as true
rebels who, under a hypocritical submission, only sought
the moment to render themselves independent and masters,
and to adroitly usurp the authority they pretended to respect
in their weakness. Such was the cause of the persecutions.

[417] What the pagans feared has happened; then everything changed its appearance, the humble Christians
changed their language, and soon one saw this pretended
kingdom of the other world become under a visible chief
the most violent despotism in this world.

[418] However, as there has always been a Prince and
civil laws, there resulted from this double power a perpetual
conflict of jurisdiction which has rendered all good polity
impossible in christian States; and one has never been able
to come to know whether one was obligated to obey the
master or the priest.

[419] Many peoples, however, even in Europe or its
vicinity, have wished to conserve or reestablish the ancient
system, but without success; the spirit of christianity has
wholly won. The sacred cult has always remained or again
become independent of the Sovereign, and without a necessary bond with the body of the State. Mohammed had very
sound views, he tied his political system together well, and

as long as the form of his government subsisted under his successors the Caliphs, this government was exactly unified, and in that regard good. But the Arabs, having become flourishing, lettered, polished, soft, and cowardly, were subjugated by barbarians: then the division between the two powers began again; although it may be less apparent among the Mohammedans than among the Christians, it is there nonetheless, especially in the sect of Ali, and there are States, such as Persia, where it is unceasingly felt.

[420] Among us, the kings of England have established themselves chiefs of the Church, as have the Czars: but, by this title, they have rendered themselves less its masters than its Ministers; they have acquired less the right to change it than the power to maintain it; they are not its legislators, they are only its Princes. Wherever the clergy forms a body,[19] it is master and legislator in its fatherland. There are then two powers, two Sovereigns, in England and in Russia, as everywhere else.

[421] Of all the christian authors, the philosopher Hobbes is the only one who has clearly seen the evil and the remedy, who has dared to propose uniting the two heads of the eagle, and bring everything back to political unity, without which no State or Government will ever be well constituted. But he should have seen that the dominating spirit of Christianity was incompatible with his system, and that the interest of the priest would always be stronger than that of the State. It is not so much what is horrible and false in

19. It is well to note that it is not so much formal assemblies, as those in France, which tie the clergy into a body, but the communion of the Churches. Communion and excommunication are the social pact of the clergy, a pact by which they will always be the master of peoples and of Kings. All the priests who communicate together are fellow citizens, be they from the two ends of the world. This invention is a masterpiece of politics. There is nothing similar among pagan priests, thus they have never constituted a body of Clergy.

his political theory as what it has that is just and true that has rendered it odious.[20]

[422] I believe that in developing the historical facts under this viewpoint, one would easily refute the opposed sentiments of Bayle and Warburton, one of whom claims that no Religion is useful to the body politic, and the other that to the contrary, Christianity is its strongest support. To the first, one could prove that no State was ever founded without Religion serving as its base, and to the second, that christian law is more injurious than useful to a firm constitution of the State. In order to make myself understood, it is only needed to give a little more precision to the overly vague ideas of Religion relative to my subject.

[423] Religion considered by its relation to the society, which is either general or particular, can also be divided into two kinds: namely, the Religion of man and that of the Citizen. The first, without temples, without altars, without rites, limited to the purely internal worship of the Supreme God and to the eternal duties of morality, is the pure and simple Religion of the Gospel, the true Theism, and what one can call the divine natural right. The other, inscribed in a single country, gives it its Gods, its proper and tutelary patrons; its has its dogmas, its rites, its external worship prescribed by the laws: outside of the single Nation that follows it, all is for it infidel, foreign, barbarous; it extends the duties and rights of man only as far as its altars. Such were all the Religions of the early peoples, to which one can give the name of divine, civil, or positive right.

[424] There is a third, more bizarre kind of Religion which, giving to men two legislations, two chiefs, two fatherlands, subjects them to contradictory duties and pre-

---

20. Note, among others, in a letter from Grotius to his brother on 11 April 1643, what this learned man approved and what he blamed in the book *De Cive*. It is true that, inclined to indulgence, he seems to pardon the author for his good points for the sake of the bad ones: but everyone is not so lenient.

vents them from being able to be at one time devout and Citizens. Such is the religion of the Lamas, such is that of the Japanese, such is Roman Christianity. One can call this the religion of the Priest. There results from it a kind of mixed unsociable right which has no name.

[425] Considered politically, these three kinds of religions all have their defects. The third is so evidently bad that it is a waste of time to amuse oneself demonstrating it. Whatever destroys social unity is worthless. All institutions which place man in contradiction with himself are worthless.

[426] The second is good insofar as it unites divine worship with the love of the laws, and by making the fatherland the object of the adoration of the Citizens it teaches them that to serve the State is to serve the tutelary God. It is one kind of theocracy, in which there should be no other pontiff but the Prince, nor other priests than the magistrates. Then to die for one's country is to go to martyrdom, to violate the laws is to be impious, and to subject a guilty man to public execration is to deliver him to the anger of the gods: *sacer esto*. [21]

[427] But it is bad in that being founded on error and on falsehood it deceives men, renders them credulous, superstitious, and drowns the true worship of the Divinity in a vain ceremonial. It is again bad when, becoming exclusive and tyrannical, it renders a people sanguinary and intolerant, so that it breathes only murder and massacre, and believes it is performing a holy action by killing whoever does not admit its gods. This places such a people in a natural state of war with all others, very detrimental to its own security.

[428] There remains then the Religion of man or Christianity, not that of today, but that of the Gospel, which is

21. A phrase from the "Twelve Tables," the earliest codification of Roman law; literally translated, it means "let him be sacred," but it was a euphemism for "let him be an outcast with whom no man would deal."—ED.

altogether different. By this holy, sublime, and true Religion, men, children of the same God, all recognize themselves as brothers, and the society which unites them is not even dissolved at death.

[429] But this Religion, having no particular relation with the body politic, leaves to the laws only the force that they derive from themselves without adding any other to them, and thus one of the great bonds of a particular society remains ineffective. What is more, far from attaching the hearts of the Citizens to the State, it detaches them as from all things of the earth; I know nothing more contrary to the social spirit.

[430] We are told that a people of true Christians would form the most perfect society that one can imagine. I see only one great difficulty in this supposition; it is that a society of true Christians would no longer be a society of men.

[431] I even say that this supposed society with all its perfection would be neither the strongest nor the most durable. By dint of being perfect, it would lack cohesion; its destructive vice would be in its very perfection.

[432] Each would fulfill his duty; the people would be subject to the laws, the chiefs would be just and moderate, the magistrates honest and incorruptible; the soldiers would despise death; there would be neither vanity nor luxury: all this is very good, but let us look further.

[433] Christianity is an entirely spiritual religion, only occupied by things of Heaven; the fatherland of the Christian is not of this world. He does his duty, it is true, but he does it with a profound indifference to the good or bad outcome of his cares. Provided he has nothing for which to reproach himself, it is of little import to him whether all fares well or poorly here below. If the State is flourishing, he hardly dares to enjoy the public felicity, for he fears to take selfish pride in the glory of his country; if the State declines, he blesses the hand of God that weighs down heavily on his people.

[434] In order that the society be peaceable and harmony be maintained, all Citizens without exception would have to be equally good Christians. But if unfortunately there is found in it a single ambitious man, a single hypocrite, a Catiline, for example, a Cromwell, such a man very certainly would have an advantage over his pious compatriots. The christian charity does not easily permit one to think ill of one's neighbor. As soon as he will have found by some ruse the art of imposing on them and securing to himself a part of the public authority, behold a man invested with dignity; God wills that he should be respected; soon he is a power; God wills that one obeys him; does the depositary of this power abuse it? He is the rod with which God punishes his children. It would violate conscience to chase out the usurper: it would be necessary to trouble the public peace, to use violence, to shed blood; all this is not accordant with the meekness of the Christian; and after all, does it matter whether one is free or serf in this vale of misery? The essential thing is to go to paradise, and resignation is only one more means toward that.

[435] Does some foreign war occur? The Citizens march to combat without distress; none among them thinks of flight; they do their duty, but without passion for victory; they know better how to die than how to conquer. Whether they are victors or vanquished, does it matter? Doesn't Providence know better than they what they need? Imagine what advantage a proud, impetuous, passionate enemy can wrest from their stoicism. Place them against those courageous people consumed with an ardent love of glory and the fatherland; suppose your Christian Republic facing Sparta or Rome: the pious Christians will be beaten, crushed, destroyed, before they have had time to know where they are, or they will owe their safety only to the scorn their enemies have for them. To my mind it was a fine oath that the soldiers of Fabius took; they did not swear to die or conquer, they swore to return as conquerors, and kept their

oath. Never would Christians have done such a thing; they would have believed they were tempting God.

[436] But I am mistaken in speaking of a Christian Republic; each of these two words excludes the other. Christianity only preaches servitude and dependence. Its spirit is too favorable to tyranny for it not to always profit by it. True Christians are made to be slaves; they know it and are hardly moved by it; this short life has too little value in their eyes.

[437] We are told Christian troops are excellent. I deny it. Let me be shown such. As for me, I do not know of any Christian Troops. I am told of the Crusades. Without disputing the valor of the Crusaders, I will note that, far from being Christians, they were soldiers of the priest, they were Citizens of the Church: they battled for its Spiritual country, which the Church had rendered temporal, one knows not how. Properly regarded, this returns us to paganism: as the Gospel does not establish a national Religion, any holy war is impossible among Christians.

[438] Under the pagan emperors Christian soldiers were brave; all the Christian authors affirm this, and I believe it: there was a competition for honor against the pagan Troops. As soon as the Emperors became Christians this competition no longer subsisted; and when the cross had driven out the eagle, all Roman valor disappeared.

[439]* But setting aside political considerations, let us return to right, and settle the principles on this important point. The right which the social pact gives to the Sovereign over the subjects does not pass, as I have said, the limits of public utility.[22] The subjects then owe no account of their

22. "In the republic," says M. d'A., "each is perfectly free in that which does not injure others." That is the invariable limit; it cannot be more exactly stated. I have not been able to refuse myself the pleasure of sometimes citing this manuscript, although it is not known to the public, in order to render honor to the memory of an illustrious and respectable man, who had preserved even in the ministry the heart of a true citizen, and upright and sound views on the government of his country.

opinions to the Sovereign except as these opinions are important to the community. Now it matters greatly to the State that each Citizen have a Religion which makes him love his duties; but the dogmas of this Religion concern neither the State nor its members except as these dogmas relate to morality and to the duties that anyone who professes it is bound to fulfill toward others. Each may have in addition whatever opinions please him, without it being the Sovereign's business to know what they are. For as the Sovereign has no competence in the other world, whatever may be the destiny of the subjects in the life to come is not its affair, provided that they are good citizens in this life.

[440]* There is then a purely civil profession of faith, the articles of which it is the business of the Sovereign to settle, not precisely as dogmas of religion, but as sentiments of sociability, without which it is impossible to be a good Citizen or faithful subject.[23] Without being able to obligate anyone to believe them, it can banish from the State anyone who does not believe them; it can banish him, not as impious, but as unsociable, as incapable of sincerely loving the laws, and justice, and of sacrificing at need his life to his duty. If anyone, after publicly acknowledging these dogmas, behaves as though he does not believe them, he should be punished by death; he has committed the greatest of crimes, he has lied before the laws.

[441] The dogmas of this civil religion ought to be simple, few in number, stated with precision, without explanations or commentaries. The existence of the Deity, powerful, intelligent, beneficent, prescient, and provident; the life to come, the happiness of the just, the punishment of the wicked, the sanctity of the social Contract and the Laws:

23. Caesar, pleading for Catiline, tried to establish the dogma of the mortality of the soul; Cato and Cicero, in order to refute him, did not amuse themselves philosophizing: they contented themselves with showing that Caesar spoke as a bad Citizen and advanced a doctrine pernicious to the State. Indeed, it was that which the Roman Senate had to judge, and not a question of theology.

these are the positive dogmas. As for the negative dogmas, I limit them to only one, intolerance: it belongs in the creeds we have excluded.

[442] Those who distinguish civil intolerance from theological intolerance are, in my opinion, mistaken. These two kinds of intolerance are inseparable. It is impossible to live in peace with people whom one believes to be damned; to love them would be to hate God who punishes them: it is absolutely necessary that they be reclaimed or tormented. Wherever theological intolerance is admitted, it is impossible that it not have some civil effect,[24] and as soon as it has any, the Sovereign is no longer Sovereign, even in temporal matters; from then on the Priests are the true masters; the Kings are only their officers.

[443] Now that there is no longer and can never be an exclusive national Religion, one should tolerate all those which tolerate the others, so far as their dogmas have nothing contrary to the duties of the Citizen. But whoever dares

---

24. Marriage, for example, being a civil contract has civil effects, without which it is impossible that society subsist. Let us suppose then that a clergy ascribe to itself alone the right of performing this act, a right it must necessarily usurp in every intolerant religion; then is it not clear that in asserting the authority of the Church it renders empty that of the prince, who will have no other subjects than those the clergy is willing to give him? Master of which people can or cannot marry, according to whether they hold or do not hold such or such a doctrine, according to whether they admit or reject such or such a formula, according to whether they are more or less devoted to it, is it not clear that by behaving prudently and keeping firm, the Church alone will dispose of inheritances, offices, citizens, and the State itself, which cannot subsist when composed only of bastards? But, it will be said, men will appeal against such abuses; they will adjourn, decree, seize temporal holdings. What a pity! The clergy, however little it may have, I do not say of courage but of good sense, will let this be done and go its way; it will quietly permit appealing, adjourning, decreeing, seizing, and will end by being the master. It is not, it seems to me, a great sacrifice to abandon a part when one is sure of taking possession of the whole.

to say: *outside of the Church there is no salvation,* ought to be chased from the State, unless the State be the Church, and the Prince be the Pontiff. Such a dogma is good only in a Theocratic Government; in any other it is pernicious. The reason for which Henry IV embraced the Roman Religion ought to make any honest man, and especially any Prince who would know how to reason, leave it.

IX. Conclusion

[444]* After having set forth the true principles of political right and attempted to found the State on its base, it would remain to support it by its external relations; this would comprise the law of peoples, commerce, the right of war and conquest, the public right, alliances, negotiations, treaties, etc. But all that forms a new object which is too vast for my limited scope; I should always have confined myself to what is nearer to me.

Discourse on
Political Economy

[1]* *Economy* or *Oeconomie* (Moral and Political). This word comes from οιχος, *house,* and from νόμος, *law,* and originally meant only the wise and legitimate government of the house, for the common good of the whole family. The sense of this term has subsequently been extended to the government of the large family, which is the state. In order to distinguish these two meanings, one refers in the latter case to *general* or *political economy;* and in the former, to *domestic* or *private economy.* It is only the first which is the question in this article. On *domestic economy,* see FATHER OF THE FAMILY.

[2]* Even if there were as close an affinity between the state and the family as several authors claim, it would not thereby follow that the rules of conduct appropriate to one of these two societies would be appropriate to the other; they differ too much in size to be administered in the same manner, and there will always be an extreme difference between domestic government, where the father can see everything by himself, and civil government, where the chief sees almost nothing except through the eyes of others. For things to become equal in this regard, the talents,

*Asterisks (*) follow the numbers of all paragraphs for which explanatory comments are to be found, with regard either to the paragraphs themselves or passages within them; these comments are to be found in the "Notes" beginning on p.217.

strength, and all the faculties of the father would have to increase in proportion to the size of the family, and the soul of a powerful monarch would have to be in comparison to that of an ordinary man as the extent of his empire is to the inheritance of a private individual.

[3] But how could the government of the state be similar to that of the family, whose foundation is so different? The father is physically much stronger than his children, and for as long as his help is necessary, the paternal power is reasonably accepted as having been established by nature. In the large family whose members are all naturally equal, political authority, purely arbitrary as to its institution, can be founded only on conventions, and the magistrate can command others only by virtue of the laws. The duties of the father are dictated to him by natural sentiments and in a tone that rarely permits him to disobey. The chiefs do not have a similar rule, and they are really accountable only to the people for what they have promised to do, and which the people may rightfully require them to carry out. Another, even more important difference is that since children have only what they receive from the father, it is evident that all rights of ownership [proprietorship] belong to him or emanate from him; it is completely opposite in the large family, where the general administration is established only to assure the private ownership anterior to it. The principal object of the work of the whole household is to conserve and increase the patrimony of the father so that he can someday divide it among his children without leaving them impoverished; in contrast, the wealth of the public treasury is only a means, often badly understood, to maintain private individuals in peace and abundance. In a word, the little family is destined to disappear, and to dissolve someday into several other, similar families; but the large family having been created to always continue in the same state, it is necessary that the first enlarge itself in order to multiply: and not only does it suffice that the second conserve itself,

but one can easily prove that every enlargement is more prejudicial than useful to it.

[4] For several reasons taken from the nature of the thing, the father ought to command in the family. First, authority ought not be equal between the father and the mother; but it is necessary that the government should be one, and that in the division of opinion, one predominant voice decide. Second, however lightly one wishes to suppose the particular indispositions of the wife; as they always necessitate intervals of inaction for her, this is a sufficient reason to exclude her from this primacy: for when the balance is perfectly equal, one straw suffices to tip it. Additionally, the husband should watch the conduct of his wife; because it is important for him to assure himself that the children whom he must recognize and sustain do not belong to anyone but himself. The wife, who does not have to fear anything similar, does not have the same right over the husband. Third, the children should obey the father, at first out of necessity, later out of gratitude; after having received fulfillment of their own needs during one half of their lives, they ought to consecrate the other half to providing for his. Fourth, regarding servants, they also owe him their services in exchange for the livelihood he gives them, unless they break the agreement when it ceases to suit them. I do not speak of slavery; because it is contrary to nature, and no right can authorize it.

[5] There is nothing of all this in political society. Far from the chief having a natural interest in the happiness of the private individuals, it is not unusual for him to seek his own in their misery. If the magistracy is hereditary, it is often a child who commands men; if it is elective, a thousand inconveniences are found in the elections, and one loses in either case all the advantages of paternity. If you have only one chief, you are at the discretion of a master who has no reason to love you; if you have several, it is necessary to bear at the same time their tyranny and their dissensions. In a

word, abuses are inevitable with dire consequences in every society, where the public interest and the laws lack natural force, and are unceasingly attacked by the personal interest and passions of the chief and the members.

[6] Although the functions of the father of the family and of the first magistrate ought to tend to the same goal, it is by such different routes; their duty and their rights are so distinct that it is not possible to confound them without forming false ideas about the fundamental laws of society and without falling into errors fatal to mankind. Indeed, if the voice of nature is the best counsel to which a good father ought to listen in order to fulfill his duties well, for the magistrate it is only a false guide which unceasingly works to separate him from his duties, and which sooner or later brings both his downfall and that of the state, if he is not restrained by the most sublime virtue. The sole precaution necessary for the father of the family is to protect himself against depravity, and to prevent his natural inclinations from becoming corrupted; but these are just what corrupts the magistrate. To do well, the father has only to consult his heart; the magistrate becomes a traitor the moment he listens to his own: his reason itself should be suspect, and he ought to follow no other rule than that of public reason, which is the law. Also, nature has made a multitude of good fathers of families: but it is doubtful whether, since the beginning of the world, human wisdom has ever made ten men capable of governing their fellows.

[7]* From all I have shown, it follows that it is with reason that one distinguishes *public economy* from *private economy*, and that the state having nothing in common with the family other than the obligation the chiefs have to render each of them happy, the same rules of conduct could not apply to the two.[1] I thought that these few lines would suffice to

---

1. In the 1782 edition, the last clause was changed to read: "neither could their rights come from the same source, nor could the same rules of conduct apply to the two."—ED.

destroy the odious system that Sir [Robert] Filmer tried to establish in the work entitled *Patriarcha,* to which two illustrious men have paid too much honor by writing books to refute it: nevertheless, this error is very ancient, since Aristotle himself judged it appropriate to challenge it with reasons which can be seen in the first book of his *Politics.*

[8]* I request my readers to distinguish clearly *political economy,* which is my topic, and which I call *government,* from the supreme authority which I call *sovereignty;* a distinction which consists in that the one has the legislative right, and in certain cases obligates the body of the nation itself, while the other has only the executive power, and is only able to obligate private individuals. See POLITICS and SOVEREIGNTY.

[9] Permit me to employ for a moment a comparison that is common and in many ways inexact, but appropriate to make myself better understood.

[10]* The body politic, taken individually, can be considered as a body, organized, living, and similar to that of a man. The sovereign power represents the head; the laws and customs are the brain, source of the nerves and seat of the understanding, the will, and the senses, of which the judges and magistrates are the organs; commerce, industry, and agriculture are the mouth and stomach, which prepare the common subsistence; public finances are the blood that a wise *economy,* in performing the functions of the heart, sends out to distribute nourishment and life throughout the body; the citizens are the body and the members who make the mechanism move, live, and work, and cannot be injured in any part without a painful impression being carried to the brain, if the animal is in a state of health.

[11] The life of each relating part is the *self* common to the whole, the reciprocal sensibility and internal relation of all the parts. What if this communication should cease, the formal unity evaporate, and the contiguous parts belong to each other only by juxtaposition? The man is dead, or the state is dissolved.

[12]* The body politic is then also a moral being which has a will; and this general will, which always tends to the conservation and the well-being of the whole and of each part, and which is the source of the laws, is for all the members of the state, by virtue of the relation to them and to it, the rule of what is just and unjust; this truth, let it be said in passing, shows with how little sense so many writers have treated as thievery the cunning prescribed to the children of Sparta to gain their frugal meal, as if everything the law orders could fail to be legitimate. See the word RIGHT, the source of this great and luminous principle, of which this article is the development.

[13] It is important to remark that this rule of justice, dependable in relation to all citizens, can be defective with regard to foreigners; and the reason for this is evident: then the will of the state, although general in relation to its members, is no longer so in relation to other states and their members, but becomes for them a private and individual will, which has its rule of justice in the law of nature, and is included in the principle established: for then the large city of the world becomes the body politic, of which the law of nature is always the general will, and of which the diverse states and peoples are only the individual members.

[14]* From these same distinctions, applied to each political society and to its members, flow the most universal and dependable rules by which one can judge of a good or bad government, and, in general, the morality of all human actions.

[15]* Every political society is composed of other, smaller societies of different kinds, each of which has its interests and its maxims; but these societies, which everyone notices because they have an external and authorized form, are not the only ones which really exist in the state; all private individuals united by a common interest comprise as many others, permanent or transient, whose force is no less real for being less apparent, and a careful observation of their diverse relationships comprises the true knowledge of customary con-

duct. It is all these tacit or formal associations which so modify the manifestations of the public will by their influence. The will of these private societies always has two relations: for the members of the association, it is a general will; for the larger society, it is a private will which is very often upright in the first regard and vicious in the second. One can be a devout priest, or brave soldier, or active practitioner of his calling, and a bad citizen. A particular decision can be advantageous to the small community and very pernicious to the large one. It is true that since private societies are always subordinate to those which contain them, one ought to obey the large one in preference to the others, for the duties of the citizen come before those of a senator, and those of a man before those of the citizen: but unfortunately, personal interest is always found in inverse proportion to that of duty, and increases as the association becomes narrower and the engagement less sacred; invincible proof that the most general will is always the most just, and that the voice of the people is indeed the voice of God.

[16]* It does not thereby follow that public decisions are always equitable; they may not be so concerning foreign affairs; I have stated the reason. Thus it is not impossible that a well-governed republic wage an unjust war. It is also not impossible that the council of a democracy pass bad decrees and condemn the innocent; but it will only happen when the people are seduced by private interests, when some clever men, by their influence and their eloquence, will succeed in substituting their own private interests for the interests of the people. Then the public decision will be one thing and the general will another. Do not cite the democracy of Athens as a counter example, because Athens was hardly a democracy, but a very tyrannical aristocracy governed by learned men and orators. Examine with care what happens in any resolution and you will see that the general will is always for the common good; but very often a secret division, a tacit confederation, occurs which eludes the natural disposition of the assembly in favor of their own private

views. Then the social body is really divided into other
bodies, whose members choose a general will, good and just
with regard to these new bodies, unjust and bad regarding
the whole from which each of them has broken away.

[17]* One sees with what ease one explains by the aid of
these principles the apparent contradictions noticed in the
conduct of many men full of scruple and honor in some
regards, deceptive and knavish in others, trampling under
foot the most sacred duties, and loyal to the death to engagements that are often illegitimate. It is thus that the most
corrupt men always render some kind of homage to the
public faith; it is thus (as remarked in the article RIGHT) that
the same brigands who are the enemies of virtue in the large
society worship its likeness in their caverns.

[18] In establishing the general will as the first principle
of public *economy* and the fundamental rule of government,
I have not believed it necessary to ask seriously whether the
magistrates belong to the people or the people to the magistrates, and whether in public affairs one should consult the
good of the state or that of the chiefs. For a long time this
question has been decided in one manner by practice and
in another by reason; in general it would be great folly to
hope that those who are in fact masters will prefer another
interest to their own. It would then also be proper to divide
public *economy* into the popular and the tyrannical. The first
is that of every state, where a unity of interest and will
between the people and the chiefs governs; the other necessarily exists wherever the government and the people have
different interests and consequently opposed wills. The
maxims of the latter are written in the archives of history
and in the satires of Machiavelli. The others are to be found
only in the writings of philosophers who dare to demand the
rights of humanity.

I

[19]* The first and most important maxim of legitimate or popular government, that is to say the one which has for its object the good of the people, is therefore, as I have said, to follow the general will in all matters; but in order to follow the general will it is necessary to know it, and above all to distinguish it well from the private will, beginning with oneself; this distinction is always difficult to make, and for making it only the most sublime virtue can provide sufficient enlightenment. Since it is necessary to be free in order to will, another, hardly lesser difficulty is to assure at the same time public liberty and the authority of the government. Seek the motives which have carried men, united by their mutual needs in the large society, to unite themselves more closely into civil societies; you will find no other than that of assuring the goods, the life, and the liberty of each member by the protection of all: now how can men be forced to defend the liberty of one among them without impairing the liberty of others? and how provide for public needs without disturbing the private ownership of those who are compelled to contribute to them? By whatever sophisms one is able to color all this, it is certain that if one is able to constrain my will, I am no longer free, and I am no longer the master of my goods if someone else can touch them. This difficulty, which must have seemed insurmountable, has been removed together with the first difficulty by the most sublime of all human institutions, or rather by a celestial inspiration which taught men to imitate here below the immutable decrees of the deity. By what inconceivable art were the means found to subject men in order to make them free? to employ in the service of the state the goods, the labor, and even the life of all its members without constraining and consulting them? to bind their will with their own approval? to let their consent prevail despite their refusal, and to force them to punish themselves when they do

what they have not willed to do? How can it be that they obey and no one commands, that they serve without having a master; so much freer indeed as under a seeming subjection, none losing any of his liberty except what may be harmful to the liberty of another? These marvels are the work of law. It is to law alone that men owe justice and liberty. It is this salutary organ of the will of all that restores in right the natural equality among men. It is this celestial voice that proclaims to each citizen the precepts of public reason, and teaches him to act according to the maxims of his own judgment, and not to be in contradiction with himself. It alone is what the chiefs should cause to speak when they command; for as soon as a man claims to subject another to his private will independent of the laws, he instantly leaves the civil state and places himself vis-à-vis the other in the pure state of nature, where obedience is never prescribed except by necessity.

[20]* The most pressing interest of the chief, even his most indispensable duty, is to watch over the observation of the laws of which he is the minister and on which all his authority is founded. If he must make others observe them, so much stronger is the reason to observe them himself, as he enjoys all of their benefit. For his example is of such force that, even if the people would permit him to free himself from the yoke of the law, he should forbear taking advantage of such a dangerous prerogative, which others would soon strive to usurp in turn and often to its detriment. In the main, as all the engagements of society are reciprocal by their nature, it is not possible to place oneself above the law without renouncing its advantages, and no one owes anything to anyone who claims he has no duty to anyone. For the same reason, no exemption from the law will ever be accorded for whatever claim in a well-administered government. Even those citizens who have most deserved recognition from the fatherland ought to be rewarded with honors and never with privileges: for the republic is at the verge of

its ruin as soon as anyone can think it fair not to obey the laws. But if ever the nobility or the military or any other order of the state should adopt such a maxim, all would be irredeemably lost.

[21] The power of the laws depends much more on their own wisdom than on the severity of their ministers, and the public will draws its greatest weight from the reason that dictated it: this is why Plato regards it as a very important precaution to always place at the head of edicts a reasoned preamble which shows their justice and utility. Indeed, the first of the laws is to respect the laws: the severity of punishments is only a vain expedient invented by little minds in order to substitute terror for the respect they are unable to obtain. One has always noted that the countries where corporal punishments are the most terrible are also those where they are most frequent; so that the cruelty of penalties only indicates the multitude of lawbreakers; punishing everything with equal severity forces the guilty to commit crimes in order to escape punishment for their mistakes.

[22] But although the government is not the master of the law, it is no small thing for it to be its guarantor and to have a thousand ways for making the law loved. The talent of reigning consists only in this. When one has force at hand, there is no art to make everyone tremble, and not much is needed to win their hearts; for long experience has taught the people to be grateful to its chiefs for all the evil they have not done to it, and to adore its chiefs when it is not hated by them. An imbecile who is obeyed is as able as anyone to punish crimes; the true statesman knows how to prevent them; it is over wills more than actions that he extends his respectable dominance. If he could make sure that everyone acted correctly, he himself would no longer have anything to do and the consummation of his works would be that he could remain idle. It is at least certain that the greatest talent of chiefs is to disguise their power in order to render it less odious, and to conduct the state

so peaceably that it seems to have no need of conductors.

[23]* I conclude then that, as the first duty of the legislator is to conform the laws to the general will, the first rule of public *economy* is that the administration should conform to the laws. This will be enough for the state not to be badly governed, if the legislator has seen, as he ought to have done, to everything required by the locality, the climate, soil, moral customs, neighborhood, and all the particular relationships of the people he was to institute. Still there remains an infinity of details, of policy and *economy,* left to the wisdom of the government; but there are always two infallible rules for conducting oneself correctly in these situations: the one is the spirit of the law, which ought to serve in deciding cases that could not have been anticipated; the other is the general will, the source and supplement of all the laws, which should always be consulted when they are lacking. How, I will be asked, can the general will be known in those cases in which it has never explained itself? Will it be necessary to assemble the entire nation at every unforeseen event? It will be less than necessary to assemble it, since it is not certain that its decision would be the expression of the general will; this method is impracticable for a large people, and it is rarely necessary when the government is well-intentioned; for the chiefs know well enough that the general will is always for the party that is most favorable to the public interest, that is to say the most equitable; thus it is only required to be just in order to be assured that the general will is followed. Often, when it is too openly flouted, it shows itself despite the terrible curb of public authority. I look as close by as I can for examples to follow in such a case. In China, the prince's constant maxim is to assign the blame to his officers in all disputes that arise between them and the people. Is bread expensive in a province? the commissioner is placed in prison; is there a riot in another? the governor is dismissed and each mandarin answers with his head for any evil that arises in his department.

It is not that the affair is not later examined in a regular
manner: but long experience has made it possible to anticipate the verdict. There is seldom any injustice to be re-
paired; and the emperor, persuaded that public clamor
never arises without reason, always discerns, among the
seditious clamors he punishes, just grievances that he re-
dresses.

[24] It is a great deal to have made order and peace reign
in all parts of the republic; it is a great deal that the state
should be tranquil and the law respected; but if one does
nothing more, it will all be more appearance than reality,
and the government will find it difficult to be obeyed if it
limits itself to obedience. If it is good to know how to
employ men as they are, it is still better to make them such
as one needs them to be. The most absolute authority is that
which penetrates to the interior of the man and exerts itself
no less on his will than on his actions. It is certain that the
peoples in the long run are what the government makes
them to be. Warriors, citizens, men, when that is what it
wants; mob and rabble when it pleases: every prince who
scorns his subjects dishonors himself by showing that he
does not know how to make them worthy of esteem. Form
men then if you would command men: if you would have
the laws obeyed, make them loved; and in order for one to
do what one ought, let it suffice that one realize one ought
to do it. This was the great art of ancient governments, in
those remote times when philosophers gave laws to peoples,
and employed their authority only to make them wise and
happy. From this came so many sumptuary laws, so many
regulations regarding moral customs, and so many public
maxims which were accepted or rejected with the greatest
care. The tyrants themselves did not forget this important
part of administration, and were as careful to corrupt the
conduct of their slaves as the magistrates were to correct the
conduct of their fellow citizens. But our modern governments which believe that they have done everything when

they have collected money do not even imagine that it should be necessary or possible to reach that point.

II

[25]* The second essential rule of public *economy* is no less important than the first. Do you wish that the general will be fulfilled? cause all private wills to relate themselves to it; and as virtue is only this conformity of the private will to the general will, to say the same thing in a word, see to it that virtue reigns.

[26] If the political men were less blinded by their ambition, they would see how it is impossible for any establishment, whatever it be, to proceed in accord with the spirit of its institution if it is not directed in accord with the law of duty; they would realize that the greatest resource of public authority is in the heart of the citizens, and that nothing can replace good customs for the maintenance of the government. Not only do good people alone know how to administer the laws but, fundamentally, honest men alone know how to obey them. He who succeeds in braving remorse will not delay in braving corporal punishment; it is less severe, less continuous, and something from which he has at least the hope of escaping; whatever precautions are taken, those who look forward only to not being punished for doing wrong hardly lack a means to elude the law or escape punishment. Then, as all private interests unite against the general interest, which is no longer that of any individual, public vices have more force to debilitate the laws than the laws have to repress the vices; the corruption of the people and the chiefs finally extends to the government, however wise it may be: the worst of all abuses is to obey the laws in appearance in order safely to violate them in deed. Soon the best laws become the most disastrous; it would be a hundred times better if they did not exist; this would still be a resource when nothing else remained. In

such a situation one uselessly adds edicts on edicts, regulations on regulations. All that serves only to introduce other abuses without correcting the first ones. The more you multiply laws, the more you render them despicable: and all the inspectors you appoint are only new lawbreakers destined to share with the old ones, or to do their pillage separately. Soon the price of virtue becomes that of brigandage: the vilest men are the most accredited; the greater they are, the more contemptible they become; their infamy glares in their high dignity, and they are dishonored by their honors. If they buy the approbation of the chiefs or the protection of women, it is in order to sell in turn justice, duty, and the state; and the people, who does not see that its vices are the first cause of its misfortunes, murmurs and cries, lamenting: "All my miseries come only from those whom I pay to protect me."

[27] It is then that the chiefs are forced to substitute for the voice of duty, which no longer speaks in the hearts, the cry of terror or the lure of an apparent interest with which they deceive their creatures. It is then that it is necessary to resort to all those petty and contemptible ruses which they call *maxims of state* and *secrets of the cabinet*. All the vigor left to the government is employed by its members to destroy and supplant one another, while the public business remains abandoned, or is pursued only to the extent that personal interest demands and directs them. Finally, the entire skill of these great political men is to fascinate the eyes of those whom they need, so much that each believes himself to work for his own interest while working for *theirs;* I say theirs, if indeed it is the true interest of chiefs to annihilate peoples in order to subject them and even to ruin them in order to assure themselves of possessing them.[2]

2. The last clause reads: *"je dis le leur, si tant est qu'en effet le véritable intérêt des chefs soit d'anéantir les peuples pour les soûmettre, et de ruiner leur propre bien pour s'en assûrer la possession."*—ED.

[28] But when the citizens love their duty, and those in whom public authority is entrusted sincerely apply themselves to nourish this love by their example and by their solicitude, all difficulties evaporate, and the administration takes on an ease which dispenses with that shadowy art whose sinister shade provides its mysterious attraction. Those vast spirits, so dangerous and so admired, all those great ministers whose glory is only its fusion with the misfortunes of the people, are no longer missed; public customs supersede the talents of the chiefs; and the more virtue reigns, the less are such talents necessary. Ambition itself is better served by duty than by usurpation; the people, convinced that its chiefs work only for its happiness, saves them by its deference from working to consolidate their power; and history shows us in a thousand places that the authority accorded to those whom it loves and by whom it is loved is a hundred times more absolute than all the tyranny of usurpers. This does not mean that the government should fear to use its power, but that it should only be used in a legitimate manner. One finds in history a thousand examples of ambitious or pusillanimous chiefs who have been undone by weakness or pride, but not one who fared badly by being only equitable. But one should confuse neither negligence with moderation, nor kindness with weakness. It is necessary to be severe in order to be just: to suffer the wickedness one has the right and the power to repress is to be wicked oneself.[3]

[29]* It is not enough to say to the citizens, be good; it is necessary to teach them how to be so; and example itself, which in this regard is the first lesson, is not the sole means that must be employed: love of the fatherland is the most

3. In the 1782 edition, the paragraph is completed by a quotation from Saint Augustine: *"Sicuti enim est aliquando misericordia puniens, ita est crudelitas parcens"* (*Letters,* 54). [In the same way that pity can sometimes punish, cruelty can pardon.]—ED.

efficacious; for as I have already said, every man is virtuous when his private will conforms in everything to the general will, and we readily want what is wanted by the people we love.

[30] It would seem that the sentiment of humanity evaporates and weakens when diffused over the whole earth, and that we could not be as touched by the calamities of Tartary or Japan as by those of a European people. Interest and commiseration must in some way be confined and compressed in order to be actuated. Now since this tendency in us can be useful only to those with whom we have to live, it is well that humane sentiments be concentrated among fellow citizens, that it take from them a new force through the habit of seeing each other and through the common interest that unites them. It is certain that the greatest wonders of virtue have been produced by love of the fatherland: this sweet and lively sentiment, which joins the force of pride[4] to the complete beauty of virtue, gives virtue an energy that, without disfiguring it, makes it the most heroic of all passions. It is what produced so many immortal actions whose brilliance dazzles our weak eyes, so many great men whose ancient virtues are taken as fables ever since patriotism has become an object of derision. This should not surprise us; the ecstasies of tender hearts appear fanciful to anyone who has not felt them; and the love of the fatherland, a hundred times more lively and delicious than that of a mistress, can also be conceived only by experiencing it: but it is easy to notice in all hearts it inflames, in all actions it inspires, this boiling and sublime ardor, which even the purest virtue does not show when separated from it. Let us dare to compare even Socrates to Cato: the one was more the philosopher, the other more the citizen. Athens was already lost, and Socrates no longer had any fatherland other than the entire world; Cato always carried his own

4. Rousseau's word is *l'amour propre.*—ED.

within his heart; he lived only for it and could not survive it. The virtue of Socrates is that of the wisest of men: but between Caesar and Pompey, Cato seems a god among mortals. The one instructs some individuals, contends against the Sophists, and dies for truth: the other defends the state, liberty, the laws, against conquerors of the world, and finally quits the earth when he no longer sees in it a fatherland to serve. A worthy student of Socrates would be the most virtuous of his contemporaries; a worthy emulator of Cato would be the greatest of them. The virtue of the first would constitute his happiness, the second would seek his in that of all. We would be instructed by one and led by the other, and that alone should decide the preference: for one has never made a people of sages, but it is not impossible to render a people happy.

[31] Do we wish peoples to be virtuous? let us begin then by making them love the fatherland: but how could they love it, if it is nothing more for them than for foreigners, and only accords them what it cannot refuse to anyone? It would be much worse if they did not even enjoy civil security, and if their goods, their life, or their liberty were placed at the discretion of powerful men, without it being possible or permitted for them to dare to invoke the laws. Then, subjected to the obligations of the civil state, without even enjoying the rights of the state of nature and without being able to employ their own strength to defend themselves, they consequently would be in the worst condition in which free men can find themselves, and the word *fatherland* could have for them only an odious or a ridiculous meaning. It should not be thought that the arm can be hurt or cut off without the pain being conveyed to the head; and it is no more credible that the general will allow a member of the state, whoever he may be, to wound or destroy another than it is to believe that the fingers of a man in full use of his reason would put out his own eyes. Personal security is so closely bound up with the public confederation that were it

not for what one should allow to human weakness, this convention would be dissolved by right, if a single citizen in the state perished who could have been saved, if a single person was wrongfully held in prison, and if one lost a single lawsuit with evident injustice: for the fundamental conventions being broken, one can no longer see what right or interest could maintain the people in the social union, unless it is retained by force alone, which itself dissolves the civil state.

[32]* Indeed, is it not the commitment of the body of the nation to provide for the conservation of the least of its members with as much care as for all the rest? and is the safety of a citizen no less the common cause than is the safety of the whole state? If we are told that it is good that a single individual perish for all, I will admire this pronouncement in the mouth of a worthy and virtuous patriot who voluntarily consecrates himself out of duty to die for the safety of his country: but if one understands this to mean that the government be permitted to sacrifice an innocent man for the safety of the multitude, I hold this maxim to be one of the most execrable that tyranny ever invented, the most spurious that could be advanced, the most dangerous one can allow, and the most directly opposed to the fundamental laws of society. Far from any individual being obligated to perish for all, all have engaged their goods and their lives for the defense of each of them, to the end that individual weakness always be protected by the public force, and each member by the whole state. After having by supposition cut off one individual after another from the people, press the partisans of this maxim to better explain what they understand by *the body of the state,* and you will see that they will reduce it in the end to a small number of men who are not the people but the officers of the people, who, having obligated themselves by a personal oath to perish for its safety, pretend to prove in this way that it is for them that the people should perish.

[33] Does one wish to find examples of the protection the

state owes its members and the respect it owes to their persons? it is only among the most illustrious and courageous nations of the earth that it is necessary to look, and only among free peoples is the worth of a man known. It is known in what perplexity the whole republic of Sparta found itself when it was a question of punishing a guilty citizen. In Macedonia, the life of a man was such an important affair that despite all the grandeur of Alexander, this powerful monarch would not have dared to kill a Macedonian criminal in cold blood, unless the accused had first appeared to defend himself before his fellow citizens and had been condemned by them. But the Romans distinguished themselves above all peoples of the earth by the regard of the government for the individual and by its scrupulous attention to respecting the inviolable rights of all members of the state. There was nothing so sacred as the life of simple citizens; nothing less than the assembly of the whole people was necessary to condemn one of them: neither the senate itself nor the consuls, in all their majesty, had this right; among the most powerful people of the world the crime and punishment of one citizen was a public desolation; and it seemed so harsh to shed blood for any crime that by the law of *Porcia* the death penalty was commuted to that of exile for all who would be willing to survive the loss of such a sweet fatherland. Everyone in Rome and in the armies breathed this love of fellow citizens for one another, and this respect for the name Roman, which raised the courage and animated the virtue of whoever had the honor to bear it. The hat of a citizen delivered from slavery, the civic crown of one who had saved the life of another, were regarded with the most pleasure in celebrations of triumphs; and it has been remarked that of the crowns by which great actions in war were honored, it was only the civic crown and those of the victors that were made of herbs and leaves; all the others were only of gold. It is thus that Rome was virtuous and became the mistress of the world. Ambitious chiefs! A herdsman governs his dogs and his flocks and is only the least of men. If it is a good thing to command, it is when those who obey us can do us honor; respect then your fellow citizens, and you will render yourselves worthy of respect; respect liberty and your power will increase every day; never pass the limits of your rights, and soon they will be without limits.

[34]* Let the fatherland then show itself to be the common mother of the citizens, let the advantages they enjoy in their country endear it to them, let the government leave them enough part in the public administration so that they feel they are at home, and let the laws be in their eyes only the guarantors of the common liberty. These rights, beautiful as they are, belong to all men; but without appearing to attack them directly, the bad will of chiefs easily reduces their effect to nothing. The law which is abused serves the powerful at the same time as an offensive weapon and as a shield against the weak, and the pretext of the public good is always the most dangerous scourge of the people. What is most necessary, and perhaps the most difficult in government, is a rigorous integrity to render justice to all, and especially to protect the poor against the tyranny of the rich. The greatest evil already has been done, when one has poor people to defend and the rich to hold in. It is only on those of moderate means that the full force of the laws is exerted; they are equally impotent against the treasures of the rich and the misery of the poor; the first eludes them, the second escapes them; the one breaks the net, the other passes through.

[35] It is then one of the most important concerns of government to prevent the extreme inequality of fortunes, not by taking treasures away from their possessors, but by removing from everyone the means of accumulating them; not by building almshouses for the poor, but by shielding citizens from becoming poor. Men unequally distributed on the territory, and crowded together in one place while other

places are being depopulated; favoring the arts of pleasure and those that are purely mechanical at the expense of useful and laborious trades; the sacrifice of agriculture to commerce; the revenue officer made necessary by the poor administration of the state's money; finally, venality pushed to such excess that respect is measured with coins, and the virtues themselves are sold at the cost of silver: such are the most obvious causes of opulence and misery, of the substitution of private for public interest, of the mutual hatred of the citizens, of their indifference to the common cause, of the corruption of the people and the weakening of all springs of government. Such are consequently the ills that are difficult to remedy when they make themselves felt, but that a wise administration should prevent in order to maintain good customs along with respect for the laws, love of the fatherland, and the vigor of the general will.

[36]* But all these precautions will be insufficient, if one does not take the matter much further. I conclude this part of the public *economy* where I should have begun it. The fatherland is not able to live without liberty, nor liberty without virtue, nor virtue without citizens: you will have all this if you create citizens; without them you will have only wicked slaves, beginning with the chiefs of the state. But to form citizens is not the affair of a day, and to have them as men one has to instruct them as children. I will be told that whoever has men to govern should not seek beyond their nature a perfection of which they are not susceptible; that he should not wish to destroy the passions in them, and that fulfilling such a project would be no more desirable than possible. I would agree all the more readily with that, for a man who had no passions would certainly be a bad citizen; but it must also be agreed that if one cannot teach men to love nothing, it is not impossible for them to learn to love one object more than another, and what is truly beautiful rather than what is deformed. If, for example, they are trained early enough never to regard their individual per-

son except by its relations to the body of the State, and not to perceive their own existence, so to speak, except as a part of its existence, they will finally be able to come to identify themselves in some way with this greater whole, to feel themselves members of the fatherland, to love it with that exquisite sentiment that every isolated man has only for himself, to elevate their souls perpetually to this great object, and to thus transform into a sublime virtue this dangerous disposition from which all our vices are born. Not only does Philosophy demonstrate the possibility of these new directions, but History furnishes a thousand brilliant examples of it: if they are so rare among us, it is because no one cares whether there are citizens, and one considers still less trying to form them early in life. It is too late to change our natural inclinations when they are set in their course and habit has joined them to pride;[5] it is too late to draw us out of ourselves, when once the *human self* concentrated in our hearts has there acquired this contemptible activity that absorbs all virtue and constitutes the life of petty souls. How could the love of the fatherland germinate in the midst of so many other passions that stifle it? and what remains for fellow citizens of a heart already divided among avarice, a mistress, and vanity?

[37]* It is from the first moment of life that one has to learn to deserve to live; and as one participates, on being born, in the rights of citizens, the instant of our birth should be the beginning of the exercise of our duties. If there are laws for maturity, there should be laws for infancy, which teach obedience to others; and as one does not allow each man's reason to be the unique arbiter of his duties, one should even less abandon to the insights and prejudices of fathers the education of their children, as it matters even more to the state than to the fathers; for according to the course of nature, the death of the father often deprives him

5. Rousseau's word is *l'amour propre.*—ED.

of the last fruits of this education, but the fatherland sooner or later feels its effects; the state abides and the family dissolves. Should the public authority take the place of the fathers, it acquires their rights in fulfilling their duties; the fathers then have less cause for complaint, as in this respect they have only changed names, and they will have in common, under the name of citizens, the same authority over their children that they separately exercised under the name of *fathers,* and they will be no less obeyed when speaking in the name of the law than they were when speaking in the name of nature. Public education under rules prescribed by the government, and under magistrates established by the sovereign, is therefore one of the fundamental maxims of popular or legitimate government. If children are raised in common in the bosom of equality, if they are imbued with the laws of the state and the maxims of the general will, if they are taught to respect them above all things, if they are surrounded by examples and by objects which constantly speak to them of the tender mother who nourishes them, of the love she has for them, of the inestimable benefits they receive from her and of what they owe in return, it cannot be doubted that they will learn to cherish each other as brothers, always to want what society wants, to substitute actions of men and citizens for the vain and sterile babble of sophists, and to become one day the defenders and the fathers of the fatherland of which they will have been the children for so long.

[38] I will not speak of the magistrates destined to preside over this education, which is certainly the most important business of the state. One knows that if such marks of public confidence were lightly accorded, if this sublime function were not, for those who had worthily fulfilled all the others, the reward of their labors, the honorable and sweet repose of their old age, and the summit of all honors, the entire enterprise would be useless and the education without success; for wherever the lesson is not sustained by authority,

and precept by example, instruction remains without fruit, and virtue itself loses its credit in the mouth of those who do not practice it. But let illustrious warriors bent under the weight of their laurels preach courage; let honest magistrates grown white in dignity on their tribunals teach justice; they will each thus develop virtuous successors and transmit from age to age, unto succeeding generations, the experience and the talents of chiefs, the courage and virtue of citizens, and the emulation common to all to live and to die for the fatherland.

[39] I know of only three people who in former times practiced public education: namely, the Cretans, the Lacedaemonians [Spartans], and the ancient Persians; among all three it was a great success, and did wonders among the last two. When the world found itself divided into nations too large to be well governed, this way was no longer practicable; and other reasons which the reader can readily see have still prevented it from being tried among any modern people. It is very remarkable that the Romans were able to do without it; but Rome was for five hundred years a continual miracle, which the world should not hope to see again. The virtue of the Romans, engendered by the horror of tyranny and the crimes of tyrants, and by the innate love of the fatherland, made all their homes into as many schools for citizens; and the unlimited power of fathers over their children placed such severity in the private realm that the father in his domestic tribunal was feared more than the magistrates as the censor of moral conduct and the avenger of the laws.

[40] It is thus that a government attentive and well-intentioned, ceaselessly vigilant to maintain or recall among the people the love of the fatherland and good moral customs, prevents from afar evils which sooner or later result from the indifference of the citizens for the fate of the republic, and contains within narrow limits that personal interest which so isolates individuals that the state is weakened by

their power and is unable to expect anything from their good will. Wherever the people loves its country, respects the laws, and lives simply, little remains to be done in order to render it happy; and in public administration, where fortune plays less of a role than it does in the fate of private individuals, wisdom is so close to happiness that the two objects are fused in each other.

III

[41]* It is not enough to have citizens and to protect them; it is also necessary to think of their subsistence; and to provide for public needs is an evident consequence of the general will, and the third essential duty of government. This duty is not, one ought to realize, to replenish the granaries of private individuals and exempt them from work, but to maintain abundance so within their reach that to acquire it, work should always be necessary and never useless. It extends to all the operations regarding the care of the public treasury and the expenses of the public administration. Thus, having spoken of the general *economy* in relation to the government of persons, it remains for us to consider it in relation to the administration of goods.

[42]* This part offers no fewer difficulties to resolve, or contradictions to remove, than the preceding one. It is certain that the right of property ownership[6] is the most sacred of all the rights of citizens, and more important in certain respects than liberty itself; either because it lies closer to the conservation of life; or because goods are more easily usurped and more difficult to defend than the person, and one ought to respect more what can be carried off more

6. Rousseau's phrase is *le droit de propriété;* insofar as the focus of this last word, from which the English "proprietor(ship)" derives, seems to be less on goods as such, *les biens,* than on the person who controls their use, the word "ownership" has generally been used for it in this essay. —ED.

easily; or finally because ownership is the true foundation of civil society and the true guarantee of the commitments of the citizens: for if goods were not answerable for persons, nothing would be so easy as to elude one's duties and to mock the laws. On the other side, it is no less certain that the maintenance of the state and the government requires costs and outlays; and as whoever accepts the end cannot refuse the means, it follows that the members of the society ought to contribute from their goods to its upkeep. Further, it is difficult to secure the property of individuals on the one hand without attacking it on the other, and it is not possible that all the rules regarding inheritance, testaments, contracts, not constrain citizens in certain ways concerning the disposition of their own goods, and consequently their right of ownership.

[43] Beyond what I have already said about the agreement which reigns between the authority of the law and the liberty of the citizen, there is an important remark to make concerning the disposition of goods that removes many of the difficulties. It is, as Puffendorf has shown, that by its nature, the right of ownership does not extend beyond the life of the proprietor, and that at the instant a man has died, his goods no longer belong to him. Thus, to prescribe to him the conditions under which he may dispose of them is at bottom less to alter his right in appearance than to extend it in fact.

[44] In general, although the institution of laws which govern the power of individuals in the disposition of their goods belongs only to the sovereign, the spirit of these laws, which the government should follow in their application, is that from father to son and from kin to kin, the family goods leaving and being alienated as little as possible. There is a sensible reason for this, in favor of the children, to whom the right of ownership would be truly useless if the father left them nothing, and who, having contributed often by their labor to the acquisition of the father's goods, are in

their own name associated with his right. But another reason, more distant and not less important, is that nothing is more fatal to habitual conduct and to the republic than continual changes of station and fortune among the citizens; such changes are the proof and source of a thousand disorders which upset and confound everything, and by which those who are raised for one thing find themselves destined for another—neither those who rise nor those who fall are able to take up the maxims or enlightenment suitable for their new status, and much less to fulfill its duties. I pass to the question of public finances.

[45] If the people governed itself, with no intermediary between the administration of the state and the citizens, they would only have to assess themselves as occasion arose in proportion to public needs and the capacities of private individuals; and as each would never lose sight of either the collection or the use of these funds, neither fraud nor abuse could slip into their management: the state would never be encumbered by debt nor the people crushed by taxes, or at least the certainty of proper use would console it for the burden of taxes. But things could not go this way; however limited the state may be, civil society is always too numerous to be governed by all its members. Necessarily, public funds pass through the hands of the chiefs, who, beyond the interest of the state, all have their private interest, which is not the last one heard. The people on its side, perceiving the greed of the chiefs with their extravagant expenditures rather than for public needs, murmurs at seeing itself deprived of necessities in order to contribute to the superfluities of others; and when once these maneuvers have embittered it to a certain point, the most honest administration could no longer be able to restore confidence. Then, if the contributions are voluntary, they produce nothing; if they are forced, they are illegitimate; and it is within this cruel alternative of either allowing the state to perish or attacking

the sacred right of ownership, which is its support, that the difficulty of a just and wise *economy* consists.

[46]* The first thing that the founder of a republic ought to do after the establishment of laws is to find sufficient capital for the maintenance of magistrates and other officers, and for all the public expenses. This capital is called *aerarium* or *public treasury* if it is in money; the *public domain* if it is in land, and this latter is preferable to the other, for reasons easy to see. Anyone who has reflected sufficiently on this matter will hardly be able to disagree with Bodin, who regarded the public domain as the most honest and the surest of all means for providing for the needs of the state; it is to be noted that the first concern of Romulus in the division of land was to set aside a third for this use. I acknowledge that it is not impossible for the product of this domain to be badly administered, and thus reduced to nothing; but it is not of the essence of the domain to be badly administered.

[47] Prior to all employment, this capital should be assigned or accepted by the assembly of the people or the estates of the country, which should then determine its use. After this solemnity, which renders these sums inalienable, they change their nature, so to say, and their revenues become so sacred that it is not only the most infamous of all thefts but a crime of high treason to divert the least of them to the detriment of their destined purpose. It is a great dishonor for Rome that the integrity of the Quaestor Cato was even questioned, and that an emperor, rewarding a singer's talents with a few coins, had to add that this money came from his family's goods and not from those of the state. But if few are found like Galba, where will we find Catos? and when once vice no longer dishonors, who among the chiefs will be scrupulous enough to abstain from touching public revenues left to their discretion, and not soon deceive themselves by pretending to confound their vain and scan-

dalous dissipations with the glory of the state, and the means of extending their authority with those of augmenting their power? It is above all in this delicate part of administration that virtue is the only effective instrument, and that the integrity of the magistrate is the only curb capable of containing his avarice. The books and all the accounts of managers serve less to disclose their infidelities than to cover them up; and prudence is never as prompt to imagine new precautions as knavery is to elude them. Leave the registers and papers aside then, and return finances to loyal hands; this is the only means by which they will be loyally managed.

[48] Once the public capital has been established, the chiefs of the state are by right its administrators; for this administration forms part of the government, always essential, though not always equally so: its influence increases in measure as those of the other parts diminish; and one can say that a government has reached its last degree of corruption when it has no other sinew than money; yet as every government tends unceasingly to slacken, this single reason shows why no state is able to subsist unless its revenues unceasingly increase.

[49] The first awareness of this increase is also the first sign of internal disorder in the state: the wise administrator, in seeking to find the money to provide for the present need, does not neglect to seek the remote cause of this new need; just as a sailor seeing water flood his vessel does not forget while starting the pumps to seek out and to close the leak.

[50] From this rule flows the most important maxim of the administration of finances, which is to work with much more care to prevent needs than to increase revenues; whatever diligence one can use, the help that comes only after the harm, and more slowly, always leaves the state worse off: while one tries to remedy a pitfall, another is already making itself felt, and the resources that are used themselves produce new pitfalls; so that in the end the nation is encum-

bered with debt, the people is ground down, the government loses all its vigor and does only little with much money. I believe that from this great well-established maxim flowed the wonders of ancient governments, which did more with their parsimony than ours do with their treasuries; and it is perhaps from this that the common conception of the word *economy* derives, which means the wise management of what one has more than ways of acquiring what one does not have.

[51]* Independent of the public domain, which yields to the state in proportion to the probity of those who regulate it, if the full force of general administration is sufficiently understood, especially when confined to legitimate means, one would be astounded at the resources the chiefs have to anticipate all the public needs without touching the goods of individuals. As they are the masters of all the state's commerce, nothing is so easy for them as to direct it in a manner which provides for everything, often without their seeming to be involved. The distribution of commodities, of money, and of merchandise in just proportions, according to the time and the place, is the true secret of finance, and the source of its riches, provided that those who administer it know how to have enough foresight, and to take an occasional apparent and current loss in order to have really immense profits in the long run. When one sees a government paying duties instead of receiving them, for the export of grain in abundant years and for its importation in years of scarcity, one needs to have such facts before one's eyes in order to believe them true, and if they had occurred long ago one would place them in the rank of fiction. Suppose that to prevent scarcity in bad years one proposed to establish public granaries: in how many countries would the maintenance of such a useful establishment not serve as a pretext for new taxes? In Geneva these granaries, established and maintained by a wise administration, serve as the public resource in bad years and the principal revenue of the

state at all times; *Alit et ditat* ["It nourishes and enriches"] is the proper and just inscription one reads on the facade of the building. In order to explain here the economic system of a good government, I have often turned my eyes to that of this republic: happy to thus find in my fatherland the example of the wisdom and happiness which I would wish to see reign in every country.

[52] If one examines how the needs of a state grow, one will find it often happens somewhat as among individuals, less by true necessity than by an increase of useless desires, and often one only increases one's expenses merely to have a pretext for increasing receipts; so the state would sometimes gain from not being rich, as this apparent wealth is fundamentally more onerous than would be poverty itself. One can hope, it is true, to hold the people in a tighter dependency, by giving them with one hand what is taken from them with the other, and this was the policy Joseph used with the Egyptians; but this vain sophism is all the more deadly to the state, as the money is not returned to the same hands from which it came, and with such maxims one only enriches the idle from the spoils of useful men.

[53]* The relish for conquest is one of the most obvious and dangerous causes of this increase. This relish, often engendered by a kind of ambition different from the one it seems to announce, is not always what it seems to be, and its true motive is not so much the apparent desire to aggrandize the nation as the hidden desire to increase the authority of the chiefs at home, with the help of increased troops and by means of the diversion that war's objectives create in the minds of the citizens.

[54] What is at least very certain is that nothing is so ground down and miserable as conquering peoples, and that their successes themselves only augment their miseries: even if history did not teach us, reason would suffice to demonstrate to us that the greater the state is, the more its expenses become proportionately heavy and onerous; for it

is necessary that all provinces furnish their quotas to the expense of the general administration; and beyond this each province must incur its contingent and cover the same expense as if it were independent. Add to this that all fortunes are made in one place and spent in another; this breaks the equilibrium between what is produced and what is consumed, and impoverishes much of the countryside to enrich a single town.

[55] Another source of the increase of public needs is tied to the preceding one. A time may come when the citizens, no longer regarding themselves as interested in the common cause, cease to be defenders of the fatherland, and when the magistrates prefer to command mercenaries rather than free men, if only to use the former at any appropriate time and place in order to better subjugate the latter. Such was the state of Rome at the end of the republic and under the emperors; for all the victories of the first Romans, and even those of Alexander, had been won by brave citizens who knew how to give their blood for the fatherland when needed, but who never sold it. Marius was the first who, in the war against Jugurtha, dishonored the legions by introducing freedmen, vagabonds, and other mercenaries into them. Having become the enemies of the people, whom they had been charged to render happy, the tyrants established settled troops, in appearance to restrain foreigners, in fact to oppress the inhabitants. In order to form these troops, it became necessary to take farmers from the land; their absence diminished the quality of food and maintaining them introduced taxes, which increased prices. This first disorder made the people murmur; it became necessary to multiply the troops to repress them, consequently increasing the misery; and the more the despair increased, the more one was constrained to increase it again to prevent its effects. On the other hand, these mercenaries, who could be valued according to the price for which they sold themselves, proud of their debasement, despising the laws that protected them

and their brothers whose bread they ate, believed themselves to be more honored to be satellites of Caesar than the defenders of Rome; committed to a blind obedience, they had as their task to hold a dagger over their fellow citizens, ready to slaughter all at the first signal. It would not be difficult to show that this was one of the principal causes of the ruin of the Roman Empire.

[56] The invention of artillery and fortifications has forced the sovereigns of Europe in our day to reestablish the use of regular troops to defend their strongholds; but with more legitimate motives, it is to be feared that the effect will be equally disastrous. It will be no less necessary to depopulate the countryside to form armies and garrisons; in order to maintain them it will be no less necessary to bear down on the people; and these dangerous establishments have been growing for some time, with such rapidity in all our areas that one can only anticipate the approaching depopulation of Europe and sooner or later the ruin of the peoples that inhabit it.

[57] Be that as it may, one ought to see that such institutions necessarily upset the true economic system, which takes the principal revenue of the state from the public domain, and leaves only the vexatious resource of subsidies and taxes, of which it remains for me to speak.

[58]* It is necessary to remember here that the foundation of the social pact is ownership, and its first condition, that each should be sustained in the peaceful enjoyment of those things which belong to him. It is true that by the same treaty each obligates himself, at least tacitly, to be assessed for the public needs; but this engagement not being prejudicial to the fundamental law, and presuming the evidence of need recognized by the contributors, one sees that to be legitimate, this assessment should be voluntary: not from an individual will, as if it were necessary to have the consent of each citizen, who only gives what he pleases, for this would be directly counter to the spirit of the confederation;

but from a general will, a majority of votes, and by a proportional rate, which leaves nothing arbitrary to the imposition of taxes.

[59]* This truth, that taxes can be legitimately established only by the consent of the people or their representatives, has been generally recognized by all philosophers and jurists who have acquired some reputation in matters of political right, without excepting Bodin himself. If some few have set down maxims contrary in appearance, however easy it is to see the particular motives which moved them to do so, they have placed so many conditions and restrictions on them that fundamentally it comes out to be exactly the same: for whether the people can refuse or the sovereign should not demand is wholly indifferent as to what is right; and if it is only a question of force, it is useless to examine whether it is legitimate or not.

[60]* The contributions taken from the people are of two kinds: the one, property taxes, which are collected on things; the other, personal taxes, which are paid by the head. One gives to them the name of *taxes* or *subsidies:* when the people fixes the sum it gives, it is called a *subsidy;* when it concedes the full product of a levy, it is a *tax.* One finds in the book *The Spirit of the Laws* that assessment by head is more accordant with servitude, and that the property levy is more congenial to liberty. That would be incontestable if the shares by head were equal; for nothing would be more disproportionate than such a levy, and it is above all in exactly observed proportions that the spirit of liberty consists. But the head-levy is exactly proportioned to the means of private individuals, as the levy in France known as the *capitation* could be, and in that manner is simultaneously both a real-property and personal tax; it is the most equitable and consequently the most suitable to free men. These proportions seem at first very easy to observe, being relative to the status each man has in the world, because the indications are always public; but avarice, credit, and fraud know

how to elude even such evidence, and it is rare that one takes account in these calculations of all the elements which should be entered into them. First of all, one should consider the relation of quantities according to which, all things being equal, he who has ten times as many goods as another ought to pay ten times more than he. Second, the relation of usage, that is to say the distinction between what is necessary and what is superfluous, should be considered. He who has only bare necessities should have to pay nothing at all; the levy on one who has abundance can, if need be, go to the full extent of everything that exceeds what is necessary for him. To this he will say that with regard to his rank, what would be superfluous for an inferior is necessary for him; but this is a lie: for a Noble has two legs just like a cowherd, and like him he has only one belly. More important, this pretended necessity is so unnecessary to his rank that if he knew how to renounce it for a laudable reason, he would be the more respected for it. The people would prostrate itself before a minister who went to the council on foot because he had sold his carriages to supply a pressing need of the state. Finally, the law prescribes magnificence to no one, and seemliness is never a reason against right.

[61] A third relation that is never counted, and which should always be counted first, is that of the usefulness each derives from the social confederation, which strongly protects the immense possessions of the rich individual and hardly permits a poor man to enjoy the cottage he has constructed with his own hands. All the advantages of society, are they not for the powerful and the rich? all the lucrative positions, are they not filled by them alone? all the favors, all the exemptions, are they not reserved for them? and the public authority, is it not in their favor? Should an important man steal from his creditors or commit other knavery, is he not always assured of impunity? The thrashings he distributes, the violent acts he commits, even the murders and assassinations of which he renders himself

guilty, are these affairs not squelched in silence, and after six months no longer in question? Should this same man be robbed, the police go into action immediately, and woe to the innocents whom he suspects. Does he travel in a dangerous place? see the escorts with him; the axle of his carriage breaks? everyone rushes to his aid; is it noisy at his door? he says a word, and all is quiet; the crowd inconveniences him? he makes a sign, and all falls into place; a wagon driver is in his way? his people are ready to assault him; and fifty honest pedestrians going about their business would be crushed rather than let one idle scoundrel be delayed in his carriage. All these niceties do not cost him a penny; they are the right[7] of the rich man, and not the price of wealth. How different is the picture of the poor man! The more humanity owes him, the more society refuses him; all doors are closed to him, even when he has a right to have them open; and if he sometimes obtains justice, it is with more difficulty than another would obtain a pardon; if work duty[8] is to be done, a militia to be raised, it is to him that one gives the preference; he always bears burdens from which his rich neighbor can afford to get himself exempted; at the least accident that happens to him, everyone avoids him; if his poor wagon turns over, far from being helped by anyone, he is to be considered happy if he avoids affronts from the flippant servants of a young duke: in a word, all the gratuitous assistance he needs is denied to him precisely because he has nothing with which to pay for it; but I hold him to be a lost man if he has the misfortune to have an honest soul, an amiable daughter, and a powerful neighbor.

[62] Another point no less important to make is that the losses of the poor are much less reparable than those of the

7. The French word is *droit;* in this context it can be construed as "privilege."—ED.

8. The French term is *des corvées,* i.e., unremunerated labor required by statute, usually among peasants.—ED.

rich, and the difficulty of acquisition is always increased with need. One does nothing with nothing; this is true in business as in Physics: money is the seed of money, and the first coin is sometimes harder to gain than the second million. There is still more: all the poor man pays is forever lost to him, and remains in or returns to the hands of the rich; and as it is to those who take part in government, or are close to it, that sooner or later the proceeds of taxes soon pass, they have, even in paying their share, an obvious interest to increase them.

[63] Let us summarize in a few words the social pact of the two stations: *You have need of me, as I am rich and you are poor; let us then reach an agreement between us: I will permit you to have the honor of serving me, on condition that you give me the little you have, for the trouble I will take to command you.*

[64] If one combines all these points with care, one will find that in order to portion out taxes in an equitable and truly proportional manner, the imposition should not be made solely by reason of the goods of the contributors but by a ratio composed of the difference of their conditions and the superfluity of their goods. This very important and very difficult operation is made every day by multitudes of honest clerks who know arithmetic, but which the Platos and the Montesquieus would not have dared to do without trembling and imploring heaven for enlightenment and integrity.

[65] Another disadvantage of personal taxation is that it makes itself felt too drastically and is levied with too much harshness; this does not prevent it from being subject to many bad debts, because it is much easier to conceal one's role and one's head from prosecution than one's possessions.

[66] Of all the other assessments, the quitrent on the land or the real estate tax has always been accepted as the most advantageous in the country where one has more regard for the quantity of the product and the surety of recovery [of

investment] than for the least infirmity of the people. Some have even dared to say that it is necessary to burden the peasant in order to rouse him from his idleness, and that he would do nothing if he had nothing to pay. But experience among all the peoples of the world disproves this ridiculous maxim: it is in Holland and England, where the farmer pays very little, and especially in China, where he pays nothing, that the land is best cultivated. On the contrary, wherever the laborer is assessed in proportion to the product of his field, he lets it lie fallow, or only reaps exactly what he needs to live. For anyone who loses the fruit of his effort, it is a gain to do nothing; and to place a fine on work is a singularly strange way of banishing idleness.

[67] The tax levy on land or grain, especially when excessive, results in two consequences so terrible that they would eventually depopulate and ruin every country where it is established.

[68] The first comes from the lack of circulation of currency, for commerce and industry attract all money from the countryside to the capitals: as the tax destroys the proportion which can still be found between the needs of the farmer and the price of his grain, money always comes and never returns; the richer the town, the more miserable the country. The proceeds of real estate taxes pass from the hands of the prince or the financier into those of artisans and merchants; and the farmer, who never receives more than the smallest part, is finally exhausted by always paying the same amount and always receiving less. How would a man be able to live if he had only veins and no arteries, or if the arteries carried blood only four inches from his heart? Chardin says that in Persia the rights of the king to commodities were also paid in commodities; this practice, which Herodotus tells us prevailed long ago in that country until the time of Darius, is able to prevent the harm of which I will speak. But unless the Persian stewards, directors, clerks, and warehousemen were a different species of people than every-

where else, I have a difficulty in believing that the least part of all these products reached the king, that the grain did not spoil in all the granaries, and that fire did not consume most of the warehouses.

[69] The second inconvenience comes from an apparent advantage, which allows mischief to aggravate before it is perceived. Grain is a commodity whose price is not raised by taxes in the country that produces it, and despite its absolute necessity, the quantity diminishes without an increase of price; this means that many people die of hunger although the grain continues to be inexpensive, and the laborer alone bears the cost of the tax he is unable to pass along in the price of the sale. We must recognize that one should not reason in the same way concerning the real estate tax as about duties on all merchandise on which the price is raised by taxes so that they are paid less by merchants than by the buyers. For these duties,[9] however high they may be, are still voluntary, and are paid by the merchant only in proportion to the merchandise he buys; and as he buys only in relation to his market, he applies the law to the individual case. But the laborer who, whether he sells or not, is constrained to pay in fixed terms for the land he cultivates, is he not the master to wait on receiving for this produce the price that he asks? and when he does not sell it to feed himself, he still would be forced to sell it to pay the quitrent tax, hence it is often the enormity of the tax that keeps the commodity at a cheap price.

[70] Notice again that the resources of commerce and industry, far from rendering the land tax more bearable through an abundance of money, only renders it more onerous. I will not insist on a perfectly obvious fact, that while the greater or lesser quantity of money in a state may give it more or less credit abroad, it in no way changes the real

9. The French word is *droits,* which in this context means "import duties."—ED.

fortune of the citizens, and has no bearing on their material comfort. I will make two important remarks: one is that unless the state has excess produce, and a large supply of money comes from foreign sales, only the towns engaged in this business profit from this abundance, and only the peasant becomes relatively poorer; the other point: as the price of all things rises with the multiplication of money, taxes also have to rise in proportion, and the laborer consequently finds himself more heavily burdened without having more resources.

[71] One should see that the land tax is truly a tax on its products. However, everyone agrees that nothing is so dangerous as a tax on grain paid by the buyer: is it not clear that this evil is a hundred times worse when this tax is paid by the farmer himself? Is this not to attack the subsistence of the state at its source? Does it not also work directly to depopulate the country and consequently to ruin it in the long run? for there is no worse scarcity for a country than that of men.

[72] In deciding about the tax base, only a true statesman is capable of raising his sights beyond the object of finances [income], to transform these onerous charges into useful adjustments of policy, and so make the people wonder whether such practices do not have the nation's good as their end rather than the mere production of tax income.

[73]* Duties on the importation of foreign merchandise which the inhabitants are eager to have but for which the country has no need, on the exportation of those products of the land[10] of which the country has no excess but which foreigners cannot do without, on the productions of useless and too lucrative arts, on the entry into the towns of things that are purely embellishments, and in general on all luxurious things, will fulfill this double purpose. It is by such taxes, which allay poverty and charge wealth, that it is necessary

10. The French word is *cru,* i.e., production of vineyards, especially. —ED.

to prevent the continual augmentation of the inequality of fortunes, the subjection to the rich of a multitude of workers and useless servants, the multiplication of idle people in the towns, and the desertion of the countryside.

[74] It is important to place between the price of things and the duties charged on them such a proportion that the greediness of individuals shall not reach fraud by the immensity of profits. It is also necessary to prevent the ease of contraband, by preferring merchandise less easy to hide. Finally, it is appropriate that the tax be paid by the one who uses the taxed article, rather than by him who sells it, who, because of the quantity of duties charged him, would have more temptations and means to defraud. This is the regular practice in China, the country where taxes are the heaviest and best paid in the world: the merchant pays nothing; the purchaser alone pays the duty, with it resulting in neither murmurs nor sedition; because the commodities necessary to life, such as rice and grain, being absolutely exempt, the people are not pressed, and the tax falls only on those comfortably situated. Moreover, all these precautions should be dictated not so much by fear of contraband as by the attention that the government ought to have to secure private individuals against the seduction of illegitimate profits, which, after having made them bad citizens, would soon make them into dishonest people.

[75] Let heavy levies be established on livery for servants, on carriages, mirrors, chandeliers, and suites of furniture, on cloth and gilding, on the courtyards and gardens of mansions, on theater performances of all kinds, on the idle professions, such as comedians, singers, actors, and, in a word, on the multitude of objects of luxury, diversion, and idleness, which strike all eyes and which can scarcely be hidden, as their sole use is to be displayed and would be without utility if not seen. One need not fear that the proceeds from such taxes would be arbitrary, for they would be on things that are not of absolute necessity; it is to not know

men well to believe that once being seduced by luxury they will never be able to renounce it; they would rather renounce necessities a hundred times and would much prefer to die from hunger than from shame. Increasing this expense will only be a new reason to sustain it, when the vanity of showing oneself as opulent will create its benefit from the price of the thing and the expense of the tax. As long as there will be rich men, they will want to distinguish themselves from the poor, and the state could not form a source of revenue less onerous or more assured than one based on this distinction.

[76] For the same reason, industry would suffer nothing from an economic order that would enrich the Public Finances, revive Agriculture, by relieving the laborer, and imperceptibly bring all fortunes to that moderate condition which is the true strength of a state. It could be, I admit, that these taxes would contribute to making some fashions disappear more rapidly; but this would never occur without substituting for them others by which the worker would profit, without anything being lost to the public treasury. In a word, let us suppose that the spirit of the government should constantly assess all taxes on the superfluous possessions of the rich; one of two things would transpire: either the rich will renounce their superfluous expenses in order to make only useful expenditures, which would return to the profit of the state; then the assessment of taxes would produce the effect of the best sumptuary laws; the outlays of the state would necessarily diminish with those of private individuals; and the public treasury will be more efficient in its receipts, as it would have much less to disburse: or if the rich diminish none of their thriftlessness, the public treasury will have in the proceeds from taxes the resources it seeks in order to be able to meet the real needs of the state. In the first case, the public treasury is enriched by the reduction in expenditures it has to make; in the second, it is still enriched, by the useless expenditures of private individuals.

[77] Let us add to all this an important distinction in matters of political right, to which governments, jealous to do everything themselves, ought to give close attention. I have said that personal tax levies and taxes on absolutely necessary things, by attacking directly the right of ownership, and consequently the true foundation of political society, are always subject to dangerous consequences, if they are not established with the express consent of the people or their representatives. It is not the same with duties on things that one can forbid oneself to use; for then, as the private individual is not being absolutely constrained to pay, his contribution can be viewed as voluntary; so that the individual consent of each of the contributors supplants the general consent and even presupposes it in some way: for why would the people be opposed to a tax that only falls upon whoever wants to pay it? It seems certain to me that anything not forbidden by the laws or contrary to moral customs, and which the government is able to prohibit, can be permitted, providing a duty is paid. If, for example, the government is able to forbid the use of carriages, it can with more reason impose a levy on carriages, a wise and useful way of disapproving their use without ending it. Then one can regard the levy as a form of reparation whose proceeds compensate for the abuse it punishes.

[78]* Someone could object perhaps that those whom Bodin calls *impostors,* that is to say those who impose or invent taxes, being in the class of the rich, will be mindful to spare others at their own expense, not to burden themselves to relieve the poor. But such ideas must be rejected. If in each nation those to whom the sovereign commits the governance of the peoples were by this very condition their enemies, there would be no point in seeking what they [the chiefs] ought to do to render them [the peoples] happy.

Notes to
*Of the Social Contract**

PREFATORY NOTE

[1] At the outset it is made clear that this is not a complete study; hence many questions (such as those of foreign policy, as noted in the final paragraph—444) remain open. The **more extensive work** is either *(a)* an early draft generally referred to as the "Geneva Manuscript," and entitled *Of the Social Contract, or Essay on the Form of the Republic,* or *(b)* a larger work, conceived under the title "Political Institutions," of which he speaks in Book IV of *The Confessions.*

The subtitle of this published version is *Principles of Political Right,* manifesting the turn of focus, from concern with specific constitutional arrangements (discussed in Roman terms in Book Four), to concern for the principles which underlie a legitimate state.

BOOK ONE

[2] The purpose of the essay is not to construct a utopian portrait of an "ideal" state; rather it is concerned to establish *practical* political principles by which to guide evaluation of a legitimate social order. Claiming to take human nature as we find it, Rousseau hopes to develop **some legitimate and certain rule,** or basic constitutional principles, which can reconcile actual human **interests** and moral standards of what is **right,** thus guiding reform.

[5–6] These two paragraphs are the key to the work. They are

---

*All unidentified references are to paragraph numbers in this essay; when preceded by "PE," to paragraph numbers in *Discourse On Political Economy;* when preceded by "E," to page numbers in *Emile;* references to other works cited are to chapter numbers, paragraphs (par.), or pages (p.).

not an argument. Rousseau sets forth here the prime theses which the entire essay is designed to work out.

[5] **Man is born free:** I.e., every human being is born with the capacity or potentiality to develop into a free person. Proceeding from the premise that man's essential attribute is the capacity for freedom, he adopts Aristotle's principle cited as the motto of the Second Discourse: "We should consider what is natural not in things which are depraved but in those which are rightly ordered according to nature" (*Politics,* I, 2).

The original French phrase, *"L'homme est né libre,"* could be translated into English with either the present or the past tense. The present-tense translation is definitional and accords with Rousseau's intent: to develop principles by which to guide political judgments; it also accords with his language elsewhere. See 9, 24, 326 for confirmation of this present-tense translation.[1]

and everywhere he is in chains: We each live under the restraints and compulsions of custom and of law (see 54).

One believes himself the master . . . they: Each of us, even the despot, is dependent on those "lower" in the social structure.[2]

I do not know: Is Rousseau here calling into question, perhaps, his earlier speculations on the origins of society?

What can render it legitimate?: Rousseau proposes to develop this mutual dependency we share as both enabling and limiting freedom in society. The concept of a legitimate society then centers about the nature of the freedom which it is held responsible for protecting and enhancing while justifying the subjection to political authority that social living entails. Working out the precise meaning(s) of freedom is then an important task for this essay (cf., e.g., 39, 56, 57, 151; PE 24, PE 36).

[6] **But the social order . . . all others:** All specific rights are social rights operative only within society; Rousseau seems to suggest here and in what follows (especially 20–33) that the only "inherent" or "inalienable" right is the right to belong to a legitimate society.

this right . . . conventions: He here announces a radical depar-

---

[1]Cf. Locke's phrase, "Man being born . . . with a title to perfect freedom" (*Second Treatise of Civil Government,* par. 87).

[2]This theme was developed by Hegel into the very influential chapter entitled "Lordship and Bondage" in his *Phenomenology of Spirit* (1807).

ture from the then-dominant view that specific rights are "natural," "inherent," or "inalienable." If all specific rights are societal, then their source can only be the social agreements or **conventions** characterizing the particular society; this word is used precisely in this sense throughout this essay (see, e.g., 20, 37–49).

[7–9] These three paragraphs are something of a summary of the opening pages of Aristotle's *Politics.* For the contrast between family and society, see PE 1–7.

[13–14] The specific text to which Rousseau seems to be referring is from *Politics,* I, 5; it reads: "But is there anyone thus intended by nature to be a slave, and for whom such a condition is expedient and right, or rather is not all slavery a violation of nature? There is no difficulty in answering this question, on grounds both of reason and of fact. For that some should rule and others be ruled is a thing not only necessary, but expedient; from the hour of their birth, some are marked out for subjection, others for rule."

[16] **into right:** Into morally justified principle; what is morally right does not depend upon external compulsion, but is an act in "good conscience" of self-commitment.

into duty: When one acts from duty or moral obligation, one acts because one determines or "wills" that one ought to do so (see 55–57).

[19] **might does not make right:** Then the *power* of the state is not the fundamental ground of our allegiance to it or of our obligation to obey its laws. Legitimate political power, Rousseau is to argue, ultimately rests, not on force, but on a moral ground that legitimatizes it, and moral obligation extends only to legitimately grounded power. To the development of these theses—the ground, justification, and limitation of political obligation—one central concern of his essay, he now turns.

[20–33] This entire chapter is a revolutionary condemnation of *all* slavery—but the implications apply far beyond the issue of chattel slavery to the most basic questions of social organization and morality.

[20] **conventions:** If our specific rights and duties do not come from "nature," and cannot be justified by the mere power of rulers, conquests, or enslavement, then they can arise only from social agreements, expressed explicitly in fundamental or constitutional laws or implicitly in accepted customs which bind a society together

and define the relationships of its citizens to it and to each other (see 6).

[22] **civil peace:** Therefore, domestic peace is not itself *the* supreme social value, and thereby is not the justification of a social order. See 86, 135, 196, 248n.

[25] **To renounce . . . duties:** Note the principle developed here that specific rights and duties are always reciprocal; they entail each other just as freedom and morality do. Freedom and the capacity for morality then go hand in hand and cannot be separated from each other (see 5, 57). The social problem then: how correlate the social needs of a society and the need for political obligations of citizens while enhancing and protecting their individual freedoms?

[26–33] Rousseau now turns from the contention that people can rightfully surrender their freedom to the historic justification of slavery as the outcome of the right of war and conquest.[3]

[29] This analysis of the nature of war—which may be read as a veiled criticism of Hobbes (see 11, 13)—presumes that a state is akin to a public or corporate person (see 46–53; PE 10–12); on the analogy of a person it can be considered as having a will, a course of action, and responsibility for its actions. It is in this sense that we distinguish between the pronouncements of a public official when he speaks as the voice of the state and when he speaks merely as a private individual. For this reason also, a war is between one state (as a collective person) and another, and is not rightfully to be taken as a personal affair between their individual subjects or citizens.

[32–33] **the state of war subsists between them:** Does it not then follow that the slave's only moral obligation is to revolt when he can? Can one even rightfully acquiesce in one's enslavement? In summary, then, on whatever ground slavery may be defended, it is unjustifiable and a society embodying the oppression of slavery is thereby illegitimate (cf. 294–98; PE 63) just because it denies to the enslaved individual the right to membership in a free or legitimate society from which all his specific rights and duties ensue.

[3]Cf. Locke's justification of slavery, *Second Treatise,* 23 and XVI, which Rousseau criticizes in 30–32.

[34–36] Picking up from 6, after the digression of 7–33, he now turns to introducing his central argument, which begins with 37. None of the previous attempts to explain the origin of society really justifies a rational social order in which freedom is esteemed. In summary of what has been discussed so far, he draws a basic distinction between a mere "aggregation" and the cohesiveness of a true social order.

[35] This gift itself is a civil act: Rousseau is distinguishing the establishment of a society itself from the social decision—by deliberate choice or tacit acceptance—of how it shall govern itself; in order for a people to determine some kind of constitutional order, there first must be some sense of social cohesiveness and mutual commitment, as exemplified, at the end, in a civil profession of faith as "sentiments of sociality" (see 440).

[37–54] These two chapters logically presuppose the thesis spelled out in 55–57. The three chapters comprising 37–57 together constitute the heart of this essay. They really are one unit and the separate discussions developed in each depend upon the others. They enunciate the basic statement of principle which the balance of the essay is largely devoted to spelling out.

The "social contract" is not discussed as a historic fact; rather it seems to be his metaphoric term for the complex of principles embodied or presupposed in a functioning legitimate social order. Perhaps the best analogy by which to understand what he is doing is to envisage a society as a club and its citizens as members: a club *is* its membership; by virtue of membership each individual gives up something, obeys its rules, and receives certain benefits or privileges in return. The "social contract" is thus the bond of membership which defines, at any instant, the accepted modes of behavior, the rights, privileges, customs, and obligations of membership, and the procedures by which disputes about them are to be resolved. To search out the *functioning* "social contract" is to search out the operating principles presupposed in a club or society (and only partly embodied in its written constitution).

[37–38] Regardless of whether we regard a "state of nature" or pre-civil society as historically true or fictionally useful, as idyllic or chaotic, it is no longer practicably possible. Civil society is, then, necessary so that each individual can contribute in an essentially cooperative endeavor to the common good—in which each person as a citizen is to find his own good.

[40] **the fundamental problem:** Rousseau explicitly states his self-imposed task. This crucial paragraph leads to 45, 55–57; it begins the resolution of the problem enunciated in 5–6.

[41] Whether explicitly stated or tacitly understood, the social contract is the requisite of membership in a given social order; should its operational principles lapse, the social freedoms (see, e.g., 321) which we have by virtue of our membership—**the conventional liberty**—can no longer be claimed and we revert to the anarchy of primitive individual liberty (see 53–56).

[42] *Every* individual, by participation in a society, gives up a supposed primitive liberty to do as he pleases; by placing himself under the basic laws of his society, he forsakes the chaos of anarchy in return for the privileges and advantages of membership. This **alienation** being equally true for each member, no one has an interest in making this social participation more burdensome than it has to be (cf. 45, 56).

[43] Rousseau is here criticizing the notion that certain specific inalienable rights which, according to some theorists, are beyond the province of social concern are somehow "innate" and are "carried" into civil society and thereby held to be absolutely inviolable.

[44] **each, in giving himself to all:** Each gives himself to the society-as-a-whole of which he is a member; he is not thereby entering into a state of slavish subservience. In contrast to others, it would seem, Rousseau does not see the social contract as an agreement by one individual with others, but rather as the entire body of citizens entering into an agreement with themselves as one unified body.[4]

[45] **the general will:** This fundamental concept, which runs through the entire essay as its guiding thread, is discussed in detail in the Introduction.

[46] **a moral and collective body . . . public person:** A collective, fictive person of imaginative reason, with a personality, will, and responsibility of its own; it is *not* the particular rulers (or, later,

---

[4]This may be regarded as a secularization of the "Covenant Theology" of the Calvinist tradition in which Rousseau was reared; derived from interpretation of Exodus 23:32–24:8, it appears again in the recurrent references to "instituting" or forming a people (e.g., SC 96, 108).

"prince") but the entire body of citizens acting as one cohesive group.

City: As the footnote makes clear, Rousseau is taking as his model the city-state of his native Geneva (although he often also looks back to the city-states of classical Greece or to the Roman Republic). In thinking through the expansion of Rousseau's focus on the city-state to the modern nation, one might well retain the notion of cohesiveness of the city-state, which he subsequently emphasizes, and the mutuality of commitment his concept of citizenship entails.

Sovereign: This word means the supreme political authority in a society. Rousseau argues that it must be popular sovereignty, i.e., the people as one collective body constitutes the supreme authority and the only legitimate source of political power. The implications he sees from this principle begin to be spelled out in 47ff., 51, 52, 66–74. The ground of this notion of popular sovereignty is the concept of the social contract as formulated in the preceding chapter (see especially 40, 42, 44, 45). The several technical terms, as defined in this paragraph, carry through the balance of the essay.

[47] reciprocal engagement: The principle of popular sovereignty is something of a "two-way street" (cf. 40, 45). As in 50, society is built on mutuality, a sense of social cohesion, and a common bond.[5]

[53] a being of reason: I.e., literally speaking, the state is not an individual person, but we think of it as if it were and as if it had the attributes of distinguishable personality; hence it is not an empirical fact but a concept which comes out of imaginative reason. See Introduction, 29 comment, 46, and the roughly equivalent terms used: "collective being," 67; "moral person," 79; and "public person," 46, 80.

[54] he shall be forced to be free: By participating in a society we not only acquire certain advantages, specific opportunities, or freedoms (which would be impossible in a solitary existence); we also incur obligations to the society. The reciprocity of rights and duties is epitomized in the dual relationship of citizenship reiterated in this chapter; it is expressed by the dual principles of the

[5]This is what the French Revolution was to call "fraternity" (although the more strictly Rousseauan slogan was "Liberty, Equality, and the Republic" —see 104).

social contract and the *general will:* the first gives us societal membership (out of which all specific rights or freedoms emerge); the second is the means whereby we, as a society, impose obligations on ourselves as members. As spelled out in 55, the entire nature of our free humanity depends upon this essential right, freedom, or opportunity to belong to a society (see 32–33 comment). Our personal freedom is not the primitive anarchy of a desert island or a pre-civil condition where each determines how to protect himself. Societal membership means that the protection of each is a community responsibility—as the society protects itself from an illiterate citizenry and children from possible parental negligence by forcing school attendance (see PE 37). Our freedoms are *in* the society and not against it, and are defined by laws applying to all. By refusing to honor social obligations expressed by the general will, we thereby bring into question the basic freedom of societal membership and the specific positive freedoms the society opens up for its citizens. By compelling the fulfillment of social obligations, the society thereby maintains itself and the responsible freedoms it makes possible for its citizens. (But note 40, 56, 57, which look to keeping the citizen from all personal dependence—and 79–88, where Rousseau seeks a principle limiting community authority over individuals.)

[55–57] The chapter title, "Of the Civil State," is what this entire essay is about. Its three paragraphs are the logical foundation of the entire work and provide the justification for 37–54. Rousseau appears to echo Aristotle by arguing that man, as a rational moral being, is essentially a social being; that the freedoms with which we are concerned are always social or civic freedoms— within a social order; that the fundamental social contract is not between a civil society and its government, but the foundation of the civil society itself. Consequently, he argues, we do not enter into society with arbitrarily designated inherent rights; rather we derive our specific rights or freedoms, together with our obligations, from the society itself.

[55] **This passage from the state of nature:** I.e., only in a civil society, not in primitive anarchy, do moral concepts arise.

It is only when . . . inclinations: Rousseau's definition of morality is based on the distinction between "impulsion" or mere appetite and moral obligation or duty. Morality is an exercise of reason, not inclination or desire; as Kant restated it later, "reason is the governor of the will." The benefits of societal membership are then spelled out, not in terms of the "negative liberty" of the absence of restraints, but in what has come to be associated with the concept of "positive freedom," the opportunities for specific individual development which society opens up for its members.[6]

transformed him . . . and a man: Reminiscent of Plato and Aristotle, man is defined as *essentially* a social being existing only in civil society. (We can, then, perhaps see this as a fundamental advance from his earlier romantic adoration of the primitive.)

[56] We should note the exchange which Rousseau is suggesting: we give up (1) natural liberty, (2) possessions, and (3) slavery to desire, characterized by a primitive condition; in return, we receive by means of civil society (1) civic liberty, (2) recognition of ownership in property, and (3) moral freedom. Adding what is said in 65, the exchange also includes that of (4) physical inequality for equality of legal right.

[57] **obedience to the law one prescribes to oneself is freedom:** If we are not to be slaves of our whims and fleeting desires, we must be able to decide rationally which of them to honor and which to disregard. This means evaluating desires in terms of what we believe *ought* to be done in conflict situations, by means of moral laws or standards we prescribe to ourselves. Only by pursuing self-prescribed moral laws do we develop coherent lives and become our own masters.

add to the preceding: If freedom is defined by law in a society, freedom is not an abstraction; it is concretized, limited, and defined in terms of specific authorizations; the maintenance of the citizen's moral freedom becomes a prime function of his society. The concomitant of this concept of morality is the social contract; their relation is reciprocal. But then we are obligated to obey the laws of our society if it meets the requirements of legitimacy—just because we are members of that society and as such accept its laws, by means of the general will, as being self-imposed obligation.[7]

[6]See, e.g., T. H. Green's essay "On the Different Senses of Freedom as Applied to Will and to the Moral Progress of Man," for an extended discussion.

[7]These three paragraphs comprise a historic preface to the reconstruction of moral philosophy proposed by Immanuel Kant, who sought to develop

[58] **is master of all their property:** I.e., society rightfully determines laws regulating the amount, title, and acceptable uses of property ownership; see Introduction.

[60] **by labor and cultivation:** Like Locke, Rousseau sees one historic source of legitimate private property as coming from labor, but unlike Locke, he sees it as coming not from a "law of nature," but from community approbation and operative within the broader context of the common needs of the community, which, in the final analysis, provides the protection for the property of the individual citizen (see 64).[8]

[63] **changes usurpation into true right:** One's rights to property ownership, as any other rights or claims, are not inherent; they are merely the specific claims which the society recognizes and protects. All specific rights, being social rights, are derived from the community, which accords its citizens specific rights and opportunities, or recognizes claims for protection just because they are deemed to serve the common good as defined by the general will. Both private and common property may be deemed socially beneficial. Recognizing no inherent rights to property claims, Rousseau argues that recognition of a specific general right is always a community decision which, by the rule of civic equality, is legitimate if applied to all. See 64, 81.

[65] **moral and legitimate equality:** Freedom presupposes legal equality of specific rights, not necessarily that of status. As Rousseau's footnote makes clear, he urges a utilitarian justification of private property and reiteration of Aristotle's advocacy of a middle-class society in which **all have something, and none of them has too much** (n.6.). See 135, 137; PE 42; Introduction.

Rousseau's founding of morality in civil society into a democratic ethic of individual moral conscience. Kant's explicit reverence for Rousseau is well known: he compared him to Newton for having provided a new foundation for morality as Newton had done for physical science, and spoke of him as "the restorer of the rights of humanity" and of his "unaffected insight into the nature and moral worth of man."

[8]Compare Locke, *Second Treatise,* V: "He that is nourished by the acorns he picks up under an oak, or the apples he gathered from the trees in the wood, has certainly appropriated them to himself. . . . That labour put a distinction between them and common; that added something to them more than Nature . . . and so they became his private right. . . . The same law of nature that does by this means give us property, does also bound that property too."

BOOK TWO

[66] **the common good:** Rousseau is equating the concept of the "common good" with the intent of the general will; as the last sentence indicates, the proper function of government is limited to this **common interest** (cf. 79–88).[1]

[67] The source of legitimate authority is the consensus or general will of the society which establishes and maintains it. Society's power, defined by its social contract, is exercised by the governing body in its name and on its behalf. See 151, 164–66.

[70] **either the will is general or it is not:** The general will is one will, not several. In contrast, "the will of all" is an aggregate total. The footnote might be construed as calling for universal citizen suffrage—but note the restricted nature of citizenship in Geneva which Rousseau frequently claimed as his model (see 338 comment).

[71–73] Rousseau is arguing against the traditional tendency to attribute sovereignty to the government, be it absolute monarchy or republic, rather than to the people as one whole (see 46–54, 104).

[72] **law:** A law is a general or universal provision which needs to be applied to particular instances, not the particular instance itself. This distinction will lead to the forthcoming distinction between sovereignty and government. Isn't Rousseau taking "law" here in its most general sense as the fundamental constitutional authorization of power rather than its particular uses in specific enactments of statutes under it? See 100.

[74] Aside from reference to events which were recent in his time, he is laying the ground for the forthcoming attack on hereditary monarchy in Book Three.

[75] **the general will is always upright:** Just because it is directed to the common good and the interest of the society as one whole; therefore, it defines the parameters within which right or justice in a given society is defined and to be had. See 66, 83, 105; PE 12; Introduction.

---

[1]Compare the opening sentence of Aristotle's *Politics:* "Every state is a community of some kind, and every community is established with a view for some good; for mankind always act in order to obtain that which they think good."

N.B. Countless commentators, working with inaccurate translations, have taken Rousseau to task for saying that "the general will is always right." But the French *droite* (= "upright") refers to what is right in the sense of lawful, legitimate, or just, *not* what is "correct," which the English word *right* would suggest in this context (see Introduction).

One wishes always his own good: Following Aristotle in drawing parallels between society and the individual, compare the opening of Aristotle's *Politics,* quoted in the footnote to the comment on 66, with the opening sentence of Aristotle's *Nicomachean Ethics.* [2]

but does not always discern it: Every legitimate society is instituted to seek out the common good which is the aim of the general will; but men do not always know how to achieve it. One central problem for an organized society is to find ways to unite the fundamental aspirations of its people with the expertise necessary to formulate public policy appropriate to furthering its attainment. See 105, 401–8 and comment; cf. PE 16.

[76] This paragraph begins the (perhaps reluctant) recognition of the fact that any actual society is composed of subgroups with interests that are not always the same. Note Rousseau's footnote, which recognizes the positive value of diverse interests; these create the tensions and potential creativity of political life. Cf. PE 15.[3]

[77] **If, when . . . the Citizens:** Is it justifiable to read this as a call not only for an informed citizenry but also for a secret ballot? Perhaps, but see—, where Rousseau seems to applaud public voice-voting (cf. 285). For the complete definition of the word "citizen," see 273.

But when factions . . . partial associations: This passage has often been interpreted as an attack on all interest groups or political parties; it can, however, be understood as an attack on the division in his time of the French *parlements* into three "estates." One

---

[2]It reads: "Every art and every inquiry, and similarly every action and pursuit, is thought to aim at some good; and for this reason the good has rightly been declared to be that at which all things aim."

[3]One might well refer to Machiavelli's observation, which the third sentence in the footnote paraphrases, that "all the laws favorable to liberty" result from the opposition of a society's inner groupings to each other. Cf. *Discourses on the First Ten Books of Livy,* I, iv.

should read this paragraph in conjunction with 78, which first opposes factional divisions but then argues that if they exist, their number should be multiplied; cf. also PE 15, which explicitly recognizes their presence.[4] (N.B. Rousseau seems to have imperceptibly shifted the discussion here from the society as such to the political state.)

Finally, when . . . : If the general will is the will of the society as one whole and *not* merely an aggregate of internal divisions, then the danger of factional control seems to be the danger he is seeking to head off, i.e., the illegitimacy of any one group, even if a majority, speaking for the whole, and perhaps also the danger of majority tyranny (see Introduction).

[78] But if there are partial associations: May this be taken, in accord with Madison, as Rousseau's rationale for the contemporary concept of political pluralism as the ground of political freedom?

[79] If the State or the City is only a moral person: In passing, we should note his equivalence of "State" and "City." But, more crucial, if the corporate individuality (see 46) of the state is cast in moral terms, then it is subject to moral predicates; as with an individual person, its moral nature is enabling only by being self-limiting in what it-wills to do by laws it imposes on itself (see 55–57).

N.B. In this chapter, Rousseau is not discussing individual rights, morality, or customs, but the essential limitation of all *political* power of the society as a whole in the functioning of the procedural stipulations and criteria of the social contract and ensuing legislation.

[80] But beyond the public person: As the footnote recognizes, this is a conceptually difficult paragraph. He is trying to emphasize the crucial distinction between our rights and obligations in our public capacity as citizens, and our private capacities

[4]Compare this with Madison's attack on the danger of factions in the Tenth *Federalist Paper:* "Among the numerous advantages promised by a well-constructed Union, none deserves to be more accurately developed than its tendency to break and control the violence of faction. . . . Liberty is to faction what air is to fire, an aliment without which it instantly expires. . . . The inference to which we are brought is, that the *causes* of faction cannot be removed, and that relief is only to be sought in the means of controlling its *effects.*"

and lives as individual people: there is more to individual life than its political aspect, even though the former may be requisite to the latter; mernbership in politically organized society is a necessary means to individual living and is *not* an end in itself—just as one's whole being is not confined to any club to which one may belong, no matter how important that club may be. Perhaps here more than elsewhere, the import of *Emile* to the whole of Rousseau's mature thought is crucial: the criterion of a good education is to develop a free being who is socially responsible while pursuing his private life, just as the reciprocal obligation of the society is to make itself an instrument for the development of its individual members.

the natural right: I.e., that potential of human nature to free development which a free society opens up for its citizens by maximizing their individual opportunities within the context of the common good of the society as a whole (see 5, 81, 439).

[81] The community does not legitimately abrogate all aspects of individual life but only those that, in its judgment, are deemed necessary to the common good—within which any individual private good is to be found. As per 82, 86, 87, 439, social utility defines the limits of the justifiable exercise of political power.

[82] **under the law of reason . . . law of nature:** Is Rousseau invoking the Leibnizian Principle of Sufficient Reason? For any burden or restraint the society places on its citizens, there must be a reason sufficient to justify the particular societal demand; is it not this rationalist principle—which sees the sufficient reason of human actions in terms of purposes or goals—which define the limits of social utility, of what is **useless to the community?**

[83] **that the general will, to be truly such:** Any legislative act must meet four conditions, only spelled out in 86: (1) it must conform to the generally conceived common good; (2) it must apply equally to all citizens laws that are general or universal; (3) it must restrict itself by rational principle to what is useful to the general welfare; and (4) it must be stable.

[84] **Thus, just as a particular will:** Basic, or constitutional, law needs particular legislative embodiments and administrative application in particular cases; such specifications are a matter for government, the agency for the society, and not for the general will itself.

the people . . . no longer acted as Sovereign: The distinction between popular sovereignty and governmental (magisterial) functions is now being developed.

This will appear contrary: Rousseau is drawing a crucial distinction—between the source of sovereignty, which is the whole people, and the governmental agency it ordains to administer its affairs. (Perhaps he is also anticipating the controversy centered on the interpretation of Book Three as to whether direct government is to be desired; cf. PE 23, 45.)

[86] **such an equality:** The civic equality that is seen as foundational to a free society is one of legal and political equality under laws that apply to all and thus assure each citizen that by participating in the general will and the social contract all will **enjoy the same rights** (cf. 83, 135, 196).

no object other than the general welfare: It is because this is the aim of the contract that, as in 75, "the general will is always upright" (cf. PE 16, 18).

So long as the subjects: Paraphrasing 42–44, Rousseau here claims that the *limitations* of the contract, discussed in the preceding paragraphs of this chapter, furnish a solution to the problem enunciated in 40.

[88] This paragraph spells out principles enunciated in 37–46.

[89–95] If one intent of the social contract is the protection of the lives of the members of the community, and if civic freedom entails responsibility, then a system of laws or statutes is necessary so that those who endanger the members of the community can be held accountable. In the light of principles enunciated in 54 and 56, this chapter provides the justification of criminal law together with some salient observations on how criminal activity reflects on the social health.

[90] **when the Prince:** This term does *not* necessarily refer to any individual (and so there is no implication of monarchical government). It *does* refer to the administrative direction (executive branch) of the government, whether it is in the hands of one man or several. (Therefore, there is no contradiction, in this very traditional usage, in referring to the "prince of the republic.")

[91–92] Citizenship means equal membership in a political society; it is this political equality that requires all legislative statutes to be universal in scope within the society. Thus one criterion of legitimate legislation is its universality. When a citizen makes himself an exception (by disobeying), he is, in effect, attacking the basic universality and political equality which is the basis of his citizenship and of the specific freedoms he enjoys because of it.

[94–95] Although Rousseau believes the society has the right to inflict capital punishment, he sees its use as something of a societal confession of failure to integrate the criminal into the society as a useful citizen; for each citizen has the potential of contributing something to the common good and *no* citizen can be rightly punished merely as an example to others (see PE 32). Widespread criminality is a visible sign that the general health of the society is amiss.

[97–98] These paragraphs underline the decisive turning away from doctrines of specificable unexceptionable rights. Whatever their merits, such doctrines provide no specific indications of concrete rights and duties *in* a given social complex—therefore, by neither explaining the dynamics of current affairs nor providing specific guidelines for practicable reforms, they are of no practical value. The only rights we do in fact enjoy are those actually prescribed by the society itself, where **all the rights are fixed by the law.** Hence he is arguing that his principles are more concrete and practical, insofar as the actual guide to specific rights and duties is that of utility for the common good (as qualified in 86).

N.B. Three different levels of justice are differentiated: (1) divine or religious; (2) moral, as delivered by reason; (3) political, which comes from moral reason as well as from the social agreements and law. Obviously, it is the third that is his concern in this essay (see 145), although, as noted especially in 55–57, it is closely related to the second. The function of political justice, based on the general will, which is always "upright," "righteous," or "just," is **to unite rights with duties and to bring justice.**

[102] One prime mark of the universality of law is that it truly be so, that **the Prince,** i.e., the public officials, are bound by the same law which binds all others.

[104] **Every legitimate Government is republican:** Here is the governmental criterion for legitimacy, the theme of the entire essay. The term "republic" comes from the Romans' *res publica* and literally means "public affair" or "public property." In contrast to contemporary use (which contrasts it to a monarchy), Rousseau uses it, in accord with traditional practice, in much the same way

as we use the word "democratic" today—to claim that the government, regardless of its form, expresses *de facto* popular sovereignty (for example, Britain, Sweden, and Japan are today regarded as democratic even if headed by royalty; in contrast, the United States and France both have a "republican" *form* of government). Rousseau's use of "republican" is reminiscent of Aristotle's distinction between "true" forms of government, which are governed for the good of the whole, and "perverted" forms, which are governed for the sake of the rulers—in each case regardless of whether the "ruler" is one, a few, or many. Rousseau's point here is that a legitimate government is that of a free society dedicated to the public interest demanded by the general will, regardless of whether the populace prefers its law to ordain as the head of its governmental agency a hereditary or an elected chief of state.[5]

[105] **system of legislation:** The problem that emerges is: what constitutional conditions are requisite for the effective expression of the general will? Such a system has to include the constitutional framework of the state (140–41) and provide for specific kinds of statutory regulations (142–44). It also needs to provide an organ to announce the general will and take account of the fact that the people always wants the good, but by itself does not always discern it (cf. 75, 401 ff.).

[106–7] As a consequence of 105, Rousseau revives the Greek concept of an author of a constitution, separate from and prior to the officials of government. This Greek Lawgiver[6] is called a Legislator. Insofar as civil society is not "natural" but rather a deliberate act of social convention, it needs a deliberately formulated system defining in advance the modes of legislation and administration to be followed, i.e., a constitution. The Legislator is the author of the constitution, not a member of the legislature set up under its provisions, which enacts the specific (statutory) laws that give it life. The Legislator need not be an individual person; it can be a collective body fulfilling this purpose, as, for example, the American Constitutional Convention, which served as a collective Legislator and as such, to use Rousseau's term, "instituted" the American Republic.

[5]In *Towards Perpetual Peace,* Kant specifies this principle of Rousseau's as "The First Definitive Article" which needs to be universalized if world peace is to become possible.

[6]Cf. Aristotle, *Politics,* II, 12.

The work of such a Legislator must, of course, be ratified by the people (cf. 112) before it can take force as an authentic expression of the general will.

[108] This paragraph, if not to be grossly misunderstood, must be read in the context of 254, 257–58, and in the light of the essential thrust of the contemporaneous *Emile,* i.e., concern for the education of the responsible individual citizen: Rousseau presumes in his *Emile* that "One must not confound what is natural in the savage state with what is natural in the civil state" (E 406). A well-founded state is concerned with the transformation of savages into citizens who, in place of living more or less self-contained lives, now find themselves in need of others for their own individual fulfillment, each needing to recognize, for his own development, his dependence on the social order of which he forms a part; thus he needs to manifest public-spiritedness, as part of his individuality, just because it is now only to be found in a **partial and moral existence.**

The paragraphs that follow point up the need for educating the citizenry in the qualities of good citizenship (cf. 114–15; PE 29, 36–38); they recognize the paradox of morality—that the norms to which we should adhere must somehow be acknowledged before we can conform ourselves to their requirements; meeting this paradox has been one of the political functions of religion (cf. 409ff., "Profession of Faith of the Savoyard Vicar," E 266–13).

[118–22] This chapter, together with the two that follow, are an elaboration of the thesis that there is a crucial relationship between a constitutional arrangement, on one hand, and the customs and historical conditions of the people it is to govern, on the other.

[123–28] The essential reason for preferring small states to large ones is that they are more cohesive and citizens are more likely to know each other (see 133), that the larger the state is, the less likely it is to reflect the sentiments of the general will and the more burdened it is likely to be with excessive administrative problems (see 244—but note the reservation in 205). Although there is recognition of external affairs (126, 444), the prime criterion appears to be that of internal social health and responsiveness to the general will.

[129–34] Continuing discussion of considerations that should enter into the formation of a new state or constitutional arrangement, he turns to the proportion of land to population; although in terms of an essentially agricultural economy, the discussion still seems somewhat relevant. The various factors considered in these chapters show the deep impact of Montesquieu on Rousseau's thinking (see 138). Noteworthy is his emphasis (130) on the consideration of possibilities by focusing not on **the actual condition of the population but on what it should naturally become;** and reiteration of the import of social unity as requisite for effective constitution.

[134] Rousseau, on invitation, wrote a proposed constitution for Corsica, shortly before its annexation by France.

[135–36] **the greatest good of all:** The aim of the general will is specified in the two prime values of any democratic society, freedom and equality under laws as institutionalized in a republican government (104). Like Aristotle, Rousseau insists on the necessary correlation of freedom and equality;[7] but it is crucial to note that equality is taken to mean political equality of rights and is explicitly valued as a means to freedom, not as an alternative to it or as an intrinsic end in itself. As he said in *Emile,* freedom is "the first of all goods" (E 84). Referring back to 5, 20–57 for the discussion of freedom or liberty, he now turns to the nature of the kind of equality requisite to it, reiterating the Aristotelian thesis that for a society to be free it must be an essentially middle-class society (cf. 65 comment; PE 73, 76).

[137] Because of the differing interests of diverse individuals, any society tends to develop gross inequalities. Doing so can be a danger to its social health; consequently one test of good legislation is that it corrects such tendencies before they become disruptive. Recognizing the interrelationship of the political and the economic, Rousseau anticipates the need for the positive state, which, in a way reminiscent of some aspects of mercantilism, oversees the economic life of the community, but in order to protect the freedoms of its members (see Introduction).

[138] Each society is uniquely individual because, despite similarities with others, each has a life, history, and situation of its own. If its constitutional arrangement is to be effective, it must be tailored to its own unique circumstances and needs. But however

[7] See Aristotle, *Politics,* VI, 2.

different in application, its legitimacy rests on its incorporation of certain fundamental principles. The task of the political theorist is to determine those general philosophic principles of political right which characterize *any legitimate* constitution; but a political theorist goes beyond his own competence in proposing a specific constitution for *all* societies (213). The insistence on the import of principle, rather than of particular statutes and practices, marks the radical difference between Rousseau and the utopianism of those who seek an ideal system for all societies regardless of history, culture, or social condition.

[139] **natural relations:** Those within the civil society (see 108 comment). What Rousseau seems to be adding to this recurrent theme of legitimacy is the pragmatic note of efficacy: i.e., legislation which is not in accord with the general will cannot be effective.

[141–45] **political laws . . . fundamental laws:** I.e., constitutional law, not specific acts of statutory legislation. As confirmed in 145, this entire discussion of law is concerned with basic constitutional arrangements and the principles they manifest, enabling a free society to function by providing for specific statutes dealing with specific problems as they arise.

Besides, in every situation: The general will is absolutely sovereign—for what outside standard can evaluate the free will of the people except the people itself (see 75, Introduction)?

[144] The customs, moral standards, and general public outlook of the citizens are seen as part of the framework of the society, which ultimately depends upon the moral fiber of its citizens as its true foundation (see 439).[8]

[145] **political laws . . . are alone relevant to my subject:** If the reader judges that Rousseau's discussion of law has not extended beyond the nature of legitimate constitutionalism, he may feel impelled to reevaluate those commentaries which appear to overlook this sentence and treat many of the foregoing discussions in terms of statutory enactments.

[8]Cf. Machiavelli, *Discourses on the First Ten Books of Livy.* I, 12, 16–18.

BOOK THREE

[146] In Books One and Two, Rousseau developed foundational concepts built into his principle of popular sovereignty, or
legitimacy. In this third book, he turns to the ways in which a
legitimate society may be governed: from a theory of free society
to some ensuing questions of government and political science.
Throughout the discussions that follow, it is crucial to remember
that a government is not the sovereign (i.e., the source of its own
authority) but only the agency or servant of the legitimate Sovereign, the people as one whole (cf. 84, which distinguishes sovereignty from magistracy).

[147] **this chapter should be read with care:** In addition to
Rousseau's reasons, we need to do so from our contemporary
outlook—because his use of political terms is generally different
from ours. Although the distinction between "sovereignty" and
"government" is generally accepted in democratic societies, his
notion of "administration" often seems to cover what we would
regard as the legislative rather than merely the executive branch
of government; and the office of the magistracy, in at least some of his
uses, could possibly be read in our terms as including members of
a legislative assembly, as well as members of an executive or judicial branch of government. (Cf. 149, 152, 153, 166; PE 8, 45).

[149] **the legislative power:** It is arguable whether Rousseau
intends the people to participate directly in the formation of statutory laws. The preceding chapter, especially 145, clearly indicates
his prime concern to be with constitutional, not statutory, law. The
act of legislative sovereignty can be construed as meaning deliberate popular acceptance of a constitutional arrangement providing
for procedures for developing and applying specific statutes to
particular cases as they arise. However one may read the degree
of popular participation commended in this process, it is clear that
administrators are necessary to administer the government (and
perhaps the constitution as well). In Rousseau's terms, one may
then regard the passing of particular statutes as one function involved in administering the constitution, an interpretation obviously in conflict with our contemporary distinction between "administrative" and "legislative."

all of whose acts can only be laws: It would seem that, by the principle of the logical coherence of the ensuing discussion, this should be read as "constitutional law" and not "statutory laws." If one may legitimately read him as converging the two, then Rousseau may be charged with some confusion and the question may be raised as to whether he has indeed stayed with his task (see 145) of only discussing *political laws.* (cf. PE 23).

[151] **subjects and the Sovereign:** I.e., the same public body in two different functions (see 46).

charged with the execution of the laws: As the agency of society, a government's specific legitimate function is the **maintenance of liberty** by means of laws.

[152] Note the specific definitions of the political terms in this and the next paragraph. **Magistrates:** I.e., a function, not the persons performing it; the terms can be applied to a chief administrator, members of an executive committee, or the people themselves in a specific function (cf. 84). **Kings:** The etymological derivation of the Latin word for "king," *rex,* is from the Latin verb *regere,* "to govern." At the heart of Rousseau's doctrine of popular sovereignty is his insistence that the traditional identification of "king" and "sovereign" is to be set aside on the ground that only the people are sovereign and it is they who may choose to have their affairs administered for them by a monarch.

[154] Perhaps one point of this long discussion of ratios is to suggest the import of keeping all aspects of a given society in proportion, of maintaining the social harmony of the whole by balancing the internal relations within the social order. It is, perhaps, a way of reiterating the Aristotelian principle of the "golden mean" between contrary extremes.

[155] Note the principle that the particular mode of government needs to be related to the condition of the society at a given time (see 138).

[163] The government, although an agency of the society, needs to reflect the composition of that society and is itself a corporate or **moral person** (see 53). (This analogy of the individual and the state is reminiscent of one that underlies the whole of Plato's *Republic* (see PE 10; Introduction).

[166] **belong exclusively to the Prince:** Note the functional use of this term and the variety of governmental functions to which it refers.

this **subordinate whole . . . the general constitution:** Although government is subordinate to its society, its unity is analogous to the problem of social unity (cf. 40).

[169] **already distinguished the State from the Sovereign:** See 46, 47, 84.

[173] From the three types of will distinguished—(1) private or particular will of individual magistrates; (2) common or corporate will of the body of rulers; (3) general will of the people as one whole—the thesis will be developed that a general tendency of governmental action is to exceed the activity of the sovereign will and thereby its legitimate limits (cf. PE 15).

[175] May this observation be taken as implicating an argument for a check-and-balance system of government (cf. 224–29)?

[176–77] If we read this in contemporary terms, we might construe the contrast drawn as between two undesirable extremes: one-man dictatorship and literal self-government in the direct democracy of a town meeting or citizen assembly (cf. 190–97).

[180] Is the point of this paragraph really the consequence of the discussion of ratios in 155–65?

[182] This mode of classifying types of governments is in accord with an old tradition widely used until recently (cf. 212).[1]

[186–89] Note reiteration of the principle, despite this multitude of governmental forms, that the form of government must in each case be suited to the conditions of the society it governs (see 152)—but in any case, it would seem that whatever the appropriate form, to be legitimate the government must be "republican" (104), regardless of the specific form of its institutions (see 138).

[190–97] The term "democracy" is taken in its traditional meaning of direct self-government by the citizenry—as contrasted to contemporary usage, which regards it as more or less synonymous with free representative government (see 104; 176–77 comments).

[191] **Legislator:** Is this term used *here* in the sense of "the sovereign people," the author of the constitution (109), or the legislative aspect of governmental magistracy (84, 149)?

[201] What Rousseau means by an **Aristocracy** of the **elective** type may conceivably be taken to mean generally what we today

[1]See Aristotle's similar, yet somewhat divergent, classifications in *Politics*, II, IV.

call "representative government"—see 203–4, which spell out practical reasons for preferring an "elective aristocracy." If, however, this is read within the context of 280–91, it could be argued that he is restricting the representative aspect of government to its strictly administrative, not legislative, functions. But then how do we square it with 84, 104, 176–77, 196–97? However that may be, recognition of this semi-representative system has been overlooked by most commentators. If one regards his judgment of direct citizen participation as either impractical or undesirable, as per 192–97, 280–91, may we understand his concept of popular sovereignty as calling for some kind of representative government on the basis of this notion of "elective aristocracy"—wherein the function of those charged with governmental magistracy is the administration of the constitution (including the enactment of statutory legislation)—as suggested in comment on 149? (Cf. PE 23, 45, 59, 77, where representative government for statutory legislation is countenanced or presumed; and *Government of Poland,* where Rousseau recommends a strict recall system for representatives in the Diet.)

[204] **govern . . . for its profit and not for their own:** I.e., Aristotle's principle of "true" government (as against its "perverted" forms), that the function of government is to govern for the good of the whole society and not that of the rulers.

[207] **as Aristotle claims:** One should consider this charge and arguments on both sides.[2]

[208–23] The length of this attack on monarchy is a reminder that it was the prevalent type of government in Rousseau's time and that it had been defended by eminent people, including England's James II (see 74), who wrote a defense of the "divine right of kings," and by Thomas Hobbes (see 11, 12, 421). This essay was written in France under Louis XV; it is thus understandable why it could not be published in France; see Introduction. (Many of the points made, however, can perhaps be read in contemporary terms by substituting, for his term "absolute monarchy," today's "totalitarian dictatorship"; see 254–58.)

[212] **Machiavelli . . . republicans:** See the various references to him in the Index, esp. 116, 248n. Note the implication, despite the previous discussion of governmental types, that Machiavelli

2See Aristotle, *Politics,* VI; cf. Montesquieu, *The Spirit of the Laws,* III, 4.

was correct in maintaining that "all states and dominions . . . are either republics or monarchies,"[3] taking the terms "republic" and "monarchy" in their traditional sense of "popular sovereignty" and "absolute monarchy" (cf. 209–10, 235).

[224–29] The concept of "mixed government," originally developed by Plato *(Laws)*, received systematic exposition under the terms "polity" and "constitutional government" in Aristotle's *Politics* (esp. IV, 11–12, V, 7). Espoused by Machiavelli in the *Discourses*, the outstanding statement of this governmental theory in Rousseau's time was Montesquieu's *The Spirit of the Laws* (esp. XI, 6), which had a powerful influence on the writing of the American Constitution.[4]

[230] **this principle established by Montesquieu:**[5] Reading this in conjunction with 108, one might wonder whether Rousseau also had in mind a loose society whose members have not been educated in citizenship.

[231] **the public person:** I.e., the state as such.

[236] For reasons stated at the outset, Rousseau, in these paragraphs, is following Montesquieu's lead and considering climatic influences on the manners and customs of different peoples in the light of the anthropological knowledge of his time.

[244] This paragraph, apt to be overlooked, is crucial to explaining Rousseau's marked bias for small, compact states—but cf. 205. In trying to assess the contemporary relevance of this preference, one might bear in mind that Rousseau knew only the agrarian societies of his time (cf. E, V). One should then ask how his specified reasons for this preference might be applicable, if at all, to a modern technological mass society and the modern systems of communication it uses (cf. 245–48).

[245] **what is . . . the best Government:** This chapter seeks an objective standard by which to answer this question. Notably, the basis for rational evaluation suggested is neither a particular form of government nor any particular interest within the society it governs. The proposed test of a governmental system is essentially pragmatic—the happiness, well-being, or prosperity to which it leads its citizens; this is summed up in the last sentence of the

[3] *The Prince*, I.
[4] See *Federalist Papers*, 9, 10, 39, 40, 71.
[5] See *The Spirit of the Laws*, XVII, 3–7.

footnote to 248 as "**not so much [the] peace as [the] liberty**" of the citizens. N.B. Liberty or freedom, not internal peace, is reiterated as the prime value of a legitimate society.

[251] **That is its natural inclination:** Rousseau's view that no form of government is permanent, that its dynamic of development goes through a more or less predictable cycle, is one that can be traced back to both Plato and Aristotle.

Squittinio della libertà veneta [fn.]: Title of an anonymous book published in 1612, which argued for the imposition of divine monarchical right on the Venetian republic.

[254] If taken together with 257–58, can we understand Rousseau to be "anticipating" what we today mean by "totalitarianism"?

Government usurps sovereignty: It is then illegitimate and the situation reverts to that described in the statement of basic principle in 16–36.

[256] **Ochlocracy:** I.e., mob rule, a condition which the emphasis on the general will (as distinguished from the will of all) is designed to forestall. (See Aristotle's discussions of these processes of governmental degeneration in his examinations of different governmental types in the *Politics.*)

[259–63] The basic analogy between the body politic and the human body, used to advance the notion of the organic theory of the state, is borrowed from Plato (cf. 163 comment; PE 9–11; Introduction).

[265–68] **The limits of the possible . . . :** Provide the proper parameters for intelligent action in developing the basic human potentiality of moral freedom (see 5, 130, 268). Note the theme appearing in succeeding paragraphs—not a simpleminded optimism but retrogression as well as progression is seen as possible in developing this essential potentiality of man.

[266–67] Rousseau here introduces and explains the reason for the extended examination of the institutions of the Roman Republic which comprises a large part of Book IV: 342–400; cf. PE 23.

[271] Perhaps a modern equivalent to this would be to let the people speak as one whole through frequent elections and referendums—but note the fear of demagoguery (cf. 105).

[275] **Estates:** "Estate" was a term common to late medieval political organization—generally meaning the classes or social or-

ders of the society; most often in the period preceding the French Revolution it was used in the sense of the "three estates," i.e., the nobility, the clergy, and the commons. See 283. (Also, is this possibly a concern in 77?)

[277] comitia: Rousseau's word is *comice,* which can be translated as "meeting," "electoral meeting," or "public assembly." In each use of words directly pertaining to Roman legal and governmental organization and practice, the standard procedure of reinstituting the Latin terms into the text has been followed (cf. 343ff.).

[280] Cf. PE 31–34.

[283] the Third Estate: See 275 comment.

[284] Sovereignty cannot be represented: See 66–69, 97–105.

The deputies of the people: See the discussion of "elective aristocracy" whose proper function, as Commissioners, is the administration of the (Constitutional) Law, 201–7 (cf. PE 45).

The English people: It is not clear just what Rousseau had in mind here; one explanation might be that Parliament is bound only by its own recognition of past precedents and not by any legal limit on its own authority, which is expressed by a principle of virtually absolute majority rule; Rousseau might also have had in mind the principle of parliamentary supremacy, and what seems to be a lack of distinction between constitutional and statutory law (cf. 71–72, 287).[6]

[287] One interpretation of the point here seems to be that although the people must sanction the constitution, i.e., "the Law," they need to delegate its administration, which includes statutory legislation, to particular individuals chosen for that purpose, i.e., "elective aristocracy" as per 201ff. or "Commissioners" as per 284. An alternative interpretation would be that he wants statutory legislation to be in the hands of the people and only believes the executive branch of government must be delegated to a few men —but then see 148.

[294] a strange manner of contracting: See 25, 33; PE 63.

[295] to go back to one's full liberty: Apparently what is meant is that by accepting an absolute master is to place oneself into slavery—a condition foreclosed at the outset, a condition carrying

[6]See Locke's *Second Treatise,* par. 134–58.

with it no moral or civic obligations and thus placing oneself in a pre-civil state of "natural liberty." See 20–33 and 32–33 comment.

[299] **the establishment of the law:** Does he mean basic constitutional law or particular statutory legislation? See 141–45, 153.

[303–4] Although he does not regard pure direct democracy as a viable way to conduct government (190–97), he apparently believes it requisite for the legitimate institution and also the periodic renewal of organized government (see 312).

Committee of the Whole: What in American practice of parliamentary procedure is instituted to allow a freer and more informal discussion of a particular issue than normally strict observance of *Robert's Rules of Order* would permit.

[308] A prime theme is that laws, and especially the basic law, must embody the customs of a people; to change laws so that they conflict with those customs is inherently dangerous, for such laws will be resisted and may well become unenforceable, thereby nurturing a disrespect for, if not an open flouting of, the laws. See 138, 144; Introduction.

[310] **The periodical assemblies:** See 96–105, 264–79; also 315–21, 374–80, 389ff.

[312–13] The act of *sovereignty* is stated in 312; the act of *magistracy* in 313.

[314] **each person can renounce:** One consequence of the social contract, explicitly presupposed, is that each citizen retains the "right to resign" without penalty—but note the reservation in the footnote and 327n. This fundamental concept, which Rousseau takes from Plato's *Crito,* 50–52, sets up a dual criterion of legitimacy: the right (if not the obligation) to advocate reform if one chooses to remain a citizen (see 321), and the right of free emigration if one chooses to leave—rights still denied to most of the world's population in this twentieth century. Is this not part of what is meant by belonging to a free society? (See 6, 16–33.) Cf. Rousseau's more extended statement in *Emile:* "For by a right nothing can abrogate, when each man attains his majority and becomes his own master, he also becomes master of renouncing the contract that connects him with the community by leaving the country in which that community is established. . . . According to rigorous standards of right, each man remains free at his own risk in whatever place he is born unless he voluntarily subjects himself to the

laws in order to acquire the right to be protected by them" (E 455–56).

BOOK FOUR

[315–444] Book Four is divided into four distinct parts: Chapters I–III (315–42) may be regarded as the conclusion of Book Three; Chapters IV–VI (343–400), seemingly following the precedent of Machiavelli's *Discourses,* seek to draw lessons for political problems from a reconsideration of the politics of the Roman Republic; Chapters VII–VIII (401–43) discuss the political implications of public morals, religious commitments, and the need for a common ideology for a cohesive legitimate society—what Rousseau terms "civil religion"; Chapter IX (444) points out that the entire essay has focused on principles requisite for a free or legitimate society without considering how it should conduct its relations with other states; he seems to imply that these principles yield guidelines for foreign policy, or "external relations," but declines to pursue them here.

[315] **the happiest people in the world:** I.e., the Swiss; see his idealized portrait of his native land in the "Dedication" of the Second Discourse.

[318] **small societies to influence the great one:** He is referring to the partial societies or subgroups which make up any actual social order (cf. 78; PE 15).

the general will is no longer the will of all: Cf. 66, 75; PE 16.

[323] **comitia:** See 277 comment for translation, and 363 for Rousseau's description.

[326] **every man being born free and master of himself:** The French original reads: *tout homme étant né libre.* This is not an inductive generalization but a statement to be taken as a first principle (see Introduction). It thus confirms the translation of the opening sentence as "Man *is* born free" (5); both versions are statements of philosophic principle and not of historical reporting. Cf. 9, 24.

[327] Compare the footnote with the "right to resign" in 314.

[328] **the greater number:** I.e., the majority; as a practical matter in most cases we have agreed to abide by majority rule (cf. 36, 70n., 331–32).

[329] **The constant will:** I.e., the general will must be continu-

ally functioning and is not to be relegated to one historic moment; only so can it maintain the goals of the society within which appropriate societal and governmental activity is circumscribed. See 54, 76: these three paragraphs together serve to define the import of Rousseau's notion of the general will as the continuing basis of civic freedom; interpretations of the essay in this volume frequently depend upon them.

[331] **In showing earlier:** See 75–78, 306–15.

I will speak of it again: See 333–42.

[335–36] **Democracy:** For the special meanings of this term as used in this essay, see 190–97, 303.

[337] **Aristocracy:** See 198–207.

[338] **our simple Citizens:** Regarding this and other references to Geneva as a prototype, note that those who participated in its government amounted to approximately six hundred people.

[341] **monarchical Government:** I.e., an absolute not a limited or constitutional monarchy in the modern sense (cf. 208–23).

[342–88] This paragraph is an introduction to the three following chapters, which elucidate Rousseau's thesis that the principle of the "assembly of the people" is practicable in a large city—as evidenced in classical Rome. Picking up from 266–67, he is looking back to the experience of the Roman Republic (the only real historic precedent for republican or free government available to him in his time); one might well refer back to Machiavelli's *Discourses* for a more detailed discussion of some of the points he touches. But cf. PE 23.

[343] **Comitia:** See 277 comment and Rousseau's description in 363.

as peoples are no longer being formed: This is an ironic lack of foresight on Rousseau's part, although it seemed true enough in his time: lack of foresight because although he anticipated the French Revolution (cf., e.g., E 194), he did not foresee that it would precipitate the rise of the modern nation-states in Europe and in due course much of the rest of the world; ironic because Rousseau is often regarded as the prophet of nationalism just because of the focus he placed on community interest and because his concept of citizenship entails that of patriotism (cf. PE, esp. 30, 40);

little did he dream that nationalism would develop into those tyrannous excesses of the twentieth century.

[345] **Curia, Curiae, Decuriae, Curiones, Decuriones:** As per 323, the Latin terms for Roman institutions have been reinstituted for Rousseau's French *Curie, Curies, Décuries, Curions, Décurions.*

[346] **Centuria:** The Latin has been reinstituted for Rousseau's French *centuries,* meaning hundred-man units (hence "centurions").

[367] Following Machiavelli and Montesquieu, and echoing Aristotle's theme of "polity," Rousseau finds a key to Rome's combination of stability and liberty in this rudimentary form of mixed government (see 224–29).

[389–400] Cf. Machiavelli.[7]

[401–8] This chapter is an introduction to the conclusion of the one that follows (439ff.). In order to appreciate the point of Chapter VII, it should be read as a way, taking up from Roman practice, by which Rousseau expresses his conviction that the operating values, customs, and general standards of approbation in a society are basic to the functioning of its political institutions. If popular sovereignty and the general will (75) are taken seriously, then the nature of public opinion is paramount. If public opinion is to guide public policy, it must be generalized and not permitted to crest in the passing passions of the moment. (Cf. 205, where it is questioned whether it is good that **the execution of the laws immediately ensues from the public will.** As the general will is to be

---

[7]*Discourses,* I, 34, 35: "it was neither the name nor the rank of the Dictator that subjected Rome to servitude, but it was the authority which citizens usurped to perpetuate themselves in the government. . . . And it is seen that the dictatorship, whenever created according to public law, and not usurped by individual authority, always proved beneficial to Rome; it is the magistracies and powers that are created by illegitimate means which harm a republic, and not those that are appointed in the regular way. . . . Dictators were appointed only for a limited term, and not in perpetuity, and their power to act was confined to the particular occasion for which they were created. . . . But the Dictator could do nothing to alter the form of the government, such as to diminish the power of the Senate or the people, or to abrogate existing institutions and create new ones. . . . Tardy measures are most dangerous when the occasion requires prompt action. . . . Thus no republic will ever be perfect if she has not by law provided for everything, having a remedy for every emergency, and fixed rules for applying it."

distinguished from the "will of all," so the basic commitments of public opinion are to be distinguished from any particularly excited expression of it.[8]

[404] **The opinions of a people:** See 144.

[406–8] The essential argument here is that political reform in any society begins with the redirection of popular praise and blame.

[409–43] This long chapter may be roughly divided into four sections: 409–15: review of the religions of the ancient world; 416–22: review of the development of Christianity in terms of its political consequences; 423–38: distinguishes three types of religion in terms of their political implications; 439–43: the point of it all—the characteristics of what Rousseau calls "civil religion."

In contemporary terms, we might describe his topic as that of the underlying ideological or value commitments which membership in a particular organized society carries with it; as such, it is the concomitant of the general will (e.g., the American commitment to the Constitution, despite any policy disagreements).

Perhaps one reason for Rousseau's term "civil religion" is the exceedingly close church-state relationship in all societies of his time (as such, 439 can be read as a call for secularization of the state; cf. 117). Two passages in *Emile* should be consulted: "The Profession of Faith of the Vicar of Savoy," E 266–313, which is generally taken as an expression of Rousseau's own religious views; and E 380–81, for a more extended statement of the reasoning behind 439–43.

[439] **The right which the social pact gives:** See 79–88, esp. 87.

but the dogmas of this Religion: Rather than religious uni-

---

[8]Cf. Alexander Hamilton, *Federalist Papers*, 71: "The republican principle demands that the deliberate sense of the community should govern the conduct of those to whom they intrust the management of their affairs; but it does not require an unqualified complaisance to every sudden breeze of passion, or to every transient impulse which the people may receive from the arts of men, who flatter their prejudices to betray their interest. It is a just observation that the people commonly *intend* the PUBLIC GOOD. This often applies to their very errors. . . . When occasions present themselves, in which the interests of the people are at variance with their inclinations, it is the duty of the persons whom they have appointed to be the guardians of those interests, to withstand the temporary delusion, in order to give them time and opportunity for more cool and sedate reflection."

formity, this can be construed as an argument for the official toleration of religious differences (see 441–42). The only limits imposed
on religious toleration are (1) that intolerance itself is unaccept-
able, and (2) that there be no interference with good citizenship.

without it being the Sovereign's business: Compare Locke.[9]

[440–41] The argument is that membership in a civil society
requires that one accept the conditions of membership, i.e., the
basic principles, value commitments, and societal goals; as reiterated before, all specific freedoms and privacies are within these
limits. This might be construed as the concomitant of the individual's "right to resign"—but as stated in the last sentence of 440,
it does have an ominous ring in the light of the tyrannies of our
time.

N.B. One reason for insisting on the belief in immortality, men-
tioned in the footnote, may be to add moral force to the moral
responsibility of citizenship (but cf. 433).[10]

[444] For some indications of the way in which Rousseau might
have pursued this further task, see his own brief *Project for Perpetual
Peace* (1761); for a more comprehensive development of these
principles, one might consult Kant's pamphlet *Toward Perpetual
Peace* (1795).

[9]*First Letter Concerning Toleration:* "Now that the whole jurisdiction of the
magistrate reaches only to these civil concernments, and that all civil power,
right and dominion, is bounded and confined to the only care of promoting
these things; and that it neither can nor ought in any manner to be extended
to the salvation of souls . . ."

[10]As he stated this in *Emile,* p. 381: "each person [should] know that an
arbiter of the fate of human beings exists . . . that the apparent happiness
of this life is nothing; that there is another life after it in which this Supreme
Being will be the rewarder of the good and the judge of the wicked."

Notes to
*Discourse on Political Economy**

—— •◆◆• ——

[1] This essay, originally published as an article in Diderot's *Encyclopédie,* vol. V, which appeared in the fall of 1755, a year after the Second Discourse, may perhaps indicate Rousseau's shift of focus from speculative history to concern with present-day problems; in any event, it clearly prefigures and helps to clarify, in terms of application, the orientation more fully worked out on a more theoretical level in *Of the Social Contract,* the first edition of which appeared in 1762, twelve years later. In contrast to the latter, the focus here is on governmental administration of laws, not on the principle of sovereignty; but it is significant that it was in this article, oriented to practical problems of justifiable administration, that Rousseau first uses the term "the general will" and first makes the distinction between "government" and "sovereignty" (cf. SC 150–53). Thus the fundamental conceptual structure worked out in *Of the Social Contract* was already present in Rousseau's thinking, and is given first expression in terms of governmental function.[1]

FATHER OF THE FAMILY: A reference to another article in the *Encyclopédie.* For Rousseau's own views on "domestic economy," one might refer to his novel *Julie, or the New Heloise.*

[2–6] Compare this extended discussion of the family structure with SC 9.

---

*All unidentified references are to paragraph numbers in this essay; when preceded by "SC," to paragraph numbers in *Of the Social Contract;* when preceded by "E" to page numbers in *Emile;* references to other works cited are to chapter numbers, paragraphs (Par.), or pages (p).

[1]"Political Economy," which was a standard term until quite recently, was defined by Adam Smith as "The act of managing the resources of a people and of its government." See *Oxford Universal Dictionary,* ed. Little et al. (Oxford University Press, 1933, 1955), p. 582, col. 3.

[7] **two illustrious men:** I.e., John Locke, in his *First Treatise on Civil Government,* and Algernon Sidney, in *Discourse Concerning Government.*

[8] **See POLITICS and SOVEREIGNTY:** Insofar as the *Encyclopédie* was not completed until 1761, it is not clear from this note whether Rousseau is merely extending the courtesy of cross-referencing anticipated articles or whether he has indeed read the manuscripts and wishes to endorse them.

[10–11] This comparison of the political to the individual body voices an old theme, in Western thought since Plato, and is used by most thinkers espousing some version of an organic theory of society (see Introduction).

[12] **general will:** Rousseau's first published use of this term, which is one central strand in *Of the Social Contract;* the definition which follows is more explicit than any in the later essay and illuminates his use of the phrase there, especially in passages such as SC 75ff.

See the word RIGHT: A reference to an article by Diderot under the heading "Natural Right," in which the distinction between "general" and "individual" will is made and it is asserted that the "general will is always good"; Rousseau acknowledges indebtedness to Diderot for his crucial term (which Diderot used in a way accordant with the tradition of natural law theory); but Rousseau radically revised its meaning in adapting it; see the definition in this paragraph and compare it with his first use of it in *Of the Social Contract,* SC 45.

[14] **good or bad government . . . morality:** It is to be noted that the standard of judgment for both are the same.

[15] **Every political society is composed of . . . smaller societies:** Despite the reluctant acceptance of political pluralism in SC 78 (cf. SC 66), notice not only its explicit acceptance here as a fact of life but that its meaning is accordant with the priority of the communal interest over the interests of subordinate groupings.

[16] **when the people are seduced:** Note the warning against the danger of demagoguery.

the public decision . . . another: Cf. use of this phrase in SC 76.

the general will is always for the common good: Cf. SC 66, 75.

Note the distinction between the will of private individuals or groups and the general will, enunciated by the distinction in SC 76 between "the will of all and the general will."

[17] **the public faith:** I.e., "civil religion" (cf. SC 439–41).

[19] **at the same time . . . the government:** Note the dual task of

a free society; cf. SC 55–57, which gives this entire paragraph a philosophic foundation.

[20] Cf. SC 96–106.

[23] **the legislator:** Cf. SC 105–16; also SC 118–34, 230–44.

[25] **that virtue reigns:** The word *virtue* is used frequently in both essays, but it does not seem to have been explicitly defined in either. It would, however, seem that what is generally meant by it, beyond the traditional individual virtues of honesty, courage, etc., is the habitual placing of the interests of the common good ahead of one's own (cf., e.g., 28–31).

[29] Rousseau is here, and in the following paragraphs, voicing a tradition, extending from Plato to Dewey, that one prime function of a responsible social order is the education of its citizens (cf. esp. 37–39).

[32] **the commitment of the body of the nation:** The principle of the reciprocity of rights and duties entails an obligation of the community to its members just as its members are obligated to the community.

sacrifice an innocent man: Participation by each citizen in the general will and the social contract endows him with a rightful claim to be protected by the power of the community; cf. 33; SC 40, 42, 47, 50. (It should be clear that charges of Rousseau's "totalitarianism" collapse in the face of this emphasis on the import of *each* individual citizen.)

[34] **the common liberty:** The preservation of which is the proper function of law.

most difficult in government: The unity of a society requires that it not be divided into two warring classes. Note here and in the balance of this essay the development of the thesis that government should properly play an economic role by fostering a middle-class society in which "all have something, and none of them has too much" (SC 65n.). (Cf. Introduction.)

[36–39] **citizens:** Note the import of citizenship and its full meaning being developed (cf. SC 46).

[37] **the education of their children:** These paragraphs are indeed prophetic—for it is only with increasing democratization that universal public education has come to be recognized as a crucial responsibility of organized society. Rousseau was one of the very first to insist that education is a prime legitimate claim of the individual citizen on his society, a completely unknown and largely inconceivable idea in his

time. Note that one prime function of such public education is development of **the courage and virtue of citizens** (see 38).

[41] This whole third section can be read as amplifying what has already been indicated in 34.

[42] **the right of . . . ownership:** Note that although private property is held to be something of a public trust (cf. SC 63), Rousseau regards private ownership essential to the health of a free society; his reasons should be noted. (See 42 n.6, 58, 77; Introduction.)

[46] Cf. SC 106ff.

[51] It would seem that what is being advocated is the role of government as a general overseer of the private economy while taking care to anticipate public emergencies and public needs; in this regard Rousseau was opposed to the Physiocrats of his time, who advocated full free trade. In a way, Rousseau's position is perhaps somewhat akin to the more traditional notion of mercantilism. (In reading these paragraphs, it is important to remember that Rousseau is thinking in terms of a preindustrial economy, and that he has been criticized for having no conception of the social benefit arising from the growth of private capital, which can be used for economic advances benefiting the society as a whole by producing new wealth for it.)

[53] **The relish for conquest . . . the chiefs at home:** One of the oldest reasons for aggressive war.

[58] **voluntary . . . from a general will:** I.e., taxation must be by general popular consent.

by a proportional rate: As spelled out further in 60 and 64, Rousseau is again being prophetic by advocating a tax system geared to the economic means of each individual; in a way, this can be seen as a forerunner of the idea of a "progressive" income tax system.

[59] **by the consent of the people or their representatives:** Here, and again in 77, "representatives" are given authority for the administration of the functions of government (apparently including the statutory legislation needed for tax laws); cf. SC 201 and comment suggesting that Rousseau's favored form of actual government is what he terms "elective aristocracy." But cf. SC 280-85.

[60] **assessment by head . . . property levy:** In accord with his principle that the rate of taxation should be in proportion to the ability to contribute to the public treasury, he is opposing a head tax (sometimes called a poll tax) in which each is assessed the same amount.

[73] In addition to proportionate taxation, he is also suggesting the

use of luxury taxes, i.e., a sales tax (see 74, 77) on luxury items. Note one important use of them aside from raising revenue: to prevent the continual augmentation of the inequality of fortunes, in accord with the principle of moderating the extremes of poverty and wealth (see SC 65n).

[78] The last sentence seems to equivocate deliberately between the way the word *sovereignty* was generally used in the eighteenth century —as the power of the ruler(s)—and the new use Rousseau is beginning to develop here (and only finally worked out in *Of the Social Contract*) —as the legitimate right of the people to ordain their own free government: for, it asks, if the ministers of the rulers are truly the enemies of the people and yet accepted as such, why bother about what is right or wrong, about what ought to be? In considering this question, it is well to remember that *On Political Economy* was written at about the same time as the Second Discourse, several years before the preliminary suggestion they both present was worked out quite explicitly in *Of the Social Contract;* indeed, this essay is the first time this new conception of "sovereignty," which Rousseau was to develop more fully in the later work, received any explicit development, and it must be then read as a preliminary statement. (Cf. 291 n.16.)

Biographical References

JEAN LE ROND D'ALEMBERT, (1717–1783): French philosopher and mathematician, and a member of the French Academy, to whom Rousseau addressed his *Letter on the Theater,* on the general relation of politics and the arts. *SC 46n.*

ALEXANDER (356–323 B.C.): Student of Aristotle; legendary leader who took Greek armies to conquer Egypt and the Middle East, diffusing Greek culture to the Indus River. *PE 33.*

ARCHIMEDES (c. 287–212 B.C.): Famed Greek scientist. *SC 210.*

M. D'A (Marquis Marc Pierre d'Argenson) (1696–1764): French minister of foreign affairs 1744–1747. Rousseau's citations are from a privately circulated manuscript which was entitled *Treatise on the Admission of Democracy in a Monarchical State, or Considerations on the Ancient and Present Government of France.* Rousseau, in his first edition, cited the author only by initial; the posthumous edition of 1782, based on Rousseau's notes, spelled out the full name. *SC 10n., 76n., 137n., 439n.*

ARISTOTLE (384–322 B.C.): Student of Plato; the Greek philosopher generally credited with bringing together the sum of classical Greek learning. His *Politics* is generally taken as a systematic defense of a free constitutional structure (which he termed "polity"); in it, he nevertheless restricted participation to free citizens, while defending the institution of slavery (I, 4–7). *SC 13, 14, 207, 257n.; PE 7.*

PIERRE BAYLE (1647–1706): Leading controversial thinker of his time; one of the first to defend the principle of religious toleration (along with Locke), and to argue for the autonomy of morality from theology (anticipating Kant). A French Calvinist, he fled, during the persecution of the Huguenots, to Rotterdam, where he edited one of the foremost intellectual journals of his time, *Nouvelles de la République des Lettres. SC 422.*

JEAN BODIN (1530–1596): French political writer who advocated religious toleration, advanced economic thought, maintained that property and family are the bases of society, and that rebellion against the reigning monarch is never justifiable. *SC 46n.; PE 46, 59, 78.*

JULIUS CAESAR (100–44 B.C.): Roman general, regarded as having destroyed the Roman Republic by becoming Rome's first emperor. *SC 251n., 440n; PE 30.*

CALIGULA (A.D. 12–41): Roman emperor known for his cruel and tyrannical reign; probably insane, he had himself declared a god just before his assassination. *SC 12, 13, 107.*

JEAN CALVIN (1509–1564): A prime leader of the Protestant Reformation, author of the *Institutes of the Christian Religion.* Born in France, he moved to Geneva in 1538 and dominated its life from 1541 until his death. Although his theology called for theocratic government, his followers were leading proponents of religious toleration and political reform. *SC 110n.*

CATO THE YOUNGER (95–46 B.C.): Roman Stoic who, as tribune, denounced Caesar as an accomplice of Catiline; after hearing of Caesar's victory in 48 B.C., he committed suicide. *SC 29n.; PE 30.*

MARCUS TULLIUS CICERO (106–43 B.C.): Roman statesman and philosopher, whose *On the Republic* is an important contribution to the development of the democratic tradition. Killed by soldiers of Mark Antony and his allies for opposing their claim to succession after Caesar's death; Rousseau cites two of his books, *Of the Duties of Office* and *Of the Laws. SC 378.*

OLIVER CROMWELL (1599–1658): Lord Protector of England, 1653–1658; presumably, Rousseau's displeasure stems from Cromwell's dissolution of the "Rump Parliament" in 1653 by military force. *SC 317, 434.*

RENÉ DESCARTES (1596–1650): French mathematician, scientist, and philosopher, whose *Discourse on Method* and *Meditations on First Philosophy* are generally regarded as the beginning of modern philosophy. *SC 126.*

SIR ROBERT FILMER (c.1590–1653): English writer who strongly supported the doctrine of the divine right of kings in several works, including *Patriarcha,* which Rousseau cites. *PE 7.*

GEORGE I (1660–1727): Duke of Hanover (and Leibniz's sponsor), who became the first Hanoverian king of England, in 1714. *SC 74.*

HUGO GROTIUS (1583–1645): Dutch jurist and statesman, generally considered one of the fathers of international law. *SC 10, 11, 21, 26, 30, 35, 74, 314, 421n.*

HENRY IV (1553–1610): King of Navarre and France, he converted to Catholicism from Calvinism in order to secure recognition as the French king. *SC 443.*

THOMAS HOBBES (1588–1679): English philosopher who espoused belief in a "state of nature" as savage anarchy with constant warfare of "each against all"; in his *Leviathan* he argued that the first necessity is domestic peace, that this necessitates a social contract whereby all individuals accept an absolute ruler, who rightfully receives complete obedience from his subjects in return for maintaining the peace. (See Rousseau on Hobbes, E 458.) *SC 11, 13, 421.*

JAMES II (1633–1701): Successor to Charles II; king of England 1658–1688, when he escaped to France during the Glorious Revolution. *SC 74.*

LOUIS XIII (1215–1270): Became king of France in 1226 and was canonized as Saint Louis in 1297. *SC 74.*

LYCURGUS (c.8th century B.C.): Traditionally regarded as the "Legislator" of the constitution of Sparta. *SC 78, 106n., 110, 120.*

NICCOLÒ MACHIAVELLI (1469–1527): Italian statesman and writer, author of *The Prince,* which outlines techniques for the seizure of political power, and *Discourses on the First Ten Books of Livy,* which sought to establish on an empirical basis the political conditions and practices requisite for political liberty. Often regarded as a father of modern political science as well as one of the first proponents of the nation-state and of modern democratic theory. *SC 78n., 116n., 212, 248n., 251n.; PE 18.*

CHARLES DE SECONDAT, BARON DE LA BRÈDE ET DE MONTESQUIEU (1689–1755): Author of a seminal work (with a direct impact on the writing of the American Constitution). Despite some criticisms, Rousseau had a high regard for him and considered his book as a key to the science of legislation. *SC 107, 137, 195, 230, 334; PE 64.*

NUMA: Mythological successor to Romulus and the originator of many Roman laws. For reasons stated in his *Government of Poland,* II, Rousseau regarded Numa, not Romulus, as the true founder of Rome. *SC 78, 343n.*

PETER THE GREAT (1672–1725): Generally regarded as the founder of the Russian Empire, he established Saint Petersburg (later to become Petrograd and then Leningrad) as Russia's Baltic "window to the

West." Rousseau's criticism of Peter's reign is in marked contrast to the general approbation expressed by Voltaire and other French Enlightenment *philosophes*. *SC 122*

PHILO (2nd Cent. B.C.): Jewish philosopher from Alexandria, who had a great influence on the development of medieval Platonism. *SC 12.*

PLATO (c.427–347 B.C.): Foremost Greek philosopher. The concept of "mixed government" was developed in his *Laws*, and the latter part of the *Crito* can be read as suggesting Rousseau's notion of the social contract. *SC 107, 118, 222; PE 21, 64.*

PLUTARCH (c.A.D. 46–120): Greek writer best known for his *Lives* of prominent Greeks and Romans. *SC 14n.*

SAMUEL FREIHERR VON PUFFENDORF (1632–1694): Author of *Elements of Universal Jurisprudence,* he was a German writer on international law, following Grotius. *PE 43.*

FRANÇOIS RABELAIS (c.1494–1553): Famous French satirist. *SC 21.*

ABBÉ DE SAINT-PIERRE (1658–1743): French writer who published *Project for Perpetual Peace* in 1713; in 1760, Rousseau wrote a commentary on this pamphlet and then his own *Project for Perpetual Peace*. *SC 341.*

TULLIUS SERVIUS (578–534 B.C.): Roman statesman who reorganized the Roman class structure and who was finally assassinated. *SC 78, 347, 349, 356, 357, 358, 368.*

SOCRATES (c.469–399 B.C.): Athenian philosopher who was Plato's teacher and celebrated as the leading figure in the Platonic Dialogues. *PE 30.*

SOLON (c.639–599 B.C.): Described by Aristotle as a "moderate democrat," he is regarded as having initiated the Athenian democratic development. *SC 78.*

TACITUS (A.D. c.55–117): Famed Roman historian. *SC 219n., 324.*

WILLIAM WARBURTON (1698–1779): English historian and churchman, bishop of Gloucester, author of *Alliance Between Church and State.* A friend of Alexander Pope, he was a vigorous opponent of the Enlightenment, as represented by David Hume, Voltaire, and the Deists generally. *SC 117, 422.*

WILLIAM OF ORANGE (1650–1702): Became William II, king of England, Scotland and Ireland, in 1689, by Act of Parliament after the Glorious Revolution *SC 74.*